Praise

Decoding

"This book is your secret decoder ring for understanding how athletes, artists, entrepreneurs, and even criminal masterminds create breakthroughs. Clear, concise, and backed by science, it's a powerful combination of analysis and storytelling that will transform the way you approach your next project."

—Daniel H. Pink, author of
When, *Drive*, and *To Sell Is Human*

"If this book was full of insights about the patterns that drive excellence across fields, it would be well worth your time. Ron Friedman has gone a step further: he actually teaches you how to detect new patterns yourself. With alluring stories and illuminating studies, he shows how we can all learn more from great achievers and innovators."

—Adam Grant, *New York Times* bestselling author of
Think Again and *Originals* and host of the TED podcast WorkLife

"A much-needed handbook for learning how success really happens. Read this book if you want to upgrade from working hard to actually producing results that matter."

—Cal Newport, the *New York Times* bestselling author of
Digital Minimalism and *Deep Work*

"Great innovators have one thing in common. They all cracked the code. In his riveting new book, Ron Friedman shows how history's most creative minds unlocked the potential of reverse engineering, and more importantly, how to apply that process strategically in today's most competitive fields. Filled with compelling, unforgettable stories, Friedman's book shows how disruptive innovations in technology, sports, art, and business have shaped our world where future innovations can be found."

—Marshall Goldsmith, *New York Times* #1 bestselling author of
Triggers, Mojo, and *What Got You Here Won't Get You There*

"*Decoding Greatness* is a playbook for success, applicable to any field you can imagine. By reverse engineering what works for others, we can all find unique ways to drive innovation. Ron Friedman is a master of how people think and work and shows us how we can apply these insights in our own lives."
—Jonah Berger, internationally bestselling author of
Contagious, Invisible Influence, and *The Catalyst*

"Psychologist Ron Friedman melds storytelling and science with a page-turning effect. I finished *Decoding Greatness* with a list of things I want to try in my own work, and I bet you will too."
—David Epstein, *New York Times* bestselling author of *Range*

"Ron Friedman brilliantly illuminates how experts in every field use reverse engineering to jumpstart their thinking and spark innovation. Clear, concise, and backed by the latest science, it's a rare combination of entertainment and enlightenment that will transform the way you approach your next project."
—Shawn Achor, *New York Times* bestselling author of
The Happiness Advantage and *Big Potential*

"We'd all like to get results and succeed faster. In this addictively readable new book, Ron Friedman shows you a smart, proven framework that actually works. Bursting with unforgettable stories, eye-opening insights, and practical strategies, it offers a genuinely new and profoundly useful perspective on how greatness is truly achieved. If you want to master your craft, this book is a must-read."
—Dorie Clark, author of *Entrepreneurial You* and executive education faculty, Duke University Fuqua School of Business

"In *Decoding Greatness*, Ron Friedman unlocks the secrets to disruptive innovation, providing a research-backed toolbox full of practical techniques that cross all fields—from business, innovation and art, to computers, music and even crime. The examples Friedman uses are as entertaining as they are unforgettable."
—Scott Barry Kaufman, PhD, author of
Transcend: The New Science of Self-Actualization

"So many professionals struggle to be original but fail to take the time to learn from the creative work of those around them. Ron Friedman has decoded the path to brilliant and innovative work and shows you how you can do the same. An essential read for anyone looking for their next big idea."

—Todd Henry, author of *The Accidental Creative* and
The Motivation Code

"Drawing on examples from Jeff Bezos to Judd Apatow, Malcolm Gladwell, and Vincent van Gogh . . . the author examines how these creative minds think and counsels readers to ask interesting questions, solicit and interpret feedback . . . develop meaningful metrics, and set goals. . . . [An] engaging prescription for getting ahead in business and life."

—*Kirkus Reviews*

"Friedman's formula for greatness is deceptively simple: find something great, then take it apart. But deconstruction is just the first step, and he uses examples of entrepreneurs, writers, musicians, chefs, athletes, and more to illustrate the rest of the process. . . . There are plenty of stories mixed in to illustrate each point clearly, and readers will leave the book inspired to start something great themselves."

—*Booklist*

"[An] empowering guide. . . . Friedman discusses how artists, chefs, athletes, and other professionals can use the process of reverse engineering to acquire new skills and spark creativity. . . . Those in need of a refresh of their problem-solving skills should give this a look."

—*Publishers Weekly*

"[Friedman] effectively balances theory with his rich collection of real-life examples, thus avoiding clichés and vague aspirations. . . . A practical and sophisticated handbook, useful for readers who wish to learn from the successful experiences of others and effectively apply the lessons to their own work and careers."

—*Library Journal, starred review*

Also by
Ron Friedman

The Best Place to Work:
The Art and Science
of Creating an
Extraordinary Workplace

Decoding Greatness

How the Best in the World
Reverse Engineer Success

Ron Friedman

Simon & Schuster Paperbacks
New York London Toronto Sydney New Delhi

Simon & Schuster Paperbacks
An imprint of Simon & Schuster
1230 Avenue of the Americas
New York, NY 10020

First Simon & Schuster trade paperback edition January 2023

SIMON & SCHUSTER PAPERBACKS and colophon are registered
trademarks of Simon & Schuster, Inc.

For information about special discounts for bulk
purchases, please contact Simon & Schuster Special Sales
at 1-866-506-1949 or business@simonandschuster.com.

The Simon & Schuster Speakers Bureau can bring authors
to your live event. For more information or to book an event,
contact the Simon & Schuster Speakers Bureau at 1-866-248-3049
or visit our website at www.simonspeakers.com.

Interior design by Lewelin Polanco

Manufactured in the United States of America

1   3   5   7   9   8   6   4   2

Library of Congress Cataloging-in-Publication Data is available.

ISBN 978-1-9821-3579-9
ISBN 978-1-9821-3580-5 (pbk)
ISBN 978-1-9821-3581-2 (ebook)

For my grandmother,
who taught me the importance of
taking risks, holding loved ones by the hand,
and injecting lemon and dill into
(nearly) every dish

Contents

Introduction

A Secret History from the Land of Innovation

By the time Steve Jobs finds out he's been betrayed, it is already far too late. The press conference is over, and the news is out. Slowly it dawns on him: Apple's head start is about to disappear.

The year is 1983, and we are in Cupertino, California. The computer company Jobs cofounded is barely seven years old. Its rise has been meteoric. In a few years, Wall Street will assess its value at more than a billion dollars. But now, just six short weeks from the release of Apple's boldest innovation yet, the Macintosh, Jobs discovers he's been scooped.

The blow arrives from more than twenty-five hundred miles away, in the lavish ballroom of New York City's famed Helmsley Palace Hotel. Onstage, standing before a gaggle of reporters, Bill Gates has just announced Microsoft's plans to develop a user-friendly operating system—one with more than a few striking similarities to the Macintosh.

Back then, computers looked nothing like today's intuitive devices. Forget the colorful graphics, clickable icons, and interactive menus. If you wanted a 1983 computer to do anything, you had to reach for a keyboard and input a rigid, text-based language to convey your instructions.

Apple's Macintosh featured two key innovations: dazzling on-screen visuals and the arrival of a mouse. No longer would users be forced to grapple with arcane computer language. On the new Mac, they could simply point and click.

Jobs couldn't wait to bring the Macintosh to market. His vision: in less than two months, his company would fundamentally disrupt the world of personal computing forever. But now here was Gates announcing the creation of this new operating system—something called Windows?

Jobs was livid. After all, Gates wasn't a competitor—he was a vendor.

It was almost too baffling to comprehend. Jobs had personally handpicked Microsoft to develop software for Apple's computers. He'd been good to Gates. He had traveled with him to conferences, invited him onstage at Apple events, treated him as a member of his inner circle. And this was how he was being repaid?

"Get Bill Gates down here," he demanded of his Microsoft handler. "Tomorrow!"

It didn't matter that Gates was at the other end of the country. Jobs got his wish.

The following day, Apple's boardroom filled with its top brass. Jobs wanted bodies—a show of force when Microsoft's team arrived. A showdown was about to take place, and he wasn't about to be outnumbered.

He need not have bothered. To everyone's surprise, Microsoft didn't send a team. Gates arrived alone, ambling awkwardly in to face the firing squad.

Jobs wasted little time tearing into him. "You're ripping us off!" he yelled, his underlings glaring, all eyes on Gates. "I trusted you, and now you're stealing from us!"

Gates took it in quietly. He paused a moment, not once looking away. Then he casually delivered a devastating line, rendering the entire room speechless: "Well, Steve, I think there's more than one way of looking at it. I think it's more like we both had this rich neighbor named Xerox, and I broke into his house to steal the TV set and found out that you had already stolen it."

Gates appreciated that Windows had not originally been his

idea. What he wasn't prepared to stand for was this notion that a mouse-driven, graphics-based operating system was the creative brainchild of Steve Jobs. It didn't matter what heroic tales Apple was peddling to the press. Gates knew the truth. The Macintosh had never been Apple's invention. It had been reverse engineered from a Rochester, New York, copier company named Xerox.

Back in the 1970s, while Steve Jobs was still in high school, Xerox faced an existential crisis. Its executives believed a paperless office was inevitable and they weren't about to wait passively for its arrival. To kick start innovation, they founded the Palo Alto Research Center, in California, calling it Xerox PARC for short. It quickly emerged as an idea powerhouse, thanks to a rare combination of generous funding, a risk-embracing culture, and geographic serendipity. Silicon Valley was brimming with brilliant engineers and Xerox PARC arrived at just the right moment to pluck them up and grant them free rein.

Among Xerox PARC's countless inventions was a personal computer most people have never heard of: the Alto. It offered many of the same features that would come to distinguish the Macintosh, like graphics that made computers easier to use and a mouse for communicating commands. Except the Alto was developed a full decade earlier.

Xerox knew the Alto had value—it just didn't realize how much. It viewed the Alto as a niche product, a high-end office gadget that might be of interest to prestigious universities and major corporations. And no wonder. With a price tag of well over $100,000 (in today's dollars) and a minimum purchase requirement of five units, Xerox's Alto was well outside the budget of even the wealthiest of Americans.

Xerox had a blind spot. Its executives, many of whom had come of age in the 1940s and '50s, considered typing the domain of secretaries. They simply could not conceive of a world in which computers were a household item. Which may explain why they were so cavalier about granting demonstrations of the Alto to many visitors, including one in 1979 to Steve Jobs.

Jobs was instantly captivated. "You're sitting on a gold mine," he told the Xerox engineer tasked with showing him the Alto. As the presentation went on, Jobs could barely sit still. He grew increasingly animated, visibly struggling to contain his excitement. At one point he blurted out, "I can't believe Xerox is not taking advantage of this."

Afterward, he jumped into his car and sped back to the office. Unlike those plodding Xerox executives, he fully recognized the significance of this invention. Jobs believed he'd been offered a glimpse of the future, and he wasn't about to wait until Xerox figured it out. "This is it!" he told his team. "We've got to do it!"

Overnight, developing a mouse-driven graphic user interface became Apple's central focus. Except they weren't trying to copy the Alto. Jobs thought he could do better. He would simplify the mouse down to a single button. He would leverage the computer's graphics capabilities to produce artistic fonts. And he would find a technological solution to slashing the Alto's exorbitant price tag, bringing personal computers to the masses.

But before he could do any of that, Jobs would debrief his team. He would share everything he remembered about the Alto, detailing its features, capabilities, and design. They were going to work backward, mapping out what it did to approximate how it had been assembled, with the goal of leveraging that information to develop a groundbreaking new machine.*

---

* If this anecdote leaves you conflicted about Jobs and Gates, a little context should help. A few facts are worth noting. First, Xerox had no intention of selling inexpensive computers to a mass market. The reason most people have never heard of the Alto isn't because Jobs stole the idea—it's because Xerox failed to recognize their technology's potential. Second, Microsoft was working on a graphic user interface before Gates saw the Macintosh. Jobs didn't know it but Gates was equally enamored with Xerox's computers. Finally, neither Jobs nor Gates wanted to simply replicate Xerox's technology. They sought to improve upon it in unique ways. Apple aimed to make computers user friendly. Microsoft prioritized making computers affordable. Both companies identified an underutilized idea and worked to make it better.

Steve Jobs's approach was not unusual. At least not in Silicon Valley, where breakthrough products are routinely conceived on a foundation of insights gleaned through reverse engineering.

The laptop I am typing this sentence on would not exist had Compaq not reverse engineered an IBM personal computer and applied their learnings to develop portable computers. The mouse I am holding reflects the influence of Steve Jobs, but it's not Xerox that deserves credit for its invention. That honor belongs to Stanford University researcher Douglas Engelbart, who in 1964 built a boxy wooden prototype that tracked movement using embedded metal disks. Xerox was no stranger to Englebart's work. His office was located a mere nine minutes away from their PARC headquarters. Even the software I am using to capture these words, Google Docs, emerged not out of thin air but following the careful analysis of existing word processing applications.

The practice of reverse engineering, of systematically taking things apart to explore their inner workings and extract important insights, is more than an intriguing feature of the tech industry. For a surprising number of innovators, it's a tendency that appears to have emerged organically, as something of a natural inclination.

When Michael Dell received an Apple II for his sixteenth birthday, he didn't so much as bother turning it on. Instead, he quietly carried it to his room, closed the door, and—to the sheer horror of his parents—dismantled it piece by piece so he could examine how it was assembled. A few short years later, he founded Dell Computers, a company that set itself apart by inviting buyers to customize their computers one component at a time. Google's Larry Page was nine when his older brother let him play around with his screwdrivers. He used them to take apart their father's power tools, just so he could peek inside. And then there's Amazon's Jeff Bezos, whose mother, Jacklyn, had always suspected there was something different about her son. She remembers the precise moment she became convinced: it was seeing her toddler attempt to take apart his crib.

Sheer curiosity is one motivator for reverse engineering. Another, more practical reason developers in tech use the practice is that in many cases, the only way to write software that's compatible with an existing operating system is to decode its underlying functionality.

Then there's the crucial role reverse engineering plays in uncovering game-changing features *before* they're announced.

Twenty-six-year-old Jane Manchun Wong is a Hong Kong–based coder. You've probably never heard of her. Online, she's a superstar. She's the brains behind one of the most-talked-about Twitter accounts in all of Silicon Valley.

Wong is a detective. She spends her days rifling through code, unearthing dormant features that app developers are secretly testing. Anytime an app updates on your phone or tablet, that update contains a new set of programming instructions. Occasionally, some segments of those instructions are made inactive for most users—except the development team. That's where Wong comes in. By poring over inactive code, she's able to detect intriguing, cutting-edge features on the horizon.

Wong's Twitter account is where founders, programmers, and technology reporters converge to discover the next big thing coming out of major companies like Facebook, Uber, Instagram, Spotify, Airbnb, Pinterest, Slack, and Venmo long before an official release. Among the many secret experiments Wong has exposed: Spotify's karaoke feature, Instagram's hiding the number of likes a post receives, and Facebook's new dating site.

Clearly, Silicon Valley is no stranger to reverse engineering. It's how tech innovators learn from their contemporaries, build upon groundbreaking ideas, and stay ahead of the curve.

What if it enabled you to do the same?

———

There's a reason reverse engineering has flourished in the world of computing. It's a field evolving at such dizzying speeds that constant, real-time learning is essential to success.

If you're hoping to thrive in the Valley, you can't afford to come across a major innovation in a magazine article or professional conference. By then, it's already too late. The only way to lead on the cutting edge is to stay on top of compelling discoveries, useful techniques, and important trends.

If those circumstances seem far removed from your profession, chances are that's about to change. In fact, it's a transformation years in the making.

In the late 1980s, a pair of Cornell and Duke University economists noticed an alarming trend. In a growing number of markets, income was becoming concentrated at the very top, among a small segment of individuals.

Economists had witnessed this phenomenon before in celebrity-rich sectors like professional sports, pop music, and blockbuster films. But this was different. Suddenly, uneven income distributions were spreading like wildfire, popping up in far less glamorous professions, like accountants, physicians, and academics.

What was causing the shift? As Robert H. Frank and Philip J. Cook explain in their 1995 book, *The Winner-Take-All Society*, technological advances are often accompanied by a troubling side effect: they increase competition for the best jobs, contributing to the rise of "winner-take-all" markets.

Frank and Cook offer the example of opera singers to illustrate how technological advances elevate competition. In the nineteenth century, opera singers were everywhere. Large, renowned opera companies were a fixture in cities all over Europe. Because travel in those days was difficult, opera companies were limited to specific locations, and if you longed to become a professional opera singer in the 1800s, your barrier to entry was relatively low. All you had to do was sing more beautifully than other performers living within a few miles of your home.

That changed dramatically in the twentieth century, when innovations in travel, recording devices, and radio communications decimated geographic boundaries. Standout performers were no longer limited to live performances in their home city—they could now be enjoyed on records, cassettes, and compact discs anytime, anywhere.

This was extraordinary news for music lovers. But it was a devastating development for average singers, who were no longer competing with just their neighbors. Now they were up against the likes of Luciano Pavarotti.

You don't have to be an economist to recognize that this line of reasoning extends well beyond the world of classical music. By making it easier for employers to find and hire exceptional performers, technological advances foster greater competition in every field.

No matter what you do for a living, you're facing significantly more competition than your colleagues did a decade back. You're no longer up against professionals only in your region. You're now competing with experts around the globe. Never before has it been simpler for clients and hiring managers to identify the best in your field and invite them to collaborate.

But there's a silver lining. Because if you do manage to differentiate yourself in valuable ways, positioning yourself as the Pavarotti of your profession, the rewards awaiting you are exponentially greater than those available to the stars of previous generations.

So, how do you achieve that level of success? One major piece of the puzzle involves cultivating the ability to learn quickly so that you can continue to master new skills.

In a world where expertise is a moving target, the ongoing pursuit of knowledge is imperative to getting ahead. Staying on top of new innovations and professional trends is no longer just for go-getters—it's a basic requirement for staying relevant.

Of course, the right kind of learning does much more than just help you stay current. It also bolsters your creativity, empowers you to pluck valuable ideas from adjacent fields, and enables you to acquire a unique combination of skills. Over time, those factors add up, multiplying your chances of making meaningful contributions and enabling you to stand out from thousands of other professionals in your field.

In the past, education was the domain of academia. Today, traditional education can't keep up. By the time an important innovation is even mentioned in a classroom or online course, chances are it's already several years old. Educational institutions were simply not designed for a world of rapid innovation.

The upshot is clear. In today's fast-moving, highly competitive landscape, enterprising professionals need a new approach. One that enables them to grow their skills on an ongoing basis, frees them up from waiting on educators, and empowers them to stay on top of vital developments in real time.

Which brings us back to the one place on Earth where the majority of professionals are self-taught: Silicon Valley.

Steve Jobs never forgave Bill Gates for Windows.

Nor was he willing to concede an inch during their showdown. No matter what zingers Gates had at the ready, Jobs was convinced: Windows would never have existed had Microsoft not been developing software for the Macintosh.

Back in Apple's boardroom, Jobs deflects Gates's stinging comment about Xerox. Changing the topic, he asks for a private demonstration of Windows. Gates consents. A few minutes in, Jobs delivers his verdict.

"Oh, it's actually really a piece of shit," he announces dismissively, feigning relief.

Gates is all too willing to allow Jobs this brief victory, this opportunity to save face. "Yes," he tells Jobs, "it's a nice little piece of shit."

Less than a decade later, Windows would dominate the market, becoming the most successful operating system in the world. Apple, meanwhile, was hanging on by a thread, its business in shambles. By 1997, Apple was on the verge of shuttering its doors when a last-minute investment, a $150 million infusion of capital, kept it afloat. That money came from none other than Bill Gates.

Still, Jobs was merciless toward Gates. He couldn't help himself, especially when invited by reporters to comment on his rival. "Bill is basically unimaginative and has never invented anything," Jobs explained to his biographer Walter Isaacson. "[It's] why I think he's more comfortable now with philanthropy than technology. He just shamelessly ripped off other people's ideas."

His bitterness notwithstanding, Jobs would eventually get the last laugh.

In 2005, both he and Gates were invited to the birthday celebration of a Microsoft engineer. Jobs was there as a favor to the engineer's wife, a longtime friend, and came grudgingly, reluctant to share an evening of wining and dining with Bill Gates. What he didn't realize was that this dinner party would fundamentally alter the future of Apple.

Eager to impress his boss, Microsoft's engineer proceeded to describe in great detail a project he was working on and how it was about to revolutionize computers. It was a tablet — one, he suggested, that could render laptops obsolete. He went on and on about the device's elegant design, its practicality, its portability. He was especially proud of a stylus that came with each unit and made it simple to use. At one point, he teasingly suggested that Jobs consider licensing his work because this device was going to change the industry.

Outwardly, Jobs played along. Inside, ideas were percolating.

The following morning, Jobs collected his team and presented them with a challenge: "I want to make a tablet, and it can't have a keyboard or a stylus." He wasn't interested in duplicating Microsoft's efforts — he was going to evolve the idea they were developing and do them one better.

Six months later, Apple had a prototype — one that enabled users to type on a glass screen using only their fingers. "This is the future," Jobs declared upon seeing it. But instead of authorizing his team to proceed with production, he threw them for a loop. He suggested they apply this touch-sensitive technology to another project, one that had stymied Apple's engineers for months. For the time being, the tablet would be shelved.

A little over a year later, Steve Jobs stepped onto the stage of the annual Macworld Conference in San Francisco and held up a new product that would turn Apple into the world's most profitable company: the iPhone.

This time, it was Bill Gates's turn to feel outmaneuvered. Years later, he would reveal his initial reaction. "Oh my God," Gates remembered thinking, "Microsoft didn't aim high enough."

The rivalry of Steve Jobs and Bill Gates contains all the elements of a Shakespearean masterpiece: flawed protagonists, endless conflict, fallen alliances, betrayal, revenge, catharsis, even a tragic, early death. At its center are two remarkable characters — Jobs, the idealistic creative visionary, and Gates, the shrewd programming savant—and it is tempting to lavish all of our attention on their personalities, shortcomings, and genius.

But what makes their story especially fascinating is not just the complexities of who they were or the decades-long battle they waged over the future of personal computing. It's the overlooked process that quietly reappears again and again in both of their stories, somehow always playing a role behind their biggest innovations: reverse engineering.

Both Jobs and Gates reaped enormous benefit from studying the works of their contemporaries, extracting crucial insights, and applying those lessons to develop new products. And they are not alone. The history of computing is not a history of independent acts of brilliance. It is the story of probing innovators learning from one another, combining ideas from multiple sources, and introducing new products and technologies that evolve from those preceding them.

And while you might assume that reverse engineering has limited value outside the world of computing, its applications are surprisingly broad, actionable, and compelling. In fact, as you'll soon discover, reverse engineering is not just a favored tool of business titans—it's one commonly utilized by literary giants, prizewinning chefs, comedy legends, Hall of Fame musicians, and championship sports teams.

More important, it's one you can apply in your field to learn from your contemporaries, extract valuable ideas, and evolve your work in exciting new directions.

This book is presented in two parts.

Part I explores how standout performers across a variety of industries reverse engineer works they admire to unlock hidden insights, acquire new skills, and spark their creativity. We'll unpack their techniques and identify practices we can all use to find patterns, discern formulas, and pinpoint precisely what makes the work we gravitate toward resonant and unique.

From there, we'll discover the inherent drawback of outright duplication and examine the importance of modifying formulas in ways that combine winning blueprints with our unique strengths. As we will soon see, in a majority of cases, copying or over-relying on established recipes is a losing strategy that rarely results in memorable outcomes. Just as dangerous, however, is ignoring proven formulas altogether and overwhelming audiences with a flood of originality. We'll investigate why that is, learn how some of the most innovative people in the world successfully evolve formulas in ways that leverage (rather than violate) an audience's expectations, and discuss ways we can apply their strategies to our own work.

Part II is about transforming knowledge into mastery. It's one thing to reverse engineer the ingredients required to produce sensational work, and quite another to execute against that knowledge effectively.

Reverse engineering outstanding examples is often accompanied by an unsettling sensation: the recognition of a divide between the work you aim to produce and the skills you currently possess. The chapters in this section offer a road map for scaling this "vision-ability gap" using a range of evidence-based strategies that empower you to master new skills.

We'll learn how a simple scoreboard can fuel improvement, why most people's definition of practice is far too limited, and why the vast majority of feedback is surprisingly detrimental. We'll discover how experts predict the future (and what that teaches us about mastery), the ideal time to ask for feedback, and the best questions to ask an expert whose success you wish to deconstruct. And we'll identify a variety of practical opportunities for stretching our skills and pushing our abilities to soaring heights without jeopardizing our career or putting our reputation on the line.

Along the way, we'll encounter some fascinating people with extraordinary tales. We'll meet a famed artist who reverse engineered his way to the top of his profession without any formal education, a president whose historic election was a testament to the power of mash-ups, and a best-selling author whose inability to emulate his idols resulted in the creation of a new literary genre.

Throughout these pages, you'll come across a range of actionable strategies grounded in cutting-edge research. We'll cover dozens of peer-reviewed studies, drawn from a wide array of fields including neuroscience, evolutionary biology, human motivation, sports psychology, learning, memory, expertise, literature, film, music, marketing, business, and computer science—all of which shed new light on ways we can decode masterful performances, elevate our skills, and produce remarkable work.

By the end of this book, you're going to have a critical new skill. One that empowers you to take apart examples you admire, pinpoint precisely what makes them work, and apply that knowledge to develop inventive, winning formulas that are uniquely your own.

Part I

The Art of Unlocking Hidden Patterns

The Mastery Detectives

Throughout our lives, we've been told two major stories about extraordinary achievement and the human capacity for greatness.

The first story is that greatness comes from talent. According to this view, we are all born with certain innate strengths. Those at the top of their field succeed by discovering an inner talent and matching it to a profession that allows them to shine.

The second story is that greatness comes from practice. From this perspective, talent gets you only so far. What really matters is an effective practice regimen and a willingness to do lots of hard work.

There is a third story about greatness, one that's not often shared. Yet it's a path to skill acquisition and mastery that's stunningly common among icons everywhere, from artists and writers to chefs and athletes to inventors and entrepreneurs.

It's called reverse engineering.

To reverse engineer is to look beyond what is evident on the surface and find a hidden structure—one that reveals both how an object was designed and, more important, how it can be re-created. It's the ability to taste an intoxicating dish and deduce its recipe, to listen to a beautiful song and discern its chord progression, to watch a horror film and grasp its narrative arc.

In industries ranging from literature and the arts to the world of business, examples abound of elite performers whose achievements would have been impossible had they not first deconstructed the work of others.

Consider filmmaker Judd Apatow. Apatow has written, directed, or produced some of the most successful comedies of his generation, including *Anchorman*, *Bridesmaids*, and *The 40-Year-Old Virgin*. How did he learn his craft? By systematically deconstructing the success of every comedian he admired.

Apatow's secret weapon was a radio show with an audience of one.

Back in high school, Apatow was a comedy fanatic, obsessing over comedians the way others his age obsessed over rock stars. He collected albums, planned his week around television appearances, and worked summers washing dishes at the local comedy club. On a whim, he joined his high school's radio station, where he noticed something peculiar: the station's teenage DJ was landing interviews with a number of surprisingly impressive bands.

That's when the idea hit him. He'd create a radio show of his own and use it to get career advice from every luminary in the field.

"I would call their agents or PR people and say I was Judd Apatow from WKWZ radio on Long Island and I was interested in interviewing their client," he later wrote. "I would neglect to mention that I was fifteen years old. Since most of those representatives were based in Los Angeles, they didn't realize that the signal to our station barely made it out of the parking lot. Then I would show up for the interview and they would realize that they had been had."

The ruse paid off handsomely. Over the next two years, Apatow interviewed the who's who of comedy—Jerry Seinfeld, Garry Shandling, John Candy, Sandra Bernhard, Howard Stern, Henny Youngman, Martin Short, "Weird Al" Yankovic, Jay Leno—on everything from how they developed their material, to how to they landed an agent, to the best way to get noticed.

In those interviews Apatow learned that seven years is the amount of time it takes to discover your voice and hit your stride, that going more than a few days without performing disrupts your delivery, and that the single most important thing a novice comedian can do to improve is to get up onstage as often as possible, if only to dull the stage fright.

Many of Apatow's recordings never aired. The radio program, of course, was beside the point. By the time he graduated high school, Apatow had assembled what he's termed a "blueprint" and "bible" for writing jokes, developing his craft, and building a career.

Interviewing your idols can be an effective strategy for uncovering their secrets (as long as you hit on the right questions—more on that in chapter 7). You don't even need to pretend you work for a radio station. In today's burgeoning world of blogs and podcasts, it's never been easier to engage experts in a conversation. But what if they're not willing to talk to you? Or worse, what if they're dead?

Not too long ago, best-selling author Joe Hill faced this very conundrum while working on a new book. His writing had stalled, and he knew precisely the type of tune-up it needed. So he turned to the work of legendary crime novelist and master of suspense Elmore Leonard.

"I put my book aside, and for about two weeks I rewrote *The Big Bounce*," Hill explained in an interview with *10-Minute Writer's Workshop*. "Every day I would open the book and write the first two pages, copying sentence by sentence, just to get the feel for his rhythms and the way he wrote dialogue and the way he suggested character in just a couple lines. . . . I only needed about two weeks with Elmore to find my way back to the kind of rhythm and the kind of jazzy, light feel you need to write a thriller. By studying his voice, I was able to find my way back to my own."

Hill was applying an approach he'd picked up from his dad, who had stumbled upon the practice back when he was six years old and stuck at home with tonsillitis. To pass the time, Hill's father took to copying comic books panel by panel, occasionally introducing his own material and riffing on the plotlines. The practice served him well. He doesn't write many comics anymore, but he has sold more than 350 million books. His name is Stephen King.

Both King and Hill were utilizing forms of copywork, a technique popularized by Benjamin Franklin and practiced by literary greats F. Scott Fitzgerald, Jack London, and Hunter Thompson. It involves studying an exceptional piece of writing, setting it aside, and then re-creating it word for word from memory, later comparing your version to the original.

Many of the painters we now celebrate as creative geniuses devoted a significant portion of their careers to copywork. Claude Monet, Pablo Picasso, Mary Cassatt, Paul Gauguin, and Paul Cézanne all developed their skills by copying the works of the French painter Eugène Delacroix. Delacroix himself spent years copying the Renaissance artists he grew up admiring. And even those Renaissance greats—Raphael, Leonardo da Vinci, Michelangelo—honed their craft by reproducing the work of their fellow artists, including one another.

What makes copywork so effective is that it forces an artist or writer to do more than simply recall content. Reproducing a piece demands that he or she pay careful attention to the organizational decisions and stylistic tendencies reflected in an original work. It is an exercise that enables novices to relive the creative journey and invites them to compare their instinctive inclinations against the choices of a master.

Ultimately, what the process reveals is decision-making patterns. And once an artist or writer's underlying code is broken, it can be defined, analyzed, and applied to producing original works.

A Primer to Reverse Engineering Books, Songs, and Photographs

Copywork is one method for revealing a hidden formula, but it's far from the only approach. Another, popular among nonfiction writers, is to leaf through the endnotes section at the back of a book and examine the original sources an author used to construct their piece. It's the writer's equivalent of enjoying a delicious meal at a restaurant and then raiding the chef's pantry to uncover the ingredients.

The index is equally prized because it helps writers unpack an author's thinking, sometimes even their own. The author Chuck Klosterman, for example, relishes the moment he gets to read the index of his new book because of how much of himself it reveals.

"Exploring the index from a book you created," he wrote in the introduction to a recent essay collection, "is like having someone split your head open with an axe so that you can peruse the contents of your brain. It's the alphabetizing of your consciousness."

Within fiction, the search for successful patterns dates all the way back to ancient Greece. In *Poetics*, Aristotle offered his analysis of what makes the best stories different. Among his conclusions: a three-part structure (beginning, middle, end) and the skillful use of surprises, especially plot twists that involve a reversal of fortune.

More recently, literary giant Kurt Vonnegut introduced a fascinating tool for exposing a story's architecture. If you read a lot of novels or watch a lot of movies, you've probably noticed that most narratives tend to follow a formula. The vast majority of stories are iterations on a small handful of plots. These include rag to riches (e.g., *Rocky*, *Oliver Twist*, *Ready Player One*), boy meets girl (e.g., *Grease*, *Jane Eyre*, most romantic comedies), and the hero's journey (e.g., *Star Wars*, *The Lion King*, *The Lord of the Rings*).

What makes each of these plots so compelling is their distinct emotional arc. The typical rags-to-riches story, like *The Karate Kid*, takes audiences on an upward journey from negative to positive emotions, as an overlooked hero goes from being an object of scorn and ridicule at the beginning to one worthy of recognition, appreciation, and praise by the end.

Contrast that to a hero's journey story like *The Wizard of Oz*, where the emotional terrain is quite different. Here, an ordinary character leads an average life when an unforeseen event thrusts her into danger. What follows is an emotional roller coaster, as the hero navigates obstacle after obstacle, overcoming impossible circumstances, mastering uncertainty, and acquiring skill and confidence along the way.

Vonnegut believed that the world's most popular stories—including those featured in the Bible, literary classics, and blockbuster films—fit neatly into one of six trajectories:

1. Rags to Riches (a rising emotional arc)
2. Riches to Rags (a falling emotional arc)

3. Man in a Hole (a fall followed by a rise)
4. Icarus (a rise followed by a fall)
5. Cinderella (rise, fall, rise)
6. Oedipus (fall, rise, fall)

To unlock a particular story's emotional arc, Vonnegut recommended a simple exercise: plot the protagonist's fortune on a graph.

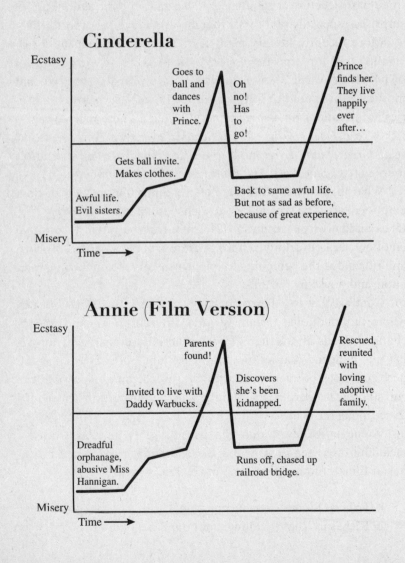

Cinderella

Ecstasy

Goes to ball and dances with Prince.

Oh no! Has to go!

Prince finds her. They live happily ever after...

Gets ball invite. Makes clothes.

Awful life. Evil sisters.

Back to same awful life. But not as sad as before, because of great experience.

Misery

Time ⟶

Annie (Film Version)

Ecstasy

Parents found!

Invited to live with Daddy Warbucks.

Discovers she's been kidnapped.

Rescued, reunited with loving adoptive family.

Dreadful orphanage, abusive Miss Hannigan.

Runs off, chased up railroad bridge.

Misery

Time ⟶

It's an illuminating activity—and not just for analyzing successful novels and movies. It's also one that writers can apply to their own work to access a 30,000-foot view of their story and pinpoint events that stall or detract from their emotional arc.

A few years ago, nearly seventy years after Vonnegut first posed his theory, data scientists crunched two enormous databases of nearly 2,000 novels and more than 6,000 movie scripts and found overwhelming support for the contention that most stories follow one of these six narrative arcs. Today, Vonnegut is best known for his provocative science fiction. But his more lasting contribution to literature may turn out to be the analytical tool he gave writers for dissecting content they admire and fine-tuning their original work.

While the hunt for winning patterns inside popular fiction has received renewed interest in recent years, it's been foundational to the education of musicians for generations. Learning to play an instrument, after all, is achieved by actively reproducing songs note for note. A novice might start with "Twinkle, Twinkle, Little Star" or "Happy Birthday to You" and later graduate to Louis Armstrong, Mozart, or Lizzo. It's a process that compels budding musicians to scrutinize a song's melody, chord progression, and arrangement.

This participatory tradition may explain why musicians are considerably more open about their efforts to reverse engineer songs than creatives in adjacent fields. To appreciate just how open, run a quick search on YouTube. If a song is even remotely popular, chances are you're a click away from a video showing you precisely how it's played on live instruments.

Not too long ago, if you wanted to learn a popular song, you had to befriend an experienced musician or visit a music store and purchase sheet music. Not anymore. Today, an app called Capo allows you to reference any song on your iPhone and instantly bring up its chords, tempo, and key.

Musicians take pride in uncovering one another's tricks—and they're not the only ones. The same can be said of enterprising photographers.

When most people look at a photo, they focus on objects. Professionals direct their attention to something entirely different: the shadows. Years of experience have taught them to scan images for clues revealing how they were constructed. The length and direction of shadows are telling: they suggest camera angle, time of day, and lens aperture. Then there's the richness and intensity of the shadows. Sharp, defined edges suggest a hard light source, while diffuse shading indicates softer lighting.

And that's just the beginning. Seasoned photographers also search for reflections, such as those that often appear in a subject's eyes, to determine where the light source was placed. They can also approximate camera lens by the level of distortion and contrast between a photo's foreground and background. All that *before* an image is imported into Photoshop for a more detailed, computer-assisted analysis.

Decoding Deliciousness

In the late 1980s, long before the days of email, an anonymous letter began arriving in mailboxes, claiming to reveal the secret recipe to Mrs. Fields brand chocolate chip cookies. The letter was purportedly sent by an irate customer who had purchased the recipe from a Mrs. Fields shop for what she thought was $2.50, only to discover on her credit card statement that she had actually been charged $250. The store, she claimed, refused to refund her payment. Distributing their recipe was her revenge.

Much to the disappointment of hundreds of home cooks, the recipe in the letter was bogus. But it did achieve one outcome: inspiring Todd Wilbur to pursue an unusual career.

Wilbur is the brains behind Top Secret Recipes, a culinary juggernaut that today includes ten best-selling books, a reality TV show, and (ironically) a proprietary line of spice blends and rubs. Wilbur was fascinated by the sensation the fake letter had sparked and dropped everything to crack the cookie recipe everyone was after. Over the course of three weeks, he transformed his kitchen into a makeshift science lab. He proceeded to bake thousands of cookies, comparing each batch to genuine Mrs. Fields cookies purchased at the store, recording detailed notes, and tweaking the recipe with each iteration until he was satisfied that he had broken the code.

Wilbur was hooked. The next target on his radar was McDonald's Big Mac, followed by Wendy's Chili and Hostess's Twinkies. Over the last twenty-five years, Wilbur has reverse engineered hundreds of fast-food recipes. His last book was pitched as "the joy of cloning," a play on the classic cookbook title.

While Wilbur's sleuthing may sound extreme, his appetite for re-creating dishes is anything but unusual. The only thing remotely unique is that he publishes his results. Decoding successful dishes is how chefs find inspiration, test their knowledge, and acquire new skills. It's an insight implicit in the guidance of James Beard Award–winning chef Michelle Bernstein, who offers this advice to the chefs she hires to work in her kitchen: Spend all your extra money on eating out.

The reason is simple: observing the greats opens your mind to fresh possibilities.

When it comes to investigating the work of other chefs, visiting restaurants is merely one option. Today it's never been easier to analyze the menus of establishments around the globe, uncover videos of chefs demonstrating their techniques, and study photographs posted online by satisfied diners.

It's when an unusual or inspiring dish is encountered that things get really interesting. This is when the inquisitive chef transforms into a cross between a private detective and research chemist. Their first mission? To uncover a dish's ingredients.

Newer chefs may begin with an internet search of related recipes, comparing a range of approaches and identifying commonalities. More experienced chefs, on the other hand, are able to leverage their extensive experience and use their palate to formulate a guess.

Next comes hypothesis testing. Are they on the right track? The first opportunity for confirmation involves playfully interrogating a restaurant's waiter. "Is that ginger, I sense?" an undercover chef might ask teasingly. Or better yet, "Can you settle a bet? I'm positive

I taste thyme, but my husband is convinced it's tarragon. Who has the better palate?"

An alternative strategy is to order a dish to go. At home, chefs can deconstruct dishes into their elemental components. The process may involve spreading a sauce across a white plate to draw a contrast between ingredients, using tweezers and a magnifying glass to enlarge its components, tasting and guessing each step of the way.

What are chefs searching for when reverse engineering the works of others? It's not simply a cloned recipe. After all, no self-respecting chef would knowingly copy the work of others and try to pass it off as their own. They are searching for novel techniques and underlying patterns that can be applied to other dishes, enriching their repertoire.

Among the many principles a discerning chef may uncover is the importance of contrasts. Memorable dishes rarely strike a single tone—they tend to feature opposites that surprise the palate and implore diners to pay closer attention. These contrasts can take the form of soft and crunchy (mesclun greens with sunflower seeds), sweet and spicy (barbecued chicken wings), dark and bright (chopped parsley and red peppercorns sprinkled over a sizzling steak), and even hot and cold (apple crisp topped with vanilla ice cream).

Other principles come from noticing that certain flavors naturally combine beautifully together. Within music, songs are built on a foundation of note combinations known as chords. Certain notes harmonize when played together, delivering a pleasing experience. A similar observation can be made of food:

> basil + mozzarella + tomato
> garlic + ginger + soy
> coconut + mint + chilies

Each represents a unique "flavor chord," a term food writer Karen Page uses to describe combinations that tend to reappear again and again across a range of dishes. By pulling back the curtain and pinpointing the flavor combinations at the heart of a dish, chefs enhance their playbook and discover new opportunities.

Chef David Chang has built a culinary empire leveraging a pattern he identified early in his culinary career. Chang is a James Beard Award–winning chef and the founder of Momofuku, a thriving conglomerate with more than forty restaurants around the globe. He calls this pattern a "Unified Theory of Deliciousness."

"When you eat something amazing, you don't just respond to the dish in front of you," he recently wrote in *Wired*. "You are almost always transported back to another moment in your life. . . . The easiest way to accomplish this is just to cook something that people have eaten a million times. But it's much more powerful to evoke those taste memories while cooking something that seems *unfamiliar*—to hold those base patterns constant while completely changing the context."

Chang's insight is that tasting a long-forgotten flavor originally experienced in youth awakens a flood of emotions, especially when it sneaks up on you out of nowhere. The secret to creating resonant dishes, according to this perspective, is going beyond serving delicious foods. It's triggering childhood memories when they're least expected.*

How does Chang apply this formula? His approach involves searching for flavor combinations that resonate within one culinary tradition and finding their corollary in a foreign cuisine. Take the dish that placed Chang's cooking squarely at the center of New York City's food scene: Momofuku's pork bun. It's a simple dish consisting of a few ingredients: steamed bread, fatty meat, and pickled cucumbers that deliver an emphatic crunch. To picky eaters, it can seem strange—a mash-up of unusual colors and strange textures— until finally, they gather the courage to take a first bite. Consciously,

---

* Nostalgia researchers would argue that Chang is leveraging the power of comfort foods. Comfort foods really do generate positive emotions and lower stress, and not just because of their (typically) fat-rich content. It's because they subtly remind us of close relationships we enjoyed as children, especially the loved ones who cooked for us in the past.

Chang is willing to bet they find it delicious. Subconsciously, the memory he hopes it sparks is that of an American classic: the BLT.

This search for underlying patterns—like the one David Chang used to place Momofuku on the map—isn't limited to artistic endeavors. It's not just writers, painters, musicians, photographers, and chefs who deconstruct the works of others in search of a hidden code. The same can be said of successful entrepreneurs.

How to Reverse Engineer a Billion-Dollar Franchise

What separates celebrity entrepreneurs like Jeff Bezos, Mark Cuban, and Richard Branson from everyone else?

Research suggests it's not just their creativity, intelligence, and drive. Successful entrepreneurs also excel at something else: pattern recognition. They possess an extraordinary capacity for identifying profitable opportunities by linking successes they've observed in the past with changes now taking place in the market.

When we think about entrepreneurs, we tend to think about creative solutions, fresh ideas, and above all originality. As it turns out, that line of thinking is exactly wrong. Studies indicate that it's novice entrepreneurs who focus on novelty. More experienced entrepreneurs—those who spend decades leading successful businesses and reliably launch profitable ventures every few years—focus on something completely different: *viability*.

Pitch your new business idea to a few friends over dinner, and the degree of enthusiasm you receive will likely hinge on your idea's originality. Run the same idea by experienced business owners, and they'll focus instead on customer demand, the logistics of production and deliverability, and projected cash flow.

Decades of experience have taught them that successful businesses fit a pattern. A few key factors tend to predict whether or not a venture will flourish. And nowhere are these patterns more evident than in the business models of other profitable companies.

What sort of patterns might a discerning entrepreneur deduce? For one thing, that winning business strategies can be applied across industries.

When San Francisco chef Steve Ells was considering launching a taqueria in the 1970s, he knew his chances of breaking through were slim. The Bay Area was flooded with Mexican eateries, and the competition was overwhelming. So he took his idea for a streamlined Mexican restaurant to a place where tacos were relatively rare: Denver. He called it Chipotle.

Ells didn't set out to establish a franchise. He was simply trying to earn enough revenue to cover his rent. But when his first restaurant was drawing lines out the door, the potential was obvious.

What makes Ells's story so compelling is that his shop's success can, in large part, be traced back to a single decision: taking a product that's popular in one location and introducing it to an entirely new geographic region. That's an approach that applies to a lot more than tacos.

By finding the underlying business strategies embedded within case studies like Chipotle, experienced entrepreneurs develop a mental database of proven blueprints. It's what enables them to quickly identify opportunities as they arise and fuels their ability to generate more moneymaking ideas than they have the bandwidth to implement.

Consider the many prompts Chipotle's case study might generate for a forward-thinking entrepreneur:

Business Blueprint

Introduce a proven product into a new market

POSSIBLE APPLICATIONS:

- *What cuisines, beverages, or desserts are popular near me that I can introduce elsewhere?*
- *What physical products are popular near me that I can introduce elsewhere?*
- *What services are popular near me that I can introduce elsewhere?*

Then, of course, there is the flip side of this equation:

- *What cuisines, beverages, or desserts are popular else-where that I can introduce near me?*
- *What physical products are popular elsewhere that I can introduce near me?*
- *What services are popular elsewhere that I can introduce near me?*

Chipotle is one of many booming chains that emerged using this blueprint. Another is Starbucks.

In the 1980s, Starbucks consisted of a handful of stores selling coffee beans to connoisseurs. One day, Starbucks' newly hired marketing director, a former Xerox salesman named Howard Schultz, visited Milan and encountered espresso bars. Schultz was riveted. There was nothing like this back home. Americans were used to tasteless supermarket coffee and so-called coffee shops that were little more than glorified diners. Could a coffeehouse culture take off in Seattle?

Starbucks' leadership had no interest in finding out. They were adamant about avoiding the hospitality business. But Schultz persisted, eventually convincing the company's CEO to allow him to run a pilot. It worked magnificently. But despite its popularity, the founders still opposed Schultz's plan for creating more stores.

Reluctantly, Schultz quit the company and opened his own espresso bar. His original foray reveals just how much his business model relied on re-creating (or transplanting) the Italian experience into Seattle. Schultz's store was called Il Giornale, after an Italian newspaper in Milan. Its baristas wore white shirts and bowties, its speakers played opera music, and its menu was loaded with Italian terms. A few years later, when Schultz's old employer was ready to sell its coffee bean business, Schultz had enough money in the bank to pounce. He merged the two businesses under the original Starbucks name.

To outside observers, entrepreneurs can seem like prodigies. They are a tornado of ideas and seemingly possess an uncanny ability to generate business ideas on demand. It's only once you start thinking in formulas that you see for yourself: entrepreneurial opportunities are everywhere.

The Secret Lives of Weapons, Drugs, and Race Cars

Not all attempts at reverse engineering are as benign as a shrewd marketer analyzing a popular franchise. Sometimes the stakes are far greater. That's because in some industries reverse engineering is a matter of life and death.

Suppose you are a world leader, and your country is embroiled in a war. A close ally has developed a devastating new weapon that fundamentally recasts the playing field in your favor. Initially, you are elated. Then it occurs to you. At the moment you are partnered on the same side. But what happens when the war is over? Will your nation truly be safe in a world where you are militarily overmatched?

Josef Stalin wrestled with these exact questions in 1944. The United States had recently debuted the B-29 Superfortress, the aircraft that would be responsible for dropping a nuclear bomb on the cities of Hiroshima and Nagasaki. It was a game changer. The Soviets had nuclear weapons in their arsenal but lacked the required delivery mechanism to make them much of a threat.

So when over the course of warfare, a B-29 made an emergency landing in the eastern Russian city of Vladivostok, Stalin's people saw an opportunity. They immediately got to work, ripping apart the plane, disassembling it into individual parts. Each component was systematically weighed, measured, and catalogued. A massive team of designers and engineers worked frantically to duplicate every square inch of the aircraft, alongside government-controlled factories tasked with manufacturing the necessary parts.

Three short years later, the Soviets debuted a long-range bomber at their annual military airshow. They called it the Tu-4. It was indistinguishable from the B-29 in virtually every way except its name.

Reverse engineering seized weaponry is hardly limited to the Russians. The history of military technological advances is teeming with stories just like it. In fact, it's a practice that's still very much alive today. In just the last decade alone, Iran's military has reportedly reverse engineered jet fighters, helicopters, missiles, "invulnerable" Humvees, and high-tech Lockheed Martin military spy drones. And those are just the weapons we know about.

While reverse engineering has led to a proliferation of deadly weapons, that's just one extreme. On the other end of the spectrum is its unmistakable contribution to the world of medicine.

Today, more than 90 percent of the medications we consume are generics—pharmaceutical drugs modeled after formulas patented by large corporations. Generic medications provide extraordinary benefits. Without them, large swaths of the world's population would lack access to lifesaving drugs.

Most consumers assume that after a drug's patent expires, its formula is made public, enabling other drug companies to reproduce the medication as a generic. But that's seldom the case. More often than not, pharmaceutical companies wage extensive legal and regulatory battles that prevent their formulations from ever seeing the light of day. Generics are rarely produced using an established formula. Rather, they are developed through a series of complex laboratory methodologies collectively known as "deformulation"—so called because they enable scientists to work backward, transforming a single tablet or pill from a finished formula into its individual chemical components.

Deformulation doesn't require decades of education or an expensive laboratory. It's available to anyone with internet access and a credit card, courtesy of the many specialized labs around the globe that boast years of experience deconstructing far more than just medications. They're prepared to uncover detailed recipes for an impressive array of products, ranging from high-end cosmetics, shampoos, and perfumes to paints, adhesives, and laundry detergents.

The fee? A modest two thousand dollars.

Decades ago, taking apart a successful product, determining its ingredients, and mapping out its precise blueprint would have required a huge investment of both time and capital. Not anymore. And while some manufacturers might bemoan the ease with which their inventions can be re-created, others have adopted a more enlightened attitude.

Take the automotive industry, where reverse engineering has played a pivotal role for generations. In 1933, after disassembling a new Chevrolet, Kiichiro Toyoda convinced his family to branch out from building weaving looms by creating an automotive development program. Three years later, they had their first car and renamed the venture Toyota (a simplified version of the family name produced by eight brushstrokes—a lucky number in Japan).

Almost a century later, Toyoda's once maverick approach has been co-opted into standard operating procedure. Today, car manufacturers routinely dissect their rivals' cars, except they don't call the process reverse engineering. They call it "competitive benchmarking."

Like Stalin's army, a team of engineers descend on a competitor's car and systematically disassemble it, part by individual part, rigorously cataloging their findings in search of technological advances, potential cost savings, and clues on an automaker's strategic direction.

What makes the automotive industry especially noteworthy is not just that all the major players in the field reverse engineer their competitors or that they openly acknowledge that reverse engineering is taking place. It's the fact that in recent years, car manufacturers have begun collectively sharing the production cost of competitive intelligence, even when it includes proprietary insights into their own products.

This arrangement is courtesy of a clever French company called A2Mac1. Founded in 1997 by a pair of car-obsessed brothers, A2Mac1 dismantles cars full-time and sells its reports as a subscription service. Their Netflix-like database includes more than six hundred car "teardowns" and contains a detailed analysis of every single component, down to the weight, geometry, and manufacturer of the tiniest bolt. A2Mac1 even allows subscribers to check out individual car parts for physical inspection and has recently taken to scanning parts in 3D so that customers can view them remotely, using virtual reality glasses.

If you've ever wondered why cars have become so much more reliable over the last two decades, A2Mac1 may deserve some portion of the credit.* By empowering automotive manufacturers to learn from one another more easily, the performance of an entire industry has been lifted considerably in a remarkably short period of time. Instead of frowning upon the practice of reverse engineering or denying that it is taking place, the automotive industry has come to realize that shared access to knowledge can actually deliver significant, industry-wide benefits.

The Wrong Way to Think About Creativity

There is a stigma associated with sifting through and unpacking the works of others, especially in fields that involve creativity. It stems from the belief that creativity requires originality and that, by definition, originality can't possibly be found inside the works of others. Creative professionals are rightly sensitive to accusations of imitation and plagiarism. And this is why, among some, there is legitimate concern that studying others closely, no matter how benign their intentions, will influence their approach, encourage duplication, and reduce them to hacks.

But these views represent the wrong way of thinking about creativity. They reflect an idealistic rigidity that is both unrealistic and counterproductive, especially in fields that evolve by the day.

First, creativity comes from blending ideas, not isolation. When we're exposed to new ideas and fresh perspectives, we are at our most generative. This is why one of the best predictors of creativity is openness to experience. Those who actively seek out novelty, embrace curiosity, and plunge down rabbit holes are far more creative than those who shut themselves off from the outside world.

Second, originality is not the same thing as creativity. Often,

---

* Over the past decade, the average price of a ten-year-old car has risen by 75 percent. Yet over the same time period, the average price of a brand-new car has increased by only 25 percent. Older cars are retaining their value for far longer than they used to.

those who introduce new concepts are locked into certain ways of thinking, preventing them from identifying important and novel applications for their "original" ideas. The business world is bursting with examples of "first movers" being outmaneuvered by scrappier, more creative rivals. As the creators of the PalmPilot, Atari, Alta Vista, Friendster, and America Online will all readily admit: being first is not the same as being best.

Finally, far from short-circuiting our creativity, reverse engineering enables us to acquire new skills, which empower us to be generative in entirely new ways. And that's important, especially given the speed with which most industries are now evolving. If reverse engineering the world's most successful blogs over a weekend enables you to launch an arresting new blog on Monday morning, blending the best practices you've identified with your niche area of expertise, you've effectively multiplied your creative capacity and reach.

Simply put: the alternative to reverse engineering isn't originality. It's operating with intellectual blinders.

To be sure, there are those who abuse the methodologies described in this book. There are companies whose entire business model consists of duplicating winning products and selling them to customers at a lower price, and there are countries that show little regard for the intellectual property of those living outside their borders.

But to focus on them would be missing the point. Because the existence of parasitic copycats does not negate the educational value of reverse engineering any more than a serial killer negates the value of a table knife.

Most professionals are not interested in copying existing products. They're after something far more crucial and valuable: a proven recipe that can be applied in a fresh context and leveraged in novel ways.

And while it's reasonable to predict that studying formulas buried within works we admire might stifle our creativity, as it turns out, the evidence suggests the opposite.

How Copying Makes You More Original

Over drinks one night, a friend invites you to a weekend drawing workshop. You're not very artsy, but you like this friend and you can use a distraction. Before you know it, you blurt out, "Why not?"

At the art studio, you're greeted with an unwelcome surprise: you and your friend will be placed in different groups. Just as you're about to object, the instructor adds that at the end of the weekend, each group's final drawings will be evaluated by a professional artist. "We're going to find out who is more creative!" Now your competitive juices are flowing. Your friend is equally excited. You're both eager to win.

The thing the instructor doesn't tell you—the twist you don't discover until after the weekend is over—is that you and your friend receive different training. While you're told to sketch object after object, drilling for three days straight, your friend's group receives similar instructions with one important variation. In addition to sketching objects, on the second day of training she is invited to copy a professional drawing and then told to resume sketching objects.

So here's the question: Which of you is more likely to be creative on the final day of the workshop? You—the one who spent all weekend drawing original works? Or your friend—who, in addition to generating her own drawings, paused to replicate the work of an established artist before resuming her original sketches?

That was the precise question at the core of a fascinating 2017 paper published in *Cognitive Science*. Takeshi Okada and Kentaro Ishibashi, creativity experts at the University of Tokyo, ran a series of experiments, including a three-day session similar to the scenario I asked you to consider. What they found poses a serious challenge to the way most of us have been taught to think about creativity.

Not only did copying an artist's drawing inspire far more creative illustrations later on, it did so by stimulating ideas that had nothing to do with the copied artist's work. In other words, copying didn't simply lead people to mimic an established approach. It unlocked a mind-set of curiosity and openness that motivated them to take their work in fresh, unanticipated directions.

Now, let's pause here and acknowledge the obvious: the idea that copying an existing work leads to more creativity is wildly counterintuitive. After all, isn't copying the very antithesis of originality? How, then, do the researchers account for this finding?

By differentiating between the act of copying and the work it subsequently inspires. In the short term, replicating a work won't result in creativity. It's *afterward* that the real magic happens.

The process of copying—of carefully analyzing a particular work, deconstructing its key components, and rebuilding it anew—is a transformative mental exercise that does wonders for our thinking. Unlike the experience we get when we passively consume a work, copying demands that we pay meticulous attention, prompting us to reflect on both subtle details and unexpected techniques.

But it's more than just heightened scrutiny. Copying also forces us to contemplate the decisions an artist made and sensitizes us to opportunities we typically overlook. In so doing, copying challenges our default approach. It opens us up to novel ways of thinking, prompting us to find creative opportunities buried within our own work.

In contrast, looking inward for creative ideas rarely gets us very far. Studies indicate that staying fixated on our own work and avoiding outside influences causes us to grow increasingly less creative over time. Psychologists have a raft of terms for the cognitive traps that result from staring at a problem for too long—the Einstellung effect, mental sets, functional fixedness—all of which can be summarized in a simple dictum: there is a price to working in isolation. Invariably, we find ourselves considering fewer options, recycling the same tired ideas again and again, or falling back on familiar solutions that have worked in the past.

It gets worse. Over time, we fall prey to unspoken assumptions about what a good solution looks like, which further limits our thinking. And the longer we spend turning over a problem in our head, the less likely we are to stumble upon a truly innovative idea.

Far from making us unoriginal, copying breaks the spell. It challenges our assumptions, relaxes our cognitive constraints, and opens us up to new perspectives. No, deconstructing works we admire doesn't weaken our creativity or lead us to produce derivative work. On the contrary: it's an essential tool for breaking down the hidden barriers that keep us stuck.

So how do you do it? How do you take apart work you admire — from your favorite podcast to a competitor's website to an Academy Award–winning film—enabling you to extract its formula and unleash your own creative juices? Is there a reliable road map for deconstructing works we wish to emulate?

And perhaps the bigger question is this: Can the practice of reverse engineering itself be reverse engineered?

Algorithmic Thinking

A lyssa Nathan was twenty-two when she met Josh Yanover. They exchanged a few shy texts, then a few more. He suggested they go out. On their first date, they visited a paint and wine studio. It went well. After some time, she noticed that the studio had emptied and employees were cleaning up. She asked one of them if they were getting ready to close. "Sweetie, we've *been* closed for forty-five minutes."

It was late, but they weren't ready to call it a night. Not even close. On a whim, they ventured out to a pizzeria Josh was crazy about, where they shared a delicious mushroom slice and their first kiss. It was the perfect date. Less than two years later, they were ready to spend the rest of their lives together and finalizing plans for their wedding.

Alyssa and Josh owe their marriage to an algorithm. They met online on the world's most popular dating app: Tinder.

Not too long ago, the idea of searching for a romantic partner on a website was considered an act of desperation. Today, that stigma has disappeared. Studies suggest that nearly 40 percent of romantic relationships now begin online and that they tend to be considerably *more* successful than those initiated in person. In other words, they are more likely to deliver the sort of riveting storybook ending experienced by Alyssa and Josh.

One reason online dating apps are so effective at pairing couples is that they utilize machine learning to identify unspoken preferences—ones people themselves may not consciously realize they possess. Each time a user like Alyssa swipes right or lingers on an image or clicks to expand a profile or responds to a text, Tinder's algorithm takes note. These actions indicate interest. The algorithm then takes all the men to whom Alyssa has devoted time and attention and analyzes the features they have in common. Are they tall or short? What's their average age? Do their profiles suggest they are outgoing and adventurous or studious and shy?

What Tinder's algorithm is searching for is a recipe—one that captures the features of Alyssa's ideal man. The better the algorithm gets at identifying Alyssa's preferences, the more effectively it can present her with suitors she deems attractive and the greater her chances of finding Mr. Right.

In recent years, algorithms like Tinder's have upended a wide swath of industries, in large part because of their ability to quickly detect patterns. The capacity to distill thousands of clicks, scrolls, and swipes into a formula and then apply that formula to predict future behavior has profound implications for the worlds of business, technology, and even romantic love.

It's also a process that shares obvious commonalities with reverse engineering. Converting a remarkable story, symphony, or photograph into a recipe similarly involves extrapolating beyond what is apparent in any single example. It requires stepping back, deducing patterns, and producing a formula.

In many ways, identifying patterns is what humans do best. In fact, for generations, it was a basic requirement of staying alive.

Over the course of human history, our ancestors relied on pattern recognition to predict all kinds of things, including where food could be found, what color plants were likely to be poisonous, and the time of day it was safe to wander the savannah. To survive in a dangerous landscape, you needed to be able to read your environment and draw inferences about what would happen next. And while excelling at pattern recognition may no longer be a matter of life and death, psychologists believe it continues to play a vital role in predicting success and constitutes a central facet of high intelligence.

And yet, as many computer scientists have noted, thanks to technological advances, we have now reached a point where the ability of computers to detect patterns far surpasses our own.

Which raises some intriguing questions: What exactly makes algorithms so good at pattern recognition? And what can they teach us to improve our ability to reverse engineer?

The short answer is a lot.

Let's start with the basics. Pattern recognition engines have four major components. The first is **data collection.** Before you can start to predict the type of men Alyssa finds attractive, you first need examples of men she likes and men she doesn't. You can get both from her reaction to a handful of profiles, and that's the first step: gathering examples.

Step two is unpacking those examples and **finding important variations.** What's *different* about these men that could be contributing to Alyssa's decisions? Obviously, there are physical features, like the men's age, weight, and height. But then there is the quality of their profile: the number of photos they post, the length of their biography, and the personality type their description conveys. The more variables you identify in this second phase, the better your chances of pinpointing a factor that prompts Alyssa's interest.

The third step involves **detecting similarities.** What do the men Alyssa finds attractive have in common? What features do they share? Now, how about the men Alyssa rejected? What differentiates them from those she liked? By comparing the characteristics of both groups—men selected against men rejected—a dating algorithm can start to identify the elements driving Alyssa's decisions.

The last step is when an algorithm applies its analyses to **generate predictions** of men Alyssa will find appealing. It's here that the options Alyssa is presented with start to look a little cuter, a little more her type. And the more Alyssa swipes, the more accurate the algorithm gets, using Alyssa's feedback to refine its predictions and improve its performance.

The Hidden Formula That Makes Your
Favorite Dish Irresistible

Given a modest number of variables, we humans do pretty well at detecting patterns. But past a certain level of complexity, our performance sinks. It's here that computer algorithms blow us out of the water. They have the bandwidth to evaluate an enormous database of features, the capacity to analyze multiple factors at the same time, and the ability to update their predictions in real time as new data are made available. They're also immune to the unconscious expectations and social pressures that can prevent us from entertaining unconventional predictions.

And those advantages add up. For a quick illustration, consider the way IBM is quietly upending the world of cooking. Not too long ago, programmers at IBM fed Watson, a machine learning program named after Thomas J. Watson, IBM's first CEO, two categories of information: research findings on foods people consider pleasing (a domain known as "hedonic psychophysics") and *Bon Appétit*'s full historical archive of recipes. They then had the program, which they named "Chef Watson," crunch the data and offer novel recipes based on patterns it had detected.

The results were remarkable. And not just because of the innovative combinations Chef Watson suggested but because of the hidden principles its algorithm had unlocked.

When we think of a successful dish, we often focus exclusively on a single factor: taste. Watson's analyses suggest that it's not taste that makes a dish irresistible—it's aroma. As it turns out, the scent of roast chicken or a hearty lobster bisque activates receptors in the nose and throat, releasing a cascade of pleasurable endorphins into the bloodstream long before we consume our first bite, sparking delight in ways we fail to register consciously.

The second insight gained from Chef Watson's findings is even more valuable, especially for chefs who are equally adept at crunching data as they are dicing vegetables. It's that aroma is, at its core, mathematical.

You don't need to go through the trouble of actually cooking a dish to determine if it produces a delightful aroma. All you need to do is fire up Excel and analyze a recipe's ingredients. Every ingredient contains certain chemicals that lend it its unique fragrance. These are called aromatic compounds. What Chef Watson's analyses reveal is that there is a hidden pattern within recipes that win awards and gushing reviews: their ingredients have lots of aromatic compounds *in common*.

Analytical, data-driven insights like these, ones that leverage complex mathematics to dig beneath the surface and uncover an invisible structure, enable Chef Watson to explain why certain foods are universally cherished. Consider pizza. According to IBM's calculations, tomatoes, mozzarella, parmesan, and baked wheat share more than one hundred different aromatic compounds, making pizza virtually irresistible to the human palate.

Watson can also apply these insights to generate new, complex, and provocative recipes that traditional chefs would never consider. Among its more compelling recommendations: a pairing of grilled asparagus with dark chocolate; roast duck with tomatoes, olives, and cherries; and chicken kabobs with strawberries, apples, and mushrooms.

Clearly, the conclusions revealed by Chef Watson's analyses would have been difficult for even the most ambitious of culinary experts to reach without the use of a powerful computer. Yet there's a lot we can learn from the programmatic approach used by algorithms like the ones driving Tinder and IBM's Watson—especially when it comes to reverse engineering work we wish to emulate.

Let's look more closely at how these algorithms unlock hidden patterns, starting with the first step: gathering examples.

Why You Need a Private Museum

It's noteworthy that the first action a computer program designed to detect patterns undertakes is not to *analyze* but to *collect*. Which is consistent with how many writers, musicians, and designers view themselves: not as master craftsmen but as collectors. They consume voraciously, pursue obsessively, and accumulate influences the way chefs hunt for ingredients.

History teaches us that a striking number of top performers appeared naturally drawn to collecting works they admired long before entering and later dominating their field. Andy Warhol collected artwork, David Bowie collected records, Julia Child collected cookbooks. Director Quentin Tarantino spent so much time consuming movies that his local video store hired him as its resident film expert to advise other customers, enabling him to watch even more movies during the day while also getting paid. Before his passing, Ernest Hemingway's library exceeded nine thousand books and was growing at a clip of nearly two hundred new titles per year, suggesting that Saul Bellow was exactly right when he observed, "A writer is a reader who is moved to emulation."

Why is collecting outstanding examples so important? Because the first step to achieving mastery is recognizing mastery in others.

For many celebrated luminaries, the journey toward mastery began as a desire for sampling works in their eventual field. Over time, that inclination led them to refine their taste, sensitizing them to elements they adore as well as conventions they despise. And much like an algorithm continues to improve by assimilating new inputs in real time, consuming examples tends to play a central role throughout a career. Novelist Tom Perrotta has been crafting stories for over thirty years. To this day, he views compulsive reading as a critical component of strong writing: "If you don't read all the time, I'm guessing you're not a writer. And that's no criticism. That's a litmus test."

Immersing yourself in examples prompts skill building in ways we don't immediately anticipate. For one thing, it enables us to absorb the conventions of a field without consciously trying. Studies indicate that simply consuming examples with an underlying structure leads you to detect their patterns, even when you're not consciously trying to learn a thing. It's a process cognitive psychologists call *implicit learning*. If you've ever found yourself captivated by the ingenuity of the first few episodes of a Netflix show, only to be bored by its formulaic predictability at the end of the season, implicit learning is likely to have played a role.

It also expands our notion of the possible. We're often told that mastery requires one thing above all else: practice. If you want to develop expertise, you need clear objectives, immediate feedback, and lots of repetition. There's a glaring problem with this formula. You can't practice an idea you've never considered. The best ideas don't emerge from hours of isolated practice. They're waiting to be found inside the work of masters.

Gathering a broad range of examples also illuminates the unique contributions of different influences. Most novel writers, for example, can appreciate that it is a rare author who proves equally adept at plot, dialogue, character development, setting, mood, and word choice. Decades of sampling a range of works has taught them that different authors excel at distinct elements. That awareness enables them to blend influences in innovative ways and empowers them to call up specific models when refining their work.

But there's another benefit to curating examples and isolating those you find compelling. Patterns are more easily found in quantity. The more remarkable examples you have to admire, study, and dissect, the easier it becomes for you to detect an underlying thread.

How to Think Like a Disruptive Innovator

So what do you do once you've gathered examples? After you've identified works you consider powerful and resonant, how do you figure out what makes them compelling?

At this point, pattern recognition algorithms unleash a flurry of analyses. They begin by searching for elements that differ from one example to the next, uncovering key features that make "successful" examples unique.

The corollary for us human pattern detectors involves playing a game that many of us enjoyed in our youth. It's called Spot the

Difference. The children's version presents two similar pictures side by side and invites viewers to identify discrepancies.

This same approach applies to unveiling patterns in examples we admire.

Here's how it works in practice. Suppose you've come across a website from a health guru you vaguely recognize. The landing page is fresh and charming and instantly draws you in. You're about to register to receive a free giveaway when you pause for a moment. "I don't usually sign up for newsletters like this," you think to yourself. "Why exactly am I drawn to this one?"

This is where the average website visitor shrugs and goes about their day. But by using Spot the Difference, you can do more than wonder. You have a concrete set of questions to begin to peel away the features that make the landing page effective.

The first and most obvious question: "How does this landing page differ from other health guru landing pages?"

Variations on this question include:

- What makes this enticing?
- What can I learn from this?
- How does this apply to a project I am working on?

Ultimately, the precise question you pose is less important than the practice of pausing when you come across a striking example and making a concerted effort to deconstruct the reasons it works.

The late Harvard Business School professor Clayton Christensen spent decades analyzing the differences between ordinary managers and disruptive innovators like Elon Musk, Reed Hastings, and Jeff Bezos. What he found is intriguing. According to Christensen's research, the personalities of managers and innovators are surprisingly comparable. Entrepreneurs are no more intelligent than middle managers, and middle managers are no less risk tolerant than entrepreneurs. The difference lies not in their *personalities* but in their *behaviors*.

On one set of behaviors, the gap between the two groups is especially striking: questioning. Compared to average managers, disruptive innovators are far more likely to act on their curiosity. It's a signature characteristic, a leading indicator of an innovative mind. Founders question; managers comply. Founders ask big-picture questions ("What's the real problem here?"), pose what-if scenarios ("What would happen if we stopped accepting cash?"), and, crucially, try to expose root causes ("What leads customers to behave this way?").

The lesson here is that taking time to question what makes a work successful should in no way feel trivial, unproductive, or academic. If you're looking to elevate your performance, questioning represents some of the most important work you can do.

Another approach that can help you spot differences involves going deep and studying a single work through multiple mediums. For example, if there is an author whose code you can't seem to crack, try listening to their audiobook for clues. Hearing authors narrate their own work reveals the voice they imagine inside their head when writing. The rhythm and cadence they utilize can convey valuable insights, and the inflection lavished on certain words can reveal an underlying intention.

Consuming text as audio is one tactic. Just as helpful: turning audio into text. If there's a speaker you admire, record their presentation and have it transcribed. If there's a show or film you want to study closely, purchase the script (or hire a transcriptionist to create one for you). If you're a musician, convert a song into notes. The more modalities you have at your fingertips, the more likely you are to identify key features that make it distinctive.

There will, however, be instances when no matter how hard you work to tease apart why an example resonates, nothing jumps out. Fortunately, there are a number of additional techniques we can use to spot the difference and identify important variations. They all stem from a single strategy that prompts us to adopt a different vantage point—one that reveals a hidden structure that's obvious only when we take a step back.

It's called *zooming out*.

How to Craft a Blueprint

In the early 1950s, a Christmas gift revolutionized professional football.

Its recipient was Wellington Mara, a World War II veteran who worked as team secretary to the National Football League's New York Giants. Mara's parents surprised him with an exciting new invention: a Polaroid camera. Instant film technology had recently made its debut and quickly became the season's hottest gift. Mara was captivated. Enamored with his newfangled contraption, he couldn't resist taking it to work.

One of the colleagues he showed it to was the team's assistant coach, Vince Lombardi.

It gave Lombardi an idea. He took Mara aside and proposed a collaboration.

From that day forward, Mara could be found at every home game near the top of the upper deck, blending in with the fans. Just before the snap of the ball, he would surreptitiously take a photo of the opposing team's formation, stuff it into a weighted sock, and wait patiently until the following play. Once fans were distracted by the action on the field, he'd chuck the sock in the direction of the Giants' bench. The intel proved invaluable. Mara's Polaroids launched the Giants on an unprecedented winning streak, landing them in the championship game (later renamed the Super Bowl) for six of the next eight years.

Today, of course, professional football teams everywhere rely on a steady stream of aerial images, delivered within seconds of a play to a color tablet. Coaches and players alike can be found studying them religiously throughout a game—and for good reason. The wide-angle shots convey information invisible to those close to the action. Nothing exposes a team's game plan faster than when opponents step back, introduce distance, and glimpse the totality of what is happening on the field.

The same principle applies to uncovering structure within works we admire. Often, zooming out to a higher level is a critical step to detecting a pattern that is impossible to recognize up close.

What does zooming out mean on a practical level? One example, used in writing, captures this approach perfectly. It's called *reverse outlining*. If you've taken even a middle school–level writing class, you'll probably remember having to write an outline. It's the process of planning a paper in advance by listing the major points you intend to address in the various sections of your piece.

Reverse outlining is traditional outlining's sneakier, more provocative cousin. It doesn't involve listing the important arguments you intend to include in the future. Rather, it entails working backward and outlining the major points contained within a completed piece.

College students are taught to reverse outline as a means of reviewing the flow and logical consistency of their essays. It's easier to evaluate the contributions of each paragraph when its main point is distilled down to a single sentence. But there's another use for reverse outlining, one that's considerably more valuable for aspiring writers: using reverse outlining to uncover the hidden structure of works by published authors.

In my second year of graduate school at the University of Rochester, I faced what seemed like an impossible task: writing my first journal article. Sure, I'd read hundreds of academic papers, and yes, I'd conducted plenty of experiments. But still, writing was a different animal. I felt about as ready to author an academic paper as I was to build a spacecraft.

What followed were weeks of agony. Endless visits to libraries and cafés, hours of staring at a menacing cursor and its endless blinks, sleepless nights. One morning, I decided to try something different. Instead of tormenting myself further and hoping that inspiration would magically strike, I devoted a few hours to rereading the articles of a highly regarded psychologist whose writing I especially admired. Perhaps his talent would rub off.

I read one article word for word, followed by a second and then a third. Eventually, I noticed something. By the fifth or sixth article, it was almost too obvious to ignore. There was a pattern contained within these articles, a structure that appeared again and again. It was evident in the way the author hooked his audience in the opening paragraphs with a surprising statistic or news story, the way he posed a provocative question before delivering a literature review of previous studies, and the dramatic flourish with which he stated his thesis, somehow making it seem logical and bold at the same time.

Fascinated by this discovery, I began reverse outlining his articles and came away with something more valuable than anything I had learned in a classroom: a blueprint for constructing academic journal articles.

Years later, I discovered that this approach isn't just applicable to crafting formal research papers. It's equally vital to developing viral online content. I was not alone. Business writer Dorie Clark has developed an entire course showing writers how to reverse engineer published articles and unlock a hidden structure. Among Clark's insights for producing viral business content: open by stating the problem in a way that gets your readers nodding along, break up a long body of text by inserting headers that pique curiosity, and close by providing provocative, counterintuitive tips that help people look smart by sharing your content.

Reverse outlining's value extends to a wide array of creative fields beyond writing. It's one that marketers can apply to reverse outline memorable advertisements and campaigns, consultants can utilize to reverse outline successful proposals and pitch decks, and live performers can use to reverse outline captivating speeches, presentations, or stand-up routines. Podcasters can use it to outline a program's structure. Directors can use it to reverse storyboard scenes.

It works because it prompts us to do something unnatural: take in the entirety of a piece all at once. That's vastly different from the way we typically experience a creative work. When we read a book or watch a movie, we can't help but focus on a small sliver of the performance—the scene unfolding in one particular moment. To the extent that we attempt to reflect on the progression of a piece as a whole, we can do so only by stitching together a string of memories which tend to be both unreliable and incomplete.

Reverse outlines eliminate that experiential limitation. By compressing staggered events into a single document, we effectively collapse time, freeing us to broaden our perspective and see a piece anew. We can finally stop staring at the brushstrokes and textures and cracks, take a few steps back, and admire the complete canvas. It's a process that places us squarely in the upper deck, sitting snugly beside Wellington Mara and his trusty Polaroid, where we can't help but notice patterns we would otherwise miss.

A second reason reverse outlines are effective at helping us detect patterns is that, ironically, they force us to ignore details. In order to distill large blocks of information down to a single sentence, we need to sacrifice massive amounts of nonessential details. We're made to adopt a more abstract view of the material, and that abstraction is critical.

When you first read *Harry Potter*, it's easy to fall in love with the magical setting, endearing characters, and engrossing plot. It's only later, while daydreaming on some lazy summer afternoon, that it dawns on you: this isn't the first time you've come across an orphan living with his aunt and uncle who is whisked away on an exciting adventure that involves discovering hidden abilities and fighting an evil villain. There's another story just like it called *Star Wars*. Now, that doesn't necessarily make J. K. Rowling's contributions any less significant or entertaining, but it does teach you something important about the patterns that emerge with the benefit of distance.

How to Illuminate Hidden Patterns Using Numbers

There's an important takeaway here: *detecting patterns requires abstraction.*

Reverse outlining isn't the only tool we have available for zooming out and finding patterns. Another involves turning ideas into numbers.

When you go to the doctor, certain measures are collected at every visit: temperature, weight, blood pressure, heart rate. These are your vitals. Each of these indicators gives your physician a read on your condition and offers clues to aspects of your health that are worth investigating.

What makes these metrics useful is that they standardize patients. They make it easy for medical professionals to compare one individual to another and, in the process, lock in on key differences.

Once you know the average vitals of a healthy person in a given age bracket, detecting aberrations becomes simple.

That's the power of quantifying features. By turning important characteristics into numbers, we can compare how often they appear from one example to the next.

In recent years, data scientists have begun using this approach to quantify the features of chart-topping songs, books, and movies. By comparing massive hits against average works, researchers believe, they can do more than just tell us why certain compositions break through. They can also use the findings to predict the commercial appeal of a new work *before* its release and pinpoint the precise elements in need of improvement.

So what do the data tell us about writing hit singles, best-selling novels, and record-breaking movies? Quite a bit, actually.

Want to break into the *Billboard* Top 10? Write a danceable song with happy lyrics, a 4/4 time signature, and avoid a large variety of instruments. Want to be a blockbuster filmmaker? Shoot a script with a broad cast of characters, little to no vulgarity, and a strong, compelling nemesis. Want to write a commercially successful novel? Be sure to start with a short opening sentence, do your best to avoid adverbs, and use language simple enough for a middle schooler to comprehend.

Data-driven insights like these are likely to grow exponentially in coming years thanks to streaming tools that capture audience experiences in real time. It used to be that feedback consisted of an audience's reaction *after* consuming a song, movie, or book. But today, Spotify captures the precise moment users hit "next" on a song, Netflix determines which episodes make a series binge-worthy, and Kindle identifies which sections of a book readers consume slowly, highlight, and altogether skip.

The good news is that you don't need thousands of data points, a doctorate in statistics, or a supercomputer to start leveraging this approach. Not even close. When it comes to finding patterns in works you admire, all you need is an openness to numbers and a willingness to explore.

It all starts with quantifying features. The more measures you have, the easier it is for you to hit upon distinguishing characteristics that make a particular work unique. What sort of metrics might be especially important? It's hard to know at first. Which is why it's best to embrace curiosity and measure everything that can be measured.

Suppose, for example, that you have an important presentation to deliver at a conference next month. You've found a TED speaker you admire whose pattern you would like to better understand. What metrics might be worth examining? A preliminary list might include:

LENGTH

- **Duration of presentation**
- **Word count**

STRUCTURE

- **For example, percentage of script devoted to:**
  - Opening
  - Thesis
  - Supporting argument 1
  - Supporting argument 2
  - Supporting argument 3
  - Conclusion

CONTENT

- **Percentage of script devoted to:**
  - Biographical stories
  - Nonbiographical stories/anecdotes
  - Persuasive arguments
  - Supporting data/facts
  - Actionable strategies

- **Number of questions/cliffhangers posed**
- **Number of jokes delivered**

- **Number of times thesis is repeated**
- **Language complexity**
  - Sentence complexity/grade level
  - Average sentence length
  - Percentage of sentences
    - ◇ Short (5 words or less)
    - ◇ Medium (6–14 words)
    - ◇ Long (15 words or more)

EMOTION

- **Audience's emotional journey** (derived by coding each paragraph for positive, negative, or neutral emotions)
  - % positive emotions
  - % neutral emotions
  - % negative emotions

DELIVERY

- **Pace**
  - Speed of delivery (words spoken per minute)

- **Body language**
  - Open vs. closed
  - % walking vs. standing

- **Slides**
  - Number of slides
  - Slides per minute
  - Average number of words per slide
  - Average number of images per slide

Once you've translated a target presentation into metrics, you can do the same for a talk you have given in the past, looking for particular categories in which your target speaker stands out. You might find that he or she poses more questions, uses simpler language, incorporates personal stories, and presents fewer slides. That tells you something important—not just about the pattern underlying the speaker's style but about the type of presentation you find impactful.

Let's apply this approach now by analyzing the single most popular TED Talk of all time: "Do Schools Kill Creativity?" delivered by the late arts scholar Sir Ken Robinson in 2006. In it, Robinson posits that formal education systems teach children to fear mistakes, short-circuiting their natural inclination to be creative.

Robinson is an arresting presenter but not for the usual reasons. His approach is unlike that of the prototypical big-stage speaker. He is earnest, professorial, stiff. But that's not the way audiences perceive him. He has them riveted every step of the way, and his metrics reveal why.

Take a look at this breakdown. See anything unusual?

LENGTH

- **Duration of presentation:** 19 minutes, 24 seconds
- **Word count:** 3,105

STRUCTURE

- **Introduction** (416 words/13%)
  - Opens by linking his topic to other presentation at the conference

- **Thesis** (51 words/2%)
  - "My contention is that creativity now is as important in education as literacy, and we should treat it with the same status."

- **Anecdotes demonstrating that children are naturally creative** (640 words/21%)
  - Little girl drawing God

- Nativity play
- Shakespeare
- Picasso

- **Education systems around the globe treat creativity as inferior** (763 words/25%)
  - Anecdote of speaker's family moving to America
  - What educational systems are designed to teach
    ◇ Subjects useful for work
    ◇ Subjects useful for entry to higher education

- **The current challenge** (154 words/5%)
  - We are producing more graduates than ever before
  - The nature of work is changing
  - Academic inflation (a high school degree is no longer sufficient)

- **How intelligence works** (308 words/10%)
  - Intelligence comes in different forms
  - Intelligence is dynamic and can adapt over time
  - Intelligence is distinctive and unique to each individual

- **Inspirational closing story** (773 words/25%)
  - Gillian Lynne the dancer
  - Link Gillian's story to other presentations at the conference
  - Restate the challenge (the narrow way education is currently defined) and link to the solution (educate the whole human being)

CONTENT

- **Percentage of script devoted to:**
  - Biographical stories: 394 words/13%
  - Nonbiographical stories/anecdotes: 674 words/22%

- Persuasive arguments: 1,608 words/52%
- Supporting data/facts: 22 words/1%
- Actionable strategies: 0 words/0%

- **Number of questions/cliffhangers posed:** 25
- **Number of jokes delivered:** 40
- **Number of times thesis is repeated:** 3
- **Language complexity**
  - Sentence complexity/grade level: 5th grade
  - Average sentence length: 11 words
  - Percentage of sentences
    - ◇ Short (5 words or less): 23%
    - ◇ Medium (6–14 words): 58%
    - ◇ Long (15 words or more): 19%

EMOTION

- **Audience's emotional journey** (derived by coding each paragraph for positive, negative, or neutral emotions)
  - % positive emotions: 36%
  - % neutral emotions: 40%
  - % negative emotions: 24%

Robinson TED Talk: Emotional Topography

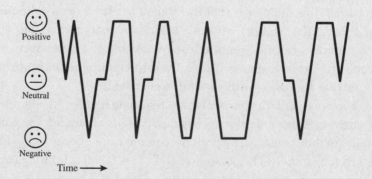

DELIVERY

- **Pace**
  - Speed of delivery: 161 words per minute

- **Body language**
  - Open vs. closed: 100% open
  - % walking vs. standing: 1% walking, 99% standing

- **Slides**
  - Number of slides: 0 slides
  - Slides per minute: N/A
  - Average number of words per slide: N/A
  - Average number of images per slide: N/A

There are a few metrics here that should immediately jump out. First, and perhaps most prominent, is the number of jokes. There are forty in a speech of less than twenty minutes, arriving at a relentless clip of more than two laugh lines per minute. Robinson is an arts education professor speaking at a prestigious, world-class conference, but his approach is completely out of place. He is performing like a stand-up comedian.

Then there's the number of questions he poses to his audience: twenty-five, which amounts to more than one question per minute. To be fair, this number is slightly inflated by Robinson's colloquial (and distinctly English) habit of tacking on "isn't it?" at the end of sentences—but its overall effect, of drawing in an audience and keeping them engaged, as if they are participating in an informal, interactive discussion with a friend, is effective.

The breakdown also reveals an astonishing metric—the number of statistics Robinson presents in support of his argument. In nearly twenty minutes onstage, he presents a grand total of one data point, almost tangentially. The persuasiveness of his talk has nothing to do with facts and everything to do with anecdotes. The metrics make this impossible to ignore. Just take a look at the percentage of his script devoted to facts: a stingy 1 percent. And how about biographical stories and anecdotes? A whopping 35 percent.

In other words, Robinson is a scholar, one of the world's most recognized experts on the topic of education. He has all kinds of riveting facts he could dispense in a heartbeat. But what does he do to captivate TED's audience and send 70 million viewers flocking to his video? He uses storytelling.

By translating Robinson's performance into metrics, we immediately gain a clear picture of the factors that make his approach distinctive. With just a cursory glance at his numbers, we perceive more about what makes it successful than most viewers do while watching him speak.

But that's not where it ends. Because these results aren't just revealing—they're instructive.

If we wanted to reproduce Robinson's formula and apply it to an entirely new topic, we could do so easily. We can even devise a template that turns Robinson's viral talk into a blueprint. All we'd need to do is reverse outline his talk and consult his metrics.

Thanks to our analysis, we now know precisely how many words to write, the portion of the script we need to devote to each section, and the emotional journey our listeners should experience. We also have a good sense for when to pose rhetorical questions, when to present a charming anecdote, and when to inject a joke.

TED Talk Skeleton à la Sir Ken Robinson

LENGTH

- **Target word count: 3,105**

STRUCTURE

- **Introduction** (13%)
  - Open by complimenting other talks at the event.
  - Highlight key takeaways that link to your presentation.

- **Thesis** (2%)
  - Transition from others' presentations to your thesis.
  - Within your thesis, identify a problem that you believe has been overlooked and advocate for an alternative point of view.
  - State your thesis clearly and concisely, in a single sentence.

- **Provide anecdotes that support your thesis** (21%)
  - Offer supporting evidence for your thesis through a series of brief, relatable, humorous anecdotes.

- **Explain how the status quo came about** (25%)
  - If possible, work in anecdotes about your childhood, children, or spouse.

- **Discuss how serious the current challenge will become** (5%)
  - Illustrate a few ways the problem you've identified will metastasize if left unchecked.

- **Transition to a solution** (10%)
  - Provide science-based insights that offer an alternative point of view on how the problem can be addressed.

- **Inspirational closing story** (25%)
  - Find a story about an individual who suffered as a result of the current problem.
  - Outline how your solution helped the individual overcome his or her challenge.
  - Highlight the incredible success the individual was able to achieve as a result of applying your solution.
  - Link the individual's story to other presentations at the conference.
  - Restate the challenge and link to the solution.

We now have a proven road map that offers detailed guidance on how to go about crafting a winning presentation in the style of the most popular talk in internet history. What's more, once we've written our script, we can go back and compare its metrics and emotional journey against those of Robinson's original TED Talk, using the results to identify the precise areas in need of fine-tuning.

Now, Robinson's approach is obviously distinctive, and not everyone has the capacity or inclination to pull off an anecdote-rich presentation with a joke every thirty seconds. Thankfully, you don't have to. All you need to do is find a different presenter whose approach aligns with your natural preferences as a speaker. Ultimately, that's the power of reverse outlining, quantifying features, and developing a template. It's a methodology that allows you to easily deconstruct a wide range of works until you find a structure that resonates, whose formula you can leverage in an entirely new way.

Using Metrics to Reveal a Business Strategy

What do the world's best websites do differently? One website that marketers often cite as a paragon of elegant, tasteful design belongs to Apple. If you've ever visited the company's home page or used the iTunes store, then you know that Apple favors clean, uncluttered layouts. But is that all there is? If we were to deconstruct Apple's home page using some of the tools introduced in this chapter, what would we learn?

Reverse outlining Apple's website is a good place to start. A recent visit revealed the following:

Apple Website: Reverse Outline

- Website menu
- [FULL PANEL]: Airpods Pro
- [FULL PANEL]: iPhone 11 Pro
- [FULL PANEL]: iPhone 11
- [HALF PANEL]: Privacy messaging/[HALF PANEL]: iWatch

- [HALF PANEL]: TV+/[HALF PANEL]: Apple credit card
- [HALF PANEL]: Apple arcade/[HALF PANEL]: iPad
- Disclaimers
- Website navigation links

Zooming out grants us a thirty-thousand-foot view of Apple's approach. But it's not until we begin to quantify features and pit the metrics we collect from Apple's website against those of other websites that we can discern a pattern that makes Apple's website distinctive.

Let's take a look at a preliminary list of metrics and how they factor in, both on Apple's website and those on the website of one of its chief competitors: Samsung.

Quantifying Websites

LAYOUT	APPLE	SAMSUNG
Number of banners	9	29
Scrolling banners	0	14
Clickable buttons (excluding menus)	18	37
Clickable buttons (including menus)	88	272
IMAGES		
Close-up images (% total)	56%	7%
Images featuring people (% total)	11%	17%
MESSAGING		
Word total	140	324
Average headline length	2.1	6.9
Focus is on features	56%	75%
Focus is on benefits	56%	25%
Mentions price	18%	52%

So, what's different about these websites?

A few discrepancies immediately jump out. For one thing, Apple's landing page contains a lot less information. There are fewer panels, shorter headlines, and less than half the total number of words. Why does Apple provide less information than its chief rival? As a brand, Apple is famously committed to simplicity, and that mantra extends to the company's marketing, which includes its website. Its website is surgically optimized for maximum simplicity.

The messaging on Apple's website is also less likely to mention price and more likely to favor emphasizing the benefits of a product over a particular feature. Apple doesn't tell you that its new AirPods include state-of-the-art noise cancellation technology. It prefers the more poetic and visceral "Magic like you've never heard before."

Apple wields this approach again and again for a variety of products, highlighting a product's benefits more than twice as often as Samsung. Why? Because Apple is appealing to emotion, not logic.

Lastly, the aesthetic differences between the two pages are obvious. The images on Apple's website are muted, the color range narrow. The panels do not enlarge when you hover. The hyperlinks do not blink. There is no movement. Everything is perfectly still. In contrast, Samsung's website is colorful, active, busy. If visiting Samsung.com feels like walking into a crowded mall, a visit to Apple.com feels like entering a museum. This, too, is intentional. Overstimulation, Apple knows, can contribute to the experience of anxiety. And anxiety is the enemy of simplicity.

Apple's decision to use fewer words, focus on emotion, and avoid overstimulation can all be gleaned from the metrics we've collected. Which highlights another benefit of quantifying features: it unveils strategy. It offers a glimpse behind the curtain and reveals what a company is aiming to achieve.

Even if you have no intention of creating a website like Apple's, there is immense value in reverse engineering the thought process that went into its construction. As this simple comparison illustrates, it is a powerful and inexpensive means of gathering intelligence.

If you are interested in designing a website that builds on Apple's model, not only do you now have direction on structure, design, and messaging, you also have metrics you can use as a benchmark. Much like that TED Talk you can now write, quantify, and compare against Sir Ken Robinson's presentation, here you can quantify your website draft and pit your metrics against Apple's. Or Tiffany's. Or Walmart's. Or any website in the world you choose, including the industry leaders in your field.

It's an approach that works by empowering you to leverage the same tools computer algorithms rely on to detect patterns and formulate predictions. By gathering examples, quantifying important variations, identifying similarities, and applying your insights to create something new, you too are formulating a prediction. One that leverages the hidden patterns that make exceptional examples so successful.

But there's a hitch.

Perhaps it's one that you've anticipated, a critique that's been nagging at you this entire time. Reverse engineering a winning formula, pinpointing the features that make it unique, and re-creating it wholesale rarely results in the power of the original. No, chances are, it will be missing something.

But what?

The Curse of Creativity

What's the secret to writing like Malcolm Gladwell? It's a puzzle that has consumed a generation of nonfiction writers. Ever since Gladwell's first book, *The Tipping Point*, debuted on the *New York Times* best-seller list in 2000, where it resided for a staggering four hundred weeks, countless writers across a range of disciplines have attempted to crack the code.

Certain patterns are obvious. There is the story-study-story-study structure that is now a fixture of popular nonfiction, the novelistic flair used to bring central characters to life, and the sticky simplicity with which complex ideas are communicated, transformed from lifeless data into irresistible dinner party ammunition.

The level of interest borders on obsessive. Run a quick online search, and you'll come across hundreds of articles, blog posts, and breakdowns, as well as a surprising number of professional courses, including a twenty-four-lesson video series delivered by Gladwell himself.

Deconstructing the Gladwellian formula unquestionably makes sense. If you want to author a successful nonfiction title, who better to study than a writer whose books have dominated the genre?

And yet there's something deeply ironic about the fixation with Gladwell's writing. At least when you consider that when he started his career, the very last person Malcolm Gladwell hoped to sound like was himself. He was preoccupied with mastering a different style, one belonging to his own literary idol.

"I began as a writer trying to write like William F. Buckley, my childhood hero," Gladwell has said, referring to the conservative American pundit who founded *National Review*. "And if you read my early writing, it was insanely derivative. All I was doing was looking for models and copying them."

Like so many of the standout performers we've encountered in this book, Gladwell's path to mastery began with a concerted effort to analyze the works of others and distill their approach into a reproducible formula. His results, as he freely admits, were a letdown—and this, too, is not unusual. In fact, it highlights a critical limitation of reverse engineering. Copying alone is rarely enough. On the contrary, it's one of the most reliable ways of ensuring that your work is not taken seriously.

One obvious reason is that it inspires work that's easily dismissed as unoriginal. In 2005, a stay-at-home mother in Arizona published a novel about a high school student who falls in love with a vampire. It took the literary world by storm. The astronomical popularity of *Twilight* launched hundreds of vampire-based young-adult titles, few of which garnered even a fraction of the fanfare lavished upon Stephenie Meyer's original series.

Nothing brings down a genre faster than a string of copycats. The reason is simple: the more often a formula is used, the more predictable and less appealing it becomes.

But there's a more nuanced explanation for why simply replicating a formula rarely yields memorable results. It's that exceptional work depends on much more than a proven recipe. It relies on a combination of factors.

At the most basic level, we have a formula on the one hand, and the person executing it on the other. Present two people with the same formula, and their results will likely differ. Why? Because they each possess distinct strengths, personalities, and biographical histories that contribute to their unique execution.

Then there is the issue of authenticity. In chapter 2, we uncovered the formula driving the world's most popular TED Talk. It includes a string of self-deprecating jokes that Sir Ken Robinson delivers flawlessly. Theoretically, anyone reading this book can now take that template and apply it to their next presentation. But let's face it, what if you're not very good at telling jokes? Or what if your topic demands a somber tone and humor is entirely inappropriate? What if you lack the academic cachet of Sir Ken Robinson and desperately require data to be persuasive?

No, you need more than the right formula. You need the right formula for the right person within the right context.

That last factor, context, can be especially tricky. All those *Twilight* clones failed to catch on not because each and every one of them was a dreadful book. They failed because readers' expectations had shifted. The moment an audience is exposed to a particular experience, it evolves. No longer are fans riveted by a once novel premise, charmed by formerly irresistible characters, or blindsided by what are now conventional plot twists. The audience has adapted, and the formula it found gripping just days earlier now feels insipid and stale.

It's a critical hurdle, one that the music industry has learned to navigate better than just about any other creative field. In music, superstar artists rarely use the same blueprint for very long. They've discovered that the safest path to staying relevant is evolving their approach by tweaking some aspect of their image, style, or sound with every album.

David Bowie was among the first to leverage this "pattern interrupt" strategy, revising both his appearance, which evolved from hippie swirls (early 1960s) to suit and tie (late 1960s) to beatnik (early 1972) to glittery makeup (1973) to high-end couture (mid-1970s), as well as his sound, which spanned a host of genres including rock and roll, glam rock, pop music, jazz fusion, and Christmas classics. Elton John, Madonna, Mariah Carey, Katy Perry, Bruno Mars, and Beyoncé have all followed suit. Today, we expect top-tier musicians to reinvent themselves over time. It's the artists who fail to adapt and trot out the same tired formula year after year that inevitably fade away.

A related principle applies in the world of business. As PayPal cofounder Peter Thiel has observed, "Every moment in business happens only once. The next Bill Gates will not build an operating system. The next Larry Page or Sergey Brin won't make a search engine. And the next Mark Zuckerberg won't create a social network. If you are copying these guys, you aren't learning from them."

Which is why simply cloning a formula that works for someone else is ultimately a failing strategy. What you need is a formula that works to compliment your unique abilities, interests, and situation.

But where exactly do you find one?

The Trouble with Too Much Creativity

You might think that the solution is to deliberately avoid the influence of others entirely and instead strive for complete originality. But this, as it turns out, is also a mistake—especially in projects geared toward a broad audience. If you're looking to write a blockbuster movie, deliver a winning presentation, or cook a memorable dish, the last thing in the world you want is a flood of novelty. Why? Because no matter how much audiences claim they want bold, innovative ideas, studies indicate that in practice, they reject them all the time.

Jennifer Mueller is a University of San Diego social psychologist whose creativity research reveals an alarming trend: the more novel the idea, the more likely it is to be rejected. Worse, we don't just quash creative suggestions—we also penalize those who raise them. Mueller's studies indicate that when we encounter highly creative ideas, not only are we likely to dismiss them, but we also perceive those proposing them as weaker leaders.

Why exactly are we so loath to embrace the new? Because novelty makes us uncomfortable, and that discomfort is unpleasant. Nowhere is this tendency more evident than at the office. At work, we vastly prefer ideas that make us feel safe and confident, especially from those in charge. When a leader exercises creativity in the workplace, it does the opposite. It introduces uncertainty and runs contrary to the reassurance we seek from those at the top.

If you're skeptical about this finding or believe it doesn't apply to you because you're a lot more receptive to new ideas than the average person, think back to the last time you encountered a new song that you absolutely loved. Now ask yourself: How novel was it, really? Did it include an instrument you've never heard before? Was it played in a rare key? Perhaps it featured an unusual rhythmic signature?

If you're like most people, hearing a song with any of these features would not only feel unpleasant, it would border on intolerable. And that's just music. The same holds true for the movies, artwork, and restaurants to which we gravitate. We like to believe that we crave novelty, but it's the familiar that we truly adore.

Just ask Thom Yorke, lead singer and songwriter for the British band Radiohead. In the late 1990s, Radiohead stood firmly at the pinnacle of the rock music scene. Its sound was timely yet distinctive: a more melodic, introspective, and complex alternative to the angsty grunge that dominated the *Billboard* charts. The band's third album, *OK Computer*, catapulted Radiohead to entirely new heights. After reaching number one, the album went platinum several times over and was voted in one UK poll to be the single greatest album of all time, ahead of anything ever put out by the Beatles.

Many artists would have felt gratified. Not Yorke. He grew restless. "I don't want to be in a rock band anymore," he announced, seemingly out of nowhere. Yorke had witnessed far too many of his contemporaries recycle the same tired tropes album after album, reducing themselves to a cliché. He feared the same fate awaited Radiohead and resolved to steer the band in an entirely different direction. He became obsessed with making Radiohead's next album, *Kid A*, a complete original. "*Kid A*," he told *Rolling Stone*, "is like getting a massive eraser out and starting again."

The first thing Yorke did was dispose of the electric guitars. In their place, he introduced moody synthesizers, electronic sequencers, and pulsing drum machines. To clear his mind of contemporary influences, he unplugged. He abandoned the city for picturesque Cornwall, where he hiked the countryside, drew sketches, and composed songs on a baby grand piano. So thorough was Yorke's commitment to evolving every element of the band's approach that even his own lyrics were considered suspect. To head off redundancy, he deliberately threw in random words, as if daring his audience to try and make sense of his songs. And to top it off, on some songs he distorted his voice through a synthesizer, rendering large portions of his nonsensical lyrics unintelligible.

Yorke was adamant. There would be no singles, no music videos. The album would speak for itself.

To say that the response was mixed would be an act of generosity. Most fans were genuinely mystified. It was as if there were two Radioheads: the beloved rock group whose catchy singles were a runaway success and now this, an experimental synthesizer troupe, hell-bent on decimating expectations. Critics were decidedly less charitable: *Rolling Stone* called the album "irritating," *Music Week* declared it "plain frustrating," and *Spin* predicted that it would be viewed as "career suicide."

Radiohead succeeded in pushing the envelope, and while there are those who admire their ambition, its defiant commitment to originality has unquestionably alienated fans. Over twenty years later, although the group is still releasing new albums, it's their 1990s music that continues to garner the most downloads and generate the majority of sales.

Too much creativity doesn't just backfire in the arts. The business world is riddled with examples of massively successful concepts that were initially spurned simply because they arrived years ahead of their time. Often it's not just the quality of the idea that matters. Just as critical is consumer receptivity.

Amazon's one-hour delivery for office supplies, books, and groceries may seem like the epitome of modern innovation—until you realize that Kozmo.com fell flat on its face trying to sell an identical service twenty years ago. The same applies to high-end food delivery platforms like Uber Eats and DoorDash. They provide precisely the same service offered by Takeout Taxi way back in 1987. It, too, went out of business. Then there's the Apple Watch, a device that provides immediate access to news, weather, traffic reports, and sports scores. All of those features were available decades ago on Microsoft's SPOT watch.

Which goes to show: sometimes quality ideas are rejected or ignored not because they lack merit. There are times when novelty is a liability. The market simply isn't capable of embracing ideas that are completely new.

All of which leads us to an impasse. Outright mimicry leads us nowhere. Absolute novelty is met with scorn. So what exactly is the right approach?

Don Draper's Guide to Winning Ideas

In 2014, a group of Harvard researchers took this "novelty paradox" head on by running a clever experiment—one that involved analyzing the type of medical research proposals that win grants.

Academic research is a cutthroat business. It's not enough to work sixty-hour weeks, churn out peer-reviewed publications, or be universally recognized as an expert in your field. To retain your job, every few years, you need to convince a panel of experts at distinguished government agencies like the National Institutes of Health that your research proposals are worth funding.

What predicts whether a proposal will win approval? To find out, the Harvard team took actual grant submissions and had them evaluated by 142 subject matter experts, including university professors and medical doctors. Each proposal was rated across a variety of metrics, including quality, feasibility, and novelty. The experts also gave each proposal a score, indicating how strongly they felt that it should receive funding.

The findings confirmed Jennifer Mueller's dictum: the more novel the proposal, the less likely the experts were to recommend funding. But there's an interesting clue buried within the data that speaks to what audiences truly want. Which proposals were most likely to receive the experts' stamp of approval? The ones that contained a small dose of novelty.

That conclusion would come as no surprise to another renowned (albeit fictional) creativity expert: Don Draper. Not long before the Harvard team conducted its study, *Mad Men* aired an episode in which the famously volatile Sterling Cooper creative director is pitched a television show in the vein of *Candid Camera*. His response captures what might be the ideal formula for popular appeal: "It's derivative with a twist. That's what they're looking for."

In other words, if outright mimicry leads us nowhere and absolute novelty is met with scorn, the solution is to steer clear of both extremes. What gets noticed is the generally familiar with a minor variation. Karim Lakhani, one of the Harvard Business School professors who conducted the grant study, has another term for this: *optimal newness*.

The idea that success is more easily achieved by those who add a novel spin to an established formula should come as welcome news. It suggests that the pressure many creators place on themselves to invent something entirely original is not just unnecessary—it's actually counterproductive. The secret to producing work with lasting significance is not absolute novelty. It's leveraging a proven formula and adding your unique twist.

Creativity Is What Happens When Ideas Have Sex

Reverse engineering provides the first half of the equation: the proven formula. The variation can come from a number of sources.

One path involves combining influences. When Quentin Tarantino's first major studio release, *Pulp Fiction*, exploded onto the movie scene in the 1990s, the director was heralded as one of the most original filmmakers of his generation. Tarantino's contributions were distinctive, but they didn't materialize out of the ether. What makes Tarantino's films unique is his penchant for injecting hallmarks of other, less popular genres—including funk music, extended fight sequences, and jarring violence—into dialogue-driven capers. In other words, he combines influences, and that combination results in a style that today is instantly recognizable as Tarantino-esque.

A similar approach is often used by musicians looking to create a unique sound. When The Doors guitarist Robby Krieger first played his bandmates the chords of a groovy song he'd recently composed, their response was underwhelming. Keyboardist Ray

Manzarek recalled dismissing the chorus as "very Sonny and Cher," which in 1967 was shorthand for "mainstream and lame." But the band was already in the studio and game for riffing on the melody. The first thing they added was a drum beat borrowed from Latin music. Next came a pair of John Coltrane–inspired jazz solos. The final piece of the puzzle was an introduction modeled after Johann Sebastian Bach. Little did they know that they had just written one of the most memorable openings in rock music history. It was Jim Morrison who came up with the song's title: "Light My Fire."

In the world of business, combining influences has a long, illustrious history. Many of the technological innovations we take for granted today, ones that have fundamentally transformed our world, are in fact simply mash-ups of widely available concepts harvested from different domains.

Steve Jobs didn't invent the MP3 player or the cell phone. But he led a team that found a way of combining the two, leading to the iPhone. Back in 1995, two Stanford University students took the way academics cite research articles and applied it to organizing information on the World Wide Web, resulting in Google. The history of innovation is so dependent on the blending of existing ideas that even books would not have come about had the wine press (which gave us ink) not been combined with the coin punch (which gave us typographic blocks for letters) to produce the world's first printer. As author Matt Ridley put it, creativity is what happens "when ideas have sex."

And so blending influences is one way of finding your twist. But it's an approach with one critical limitation: your ability to locate unique influences. Combining influences works best for those who, like Quentin Tarantino, hunt for inspiration outside the cultural mainstream and import the elements they love best.

Another path to finding your twist: borrow an approach that resonates in another domain, and apply it to your own. Less than a decade before seemingly coming out of nowhere to capture the United States presidency in 2008, Barack Obama was immersed in an uphill political battle in Chicago, doing everything he could to persuade voters to elect him to Congress. There was just one problem: he was a dreadful speaker. As a former law professor, he was accustomed to lecturing audiences, not engaging them, and had an off-putting habit of incorporating complex, academic ideas that sailed over voters' heads. His speeches left them feeling cold. Obama's campaign staff begged him to abandon the professorial jargon and ramp up the emotion. But Obama was obstinate, leading his consultant Ron Davis to snap, "Motherfucker, you ain't goin' anywhere. You ain't gonna get elected dogcatcher. You're full of yourself. You have to let the air out."

The pleas fell on deaf ears. Obama went on to get trounced that November, losing by an embarrassing margin of more than two to one. The race left him broke, marginalized, and rudderless. For a time, he considered leaving politics. Then an adviser suggested that he spend some time in Chicago's churches, paying close attention to the way preachers get their message across and inspire their audience.

By the time Obama declared his candidacy for the US Senate just a few years later, his speaking style was transformed. Instead of communicating in abstractions, he was now telling stories, quoting the Bible, and using repetition to drive home his points. But it was more than just his words; it was also the way he was delivering them. Obama had learned to speak loudly at some points and softly at others, to modulate his tone and subtly convey emotion, to emphasize important arguments with a calm, deliberate pause. By adapting techniques commonly used in churches and importing them into the political arena, Obama was able to evolve his speaking style and establish himself as a unique political force.

Within the business world, surveying adjacent fields for fresh ideas is surprisingly common. When Steve Jobs was working with Steve Wozniak to build the Apple II, he wanted more than a trailblazing computer. He wanted a device that looked the part. But he didn't look at other computers for inspiration. Instead, he drove to Macy's and surveyed kitchen appliances, where Cuisinart's food processor caught his eye. Its plastic molding gave him the idea for what was a revolutionary computer design at the time: a single, self-contained unit that required no assembly (and would therefore also be difficult to take apart).

Jobs wasn't the only entrepreneur with a habit of scavenging outside his field for innovative ideas. The same is true of Steve Case, chairman of the world's first major social media platform, America Online (AOL). Case recognized early on that, like telephones, the value of AOL's service was largely dependent on the number of people using it. To succeed, he needed to amass a substantial network quickly or risk losing the few users who had already signed up. To grow AOL's numbers, Case leveraged a tactic commonly employed in the laundry detergent market: free samples.

If you grew up in the 1990s, you will recall those ubiquitous compact disks with a yellow stick figure arriving in your mailbox every few days, courtesy of America Online. Under Case's charge, AOL spent upward of $300 million on free trials, giving away hours of internet access to millions of consumers in his quest to attract new users. That might seem like a staggering expense until you factor in that in 2015, Case sold AOL for a jaw-dropping $4.4 billion. Even more impressive: it is entirely possible that AOL would have sold for nothing at all had Case not applied a marketing strategy that no one in the software field had seriously considered before.

The Magic of "Inexperienced Experience"

In the early 1960s, Stan Lee was about to give up on writing comics. Back then, conventional wisdom held that comic book fans craved simple heroes and intense fight scenes. Lee was fed up with churning out the same tired plot over and over. It didn't matter that he was on the cusp of turning forty or that he was qualified to do little else. He was ready to take his chances on a new career.

Just before handing in his notice, Lee consulted with his wife, Joan. The advice she gave him is the reason superheroes like Spider-Man, the Incredible Hulk, Thor, and the X-Men are now household names. "My wife said if you're going to quit," Lee recounted years later at Comic-Con, an annual convention inspired largely by his groundbreaking work, "why don't you just do one book the way you want to do it. Get it out of your system. The worst that will happen is that he'll fire you but you want to quit anyway."

He took her advice. And what was it that the newly emboldened Lee finally had license to do? Write about the one thing no comic book aficionado was expecting: superheroes with flaws. At the time, this was a daring twist, far afield from the traditional approach, which glorified perfection. Superman, a character who was friendly, optimistic, and wise, dominated the industry. Lee kept the physical prowess but added an important variation: emotional vulnerability.

Starting with the Fantastic Four, Lee introduced superheroes who got angry, sulked, struggled, bickered, and pursued vendettas. Much to his publisher's surprise, audiences loved them. Lee was finally free to develop more imperfect characters and craft the type of challenging storylines he actually wanted to read.

Today, the Fantastic Four are among Marvel's lesser-known properties, though not because the work has failed to stand the test of time. It's because Lee's later comics achieved an unprecedented level of success, turning Marvel into a billion-dollar franchise.

What's fascinating about the Marvel franchise is not just its extraordinary ability to seemingly print money every summer (and sometimes Thanksgiving) or that its revenue has risen exponentially over the past thirteen years—it's that its movies continue to draw rave reviews from both die-hard fans and highbrow critics despite relying on a formula.

Every Marvel movie contains certain features, many of which can be traced back to Stan Lee's original influence, that together constitute a pattern.

Often, there's a hero who acquires a supernatural ability that he or she must learn to control. There's the string of rapid fire one-liners and sarcastic quips, especially when characters are facing mortal danger. There's the incessant hero infighting (think Captain America versus Iron Man, Antman versus the Wasp, Thor versus Hulk) that makes up much of each film. In Marvel movies, it's not uncommon for heroes to spend more time verbally jousting with their "friends" than physically battling their enemies. Then there's the contrast of small but sassy women paired with powerful but insecure men, the innocent romances that never quite progress, the stream of wry pop culture references, the climactic CGI-driven battle scene that brings the film to its conclusion, and the postcredits preview of a future Marvel film.

When you see it spelled out in a single paragraph, it seems pretty formulaic, doesn't it?

Which raises some intriguing questions: How exactly does Marvel manage to captivate moviegoers year after year? How is it able to present the same characters, storylines, and themes without boring viewers? And what does its process teach us about taking a proven recipe and making it feel fresh?

In 2019, creativity researchers led by INSEAD's Spencer Harrison attempted to answer these very questions by conducting an extensive study into Marvel's approach. Harrison's team pored through hundreds of interviews with the Marvel employees—everyone from actors to directors and producers—analyzed movie scripts, and studied critical analyses of each film. Among their key findings is an insight that applies to far more than Hollywood filmmakers.

One of the ways Marvel has managed to prevent a formula from feeling stale is by introducing a novel element into its films: a director whose expertise lies *outside* the superhero genre. Instead of relying on the same accomplished team over and over again, Marvel deliberately places a leader with limited genre exposure at the helm for the purpose of introducing a fresh perspective. Harrison calls this approach "inexperienced experience."

If you've watched your share of Marvel films, you may have noticed that *Thor: Ragnarok* is way funnier than *Thor: The Dark World*. That's because the latter was directed by a *Game of Thrones* alumnus while the former was directed by an improv comic. By relying on a core team with a proven recipe and adding an outsider to the group, Marvel is able to tweak its approach just enough for each new movie to feel relatively novel.

One clear application we can draw from Marvel's approach is to inject new team members and marshal their influence to evolve a formula in a new direction. Instead of enjoying the comfort of working with the same team of colleagues, no matter how successful you might be, if you're looking to produce creative work, it pays to seek out new team members every few projects. That can take the form of introducing new colleagues into an existing group, making a new hire, or engaging an outside freelancer or consultant on a project basis.

If you work alone, Marvel's solution may appear not to apply to you. Except that's not exactly true because the influence of other people can still be strategically harnessed, even when they're not technically members of your team.

It is often said that the person you are today is largely determined by the five people with whom you spend the most time. It's because our close friends, colleagues, and family have the power to shape our beliefs and expectations in subtle ways that we often fail to appreciate. All of us have some control over how we spend our time and with whom we surround ourselves, yet we rarely consider changing our social circle as a tool for sparking creative ideas. We should.

Seen in this light, one opportunity we undervalue is the practice of networking. Many of us have been taught to view networking as a transactional tool in the service of business development and career advancement. But not everyone views networking this way. Clayton Christensen, the late Harvard Business School professor we met briefly in the last chapter, found that while executives use networking to sell themselves and their company or to strategically befriend those with access to valuable resources, entrepreneurs go about it differently. They use networking as a means for gathering valuable insights and cutting-edge ideas.

Imagine if you could abandon the inauthentic, self-serving motives that lead so many of us to despise networking and instead simply aim to connect with a few thought-provoking people and gather one or two stimulating ideas. By actively seeking out and curating a diverse network of friends and colleagues from a wide range of disciplines, anyone can increase the odds of finding novel ideas worth incorporating into their work.

Of course, there will be times when reaching those whose influence you consider most valuable will prove impossible. Suppose, for example, that you've agreed to deliver a wedding toast and you want it to be charming, witty, and incisive. You know the perfect model for the occasion: comedian Stephen Colbert. Obviously, phoning CBS and requesting Colbert's assistance is unlikely to get you very far. You consider reverse outlining his monologues and realize that doing so lends limited value because his performances are so specific to news stories.

Fortunately, there is one other option for injecting Colbert's point of view into your wedding toast. It involves posing questions that lead you to reflect on how Colbert would tackle specific elements of your speech.

For example, how would Stephen Colbert start a wedding toast? Posing that simple question nudges you toward a very particular state of mind, placing his influence in the forefront of your consciousness and making you more likely to create material that is consistent with his approach. In contrast, asking yourself how the Dalai Lama, or Oprah Winfrey, or Donald Trump would start a wedding toast all pull you in very different directions.

And indeed, research shows that simply calling to mind a specific influence shifts our mind-set and changes our behavior. And it's not just celebrities—it's an effect that also extends to brands. Studies have found, for example, that seeing a Disney logo prompts people to behave more honestly, exposure to a Gatorade bottle motivates people to invest more effort, and reminders of Red Bull propels people to act more aggressively.

What these examples demonstrate is the vast potential of calling to mind a specific influence when crafting original work. By actively reflecting on a particular model, we spark ideas that blend its attributes with our thinking, stimulating our creativity.

Channeling personas is an approach that can be especially effective in the world of business. Consider the case of Stephanie, a marketing manager who is struggling to come up with a new promotion for the holiday season. Instead of rifling through last year's campaign or racking her brain to somehow think up something new, Stephanie can channel the work of an acclaimed brand in an entirely different industry.

Here, the question we posed earlier ("How would Stephen Colbert start a wedding toast?") becomes "How would Amazon launch this product?" or "How would Target feature this on display?" or "How would Kim Kardashian make this offer go viral?" Each of these prompts provides a unique launching point for ideas, sparking strategies, tactics, and techniques that might otherwise have gone overlooked. They also grant Stephanie creative license to consider opportunities that her company's history and status may have prevented her from seeing.

The Unexpected Power of Willful Ignorance

So far, we've identified three strategies for taking a proven formula and adding a unique twist. We've explored the benefits of (1) blending several influences together, (2) finding ideas in outside genres and industries and importing them into your own, and (3) shifting the composition of your team and network (both physically and virtually).

The fourth strategy involves being proudly selective about the information you consume and intentionally *excluding* influences.

Being choosy about what you pay attention to and what you ignore is a vital precursor to differentiating yourself from others in your field. As Steve Jobs famously pointed out, "Creativity is just connecting things." What Jobs left out is the strategic implications of this astute observation: if you want to stand apart from the other chefs, it helps to cook with different ingredients.

And yet many creative professionals subscribe to the same newsletters, listen to the same podcasts, and read the same books. Whether their motivation is genuine interest or simply the pressure to keep up is ultimately irrelevant. The result is the same: originality becomes harder to achieve. Being selective about your influences is the antidote to creative homogeneity.

Which leads us to the second reason for paring down the content you allow in: it lends the materials you do consume more weight. Bandwidth is a zero-sum game. The more dispersed your attention, the weaker the impact of any one influence. By weeding out unhelpful inputs, you amplify the attention received by influences that are truly valuable. No longer are essential classics crowded out by a noisy stream of mediocre content.

It also makes you more resistant to fads. Your creativity is largely determined by what you pay attention to, and if what you pay attention to are fleeting trends or the latest craze, the work you produce is likely to have a short-lived expiration date. In contrast, digging deeper into classical works that have stood the test of time and incorporating those influences into your approach can inspire a unique spin that is more likely to endure.

For all of these reasons, a surprising number of successful creatives have adopted the practice of strategically ignoring certain influences, recognizing that there are times when consuming less results in a more distinctive approach. Rock legend Tom Petty, for example, was keenly aware that his melodic blend of folk, country, and pop was not unique. In fact, it shared an uncomfortable degree of overlap with the work of another popular musician of the time, Bruce Springsteen. Which was why, throughout his career, Petty was adamant about avoiding Springsteen's music to prevent intensifying the resemblance.

In the decades before his passing, Van Halen's chief songwriter, the late Eddie Van Halen, eliminated modern music from his listening regimen entirely. What did he listen to instead? Yo-Yo Ma. "I couldn't make a contemporary record if I wanted to. . . ," Van Halen confessed to *Billboard* in 2015. "Because I don't know what contemporary music sounds like."

Comedian Bill Maher has a weekly news program on HBO. The same is true of British comedian John Oliver. Yet Maher hasn't watched a single episode of Oliver's show—nor does he ever intend to. He deliberately ignores Oliver's work in order to avoid its influence. The same is true of Jimmy Fallon, the host of NBC's *The Tonight Show*. Fallon steers clear of both Maher and Oliver, as well as every other news-based comedian, recognizing that his creativity is shaped by the material he consumes.

Even movie producer Judd Apatow, the comedy enthusiast we met earlier, avoids the work of other comedians when he is writing films. It's not solely to eliminate their influence, it's also to shield his confidence. The last thing he wants when he's writing is the nagging feeling that everything he is working on has already been done before.

Choosing to pursue a strategy of "willful ignorance" does not mean consuming nothing new and waiting for creativity to strike. It means being more selective about the works you pay attention to, with an eye for inputs that serve and diversify your work. That can mean favoring the classics over the new and even going back and reexamining exceptional works you've enjoyed in the past more deliberately.

Many people assume that consuming the same work more than once provides, at best, limited value. If you've already read a book or seen a movie, what's the point of reliving the experience again, right? Well, as it turns out, that's not at all the attitude of successful authors. In fact, a surprising number of award-winning writers invest more time rereading old books every year than they do absorbing new ones. Why? Because reading and rereading offer distinct benefits.

Expert writers know that their focus shifts each time they read a book. The first reading centers on plot: What's the big-picture idea? What's the overall emotional arc? What's happening and to whom? In later readings, however, the storyline is no longer enough to hold our attention, and it's here that we start to unlock important structural clues and unpack a writer's technique. This is when readers naturally become better attuned to easily overlooked elements like word selection, character development, and crucial details an author chooses to leave out. As Booker Prize–winning writer John Banville has observed, "The more often we read a favorite classic the more of its secrets it gives up: each time we revisit it we see more clearly the cogs and flywheels of the writer's technique behind what at first had been its opaque and burnished surface."

Revisiting the classics also serves another crucial function: it reminds us of winning strategies that have been prematurely discarded in the present age and are just waiting to be revived. Adding a classical influence to a current project is another fruitful path to revitalizing a proven formula. It's one that musicians leverage all the time. Bands like Daft Punk and Arcade Fire routinely draw from older influences, from classical music to dancehall disco, both as a means of giving their new songs a distinctive flourish and evolving their sound in unexpected directions.

It's a theme that's as relevant to the world of business as it is to the arts. Consider all the marketing strategies that have gone by the wayside thanks to the rise of online advertising. Not too long ago, a local business might promote itself by printing flyers, publishing yellow pages ads, and airing radio jingles. Today, most companies would scoff at these tactics, believing their marketing dollars are better spent on internet-based communications. But not everyone is following the herd. Shrewd marketers in a range of fields are discovering that the many so-called outdated advertising strategies of yore can still be remarkably effective at setting them apart from their competitors.

Take direct mail. On the surface, designing a successful mailer is both expensive and time consuming. You need to hire a writer and a designer and somehow procure a list of addresses. Then there's the cost of printing and postage. When you consider that email costs a fraction of the price, investing in email blasts seems like a no-brainer. But is it?

Let's look at the numbers. The average American worker is deluged with more than 120 emails a day, for a total of more than 840 emails per week. And how many pieces of physical mail does that worker find in their mailbox over that same time period? Eighteen. So yes, direct mail is not cheap. But the chances of it attracting attention are exponentially higher than those of even the most thoughtfully composed email.

That insight hasn't escaped the notice of the world's savviest marketers, including those leading the charge at internet giants Amazon, Apple, and Google, all of which continue to use direct mail when spreading a message quickly is mission critical.

We tend to think that progress requires embracing the new. But sometimes you have to look backward to see ahead.

The Art of Elevating an Overlooked Ingredient

In the late 1950s, Roy Orbison's career was going exactly nowhere. He was barely scraping by, spending his days writing country songs no one wanted to buy, and wasting his nights hunting for paying gigs at dive bars and drive-in movie theaters. Just a few years back,

Orbison's band, the Teen Kings, had scored a minor top-100 hit called "Ooby Dooby." But that seemed like ages ago. The group had disintegrated after a fight had broken out over songwriting credits. And now Orbison was back on his own, pounding the pavement, desperately trying to stay afloat with a wife and baby boy waiting for him in their crowded Odessa, Texas, apartment.

Orbison looked nothing like the typical rock-and-roll star. He was shy and reserved and wore thick, Coke-bottle bifocals, and even then could barely see. When he took the stage, he stood perfectly still, as if he were terrified that the slightest movement might attract unwanted attention.

Around this time Orbison ran into another struggling songwriter named Joe Melson, who suggested that they write songs together. The two quickly gelled and together composed a landmark ballad that would launch Orbison's career, elevating him from awkward country bumpkin into international sensation. It was called "Only the Lonely."

On paper, "Only the Lonely" was nothing special. Orbison and Melson themselves weren't convinced the song was a hit. They even tried to sell it, pitching it first to Elvis Presley and later to the Everly Brothers. Both acts quickly passed. Yet when Orbison's single was released in May of 1960, the response was electric. Orbison, at the time a complete unknown, found himself with one of the most popular songs in the world.

What made "Only the Lonely" so distinctive was not its composition. It wasn't its structure, melody, or heartbreaking yet hopeful message. It wasn't even Orbison's delicate voice, which legions of record producers had already listened to and dismissed. The secret was in its arrangement, the way its individual components were organized.

Unlike other popular songs of the time, "Only the Lonely" plucked an element that was typically buried in the background of a musical composition and placed it squarely in the foreground, granting it center stage. That element? The backing vocals.

"Only the Lonely" begins with an unforgettable line, delivered not by Orbison but by his backup singers: "Dum-Dum-Dum-Dum-Be-Doo-Wah."

It was Orbison's idea to give the backing vocals a starring role, but it was his sound engineer, Bill Porter, who brought it to life. Instead of recording the musical instruments first and then layering the vocals on top, Porter experimented with a different approach. He abandoned the traditional model and began by recording the soft, close-miked whisper of the backing vocalists. Then he mixed the musical instruments around their track so that their singing would not lose its potency. The result was haunting and became a central feature of Orbison's trademark sound.

The method Orbison used to differentiate his songs, taking an element that is typically buried in the background and making it a central feature of his approach, represents the fifth path to finding your creative twist. It involves seizing an ingredient already contained within an existing formula and elevating its status, making it a distinguishing feature.

Orbison's compelling use of backing vocals offers one example. Another can be found in one of the most successful television shows of all time: *Seinfeld*. There's a lot that distinguishes *Seinfeld* from other comedies of its era. There are the unforgettable characters, interweaving storylines, flagrant self-centeredness. But there's also something else: the starring role of minutiae.

Unlike other sitcoms, *Seinfeld* took minor irritations—the kind experienced daily by every human being on the planet—and elevated them to soaring heights, transforming them into a central feature of the show's plot. Each episode presented a parade of petty aggravations: low talkers, high talkers, close talkers, telemarketers, unrelenting body odor, dreadful customer service, forgotten parking spots, and unwelcome neighbors.

What's the appropriate method of consuming a chocolate bar? How many times are you allowed to dip a single chip into a communal bowl of salsa? Are restroom users obligated to share toilet paper with people in adjacent stalls? These are the sorts of incisive, hard-hitting questions that *Seinfeld* tackled each week with Talmudic fervor.

By taking trivial interactions, the kind that occur in the background of most lives and strategically moving them to the foreground of the show's plot, *Seinfeld* was able to create something genuinely unique: a so-called show about nothing. Except it wasn't nothing. It was simply the storylines other shows had chosen to ignore.

Taking an unnoticed ingredient and placing it squarely in the limelight is an approach that is at the heart of a number of notable advertising campaigns. There is perhaps no better example than the campaign that propelled Absolut from an obscure Swedish novelty to the worldwide vodka leader. When Absolut first entered the global market in 1979, its prospects were dim. In the United States, the vodka market was dominated by Russian brands with aggressively Soviet names like Smirnoff and Stolichnaya. It didn't seem as though Absolut had many options. It could try to set itself apart by its place of origin, though at the time most Americans had no idea that Swedes even made vodka, let alone that it might be any good. Competing on taste was also going to be tricky. Vodka's flavor is subtle. Even the most knowledgeable drinkers have a hard time reliably distinguishing between brands.

So how did Absolut manage to differentiate itself and soar to the top of the US vodka market? By highlighting an overlooked element of the vodka-drinking experience that hovered in the background and elevating its status, making it a central feature of Absolut's advertising campaign: the shape of its bottle.

If you've picked up a magazine or driven by a bus stop in the past year, Absolut's ads will be familiar to you. The company has been running variations of the same campaign for close to forty years now. It involves an image of a desirable destination, activity, or event photoshopped into the shape of an Absolut bottle and accompanied by a two-word headline: "Absolut [fill in the blank]." The first iteration of the ad, which appeared in 1980, featured an Absolut bottle with a halo over it and the headline "Absolut perfection." Over the years, the campaign has grown more abstract, abandoning the literal bottle but keeping its outline, granting Absolut's creative team infinite flexibility to insert itself into countless relevant and seductive topics.

Like Roy Orbison and *Seinfeld*, Absolut distinguished itself by taking what had once been considered a tangential feature of the vodka-drinking experience and making it not only relevant but unforgettable.

But that's not where the Absolut story ends. About a decade after Absolut debuted its iconic advertising campaign, its distribu tor, Carillon Importers, lost the rights to sell Absolut. The news hit Carillon's president, Michel Roux, especially hard. Roux had been instrumental in developing Absolut's creative strike, had personally recruited artists like Andy Warhol to design its ads, and considered Absolut's success the crown jewel of his career. "I grew this baby, cared for it and gave it a good deal of tender love," he confessed to reporters in an era before executive statements were sanitized. "I sure hope its new parent will take good care of it . . . ."

When Absolut abandoned Carillon for a larger distributor, Roux was at a loss. Until he had an epiphany. Not long after surrendering his favorite brand, it occurred to Roux that the formula that had turned Absolut into the United States' best-selling vodka could be resurrected. Not in vodka, of course; that market was spoken for. But there were plenty of other beverages that had yet to highlight a bottle's design as a means of distinguishing themselves to consumers.

Roux did not have to look far to find his first target. As a nationwide distributor, Carillon controlled a wide roster of spirits and liquors. A mere two years later, he was ready with his first release. In 1986, Roux helped introduce a sleek, eye-catching blue bottle that mesmerized customers and single-handedly reignited what had been a dormant gin market. Roux's creation was called Bombay Sapphire.

When Weakness Becomes a Strength

The final path to finding a twist is often accidental. It's a variation introduced by those not striving for originality at all.

When singer Amy Winehouse and songwriter Mark Ronson first began collaborating in 2006, they weren't trying to be distinct. Quite the opposite. They were deliberately trying to re-create the soulful sound of 1960s Motown.

As Ronson explained to NPR's Guy Raz, "I had no idea how to re-create that sound or that vibe. I had never done anything like it up to that point. But I was just so enamored with [Amy] and what she wanted to do that I was like, 'However it happens, I'm going to find out how to do it, even if we get it wrong.' And I think we did get it wrong—just enough to make it its own new thing—which is kind of what you want to do."

Winehouse and Ronson did their best to mimic legendary groups like The Temptations and The Supremes. You can hear it in their songs. All the elements are there: the melodic bass lines, the echoey reverb, the playful rattle of the tambourine. But as a hip-hop DJ, Ronson couldn't help layering on a flurry of electronic beats, while Winehouse's biting, somber lyrics strayed far from the cheerful Motown script. The resulting classics, including "Rehab," "You Know I'm No Good," and "Back to Black," were unique *despite* Winehouse and Ronson's efforts to model their work after an established formula.

What makes those early Winehouse hits so striking?

Like so many of the examples we've explored in this chapter, their allure is explained by a simple blueprint: a proven formula with a novel twist. And how exactly was that twist introduced? Here, Winehouse and Ronson offer an unusual path. One that involves *trying* to apply a proven formula and somehow falling short, forcing you to compensate in a way that results in accidental innovation.

Culinary legend Jacques Pépin has noticed a similar pattern in the world of cooking. Pépin has authored countless cookbooks, yet he believes that no printed recipe is ever perfect—nor can it be. That's because there will always be an unpredictable factor that contributes to the execution of a dish: the influence of the chef. All chefs invariably bring their unique experiences, beliefs, and biases to their cooking, and those tendencies shape the dishes they produce, whether they intend to or not.

Pépin has devoted a significant portion of his career to teaching in the classroom, which is where he noticed that chefs can't help but inject themselves into each dish. "I would ask fifteen students to cook a salad, a boiled potato, and a roast chicken, and would always tell them, 'You want to blow my mind? You want to be different? Please don't.' No matter what, I will have fifteen different chickens—with three practically perfect, three undercooked, three cold, three burned, and three whatever, but they are going to be different. You actually don't have to torture yourself to be different. If you cook with your gut, you are different."

You might think that Pépin would urge his students to limit their impulses and stick to proven recipes more carefully. But that's not at all what he recommends. Instead, he tells aspiring chefs to follow a recipe exactly once. The next step is to embrace their influences by iterating on the original instructions. The chef's job is not to copy. It is to reimagine and adjust, "massaging [recipes] to their aesthetic and sense of taste."

About a decade before Winehouse and Ronson started writing songs together, Malcolm Gladwell left the *Washington Post* to join the staff of the *New Yorker*. It was a jarring move for Gladwell, who had invested ten years mastering a particular style of writing: the newspaper article. This was not what the *New Yorker* had hired him to do. "All of a sudden you need to write things that are anywhere between three and five times longer than anything you've ever written before in your life," Gladwell recounted on the *Longform* podcast. "In a newspaper, everything is about compression: How can I represent something as quickly and simply as possible? And most of what you report, you never use. So then you have to go to a mind-set which is about expansion: How can I tell the story in a way that is worthy of six thousand words?"

Suddenly, Gladwell, who had been used to writing four-paragraph stories, needed to keep readers entertained for more than an hour. At first, he wasn't quite sure how. His role required that he adapt to the demands of longform writing. Eventually he settled on an approach. "My thing was, well, I'm going to try and mix up ideas and narrative because I don't know how to fill the space any other way, you know? I don't have enough faith in my ability to just tell a story."

That's a stunning admission that many writers would do well to keep in mind. Gladwell did not set out to be unique. His originality came about as a direct result of his inability to write a typical *New*

Yorker story. He was compensating, and it was through that compensation that something remarkable and innovative emerged.

Not too long ago, Gladwell published a book called *David and Goliath*. In it he argued that when it comes to advantages and disadvantages, looks can be deceiving. Often, what appears to be a strength is actually a weakness, and what appears to be a weakness is actually a strength. Gladwell's thesis wasn't intended as a commentary on his career, but it would be hard to find a more fitting example of an apparent weakness evolving into an unexpected strength.

We began this chapter with a question: What's the secret to writing like the most influential nonfiction author of the twenty-first century? But perhaps that's the wrong question. Yes, reverse engineering can reveal important patterns embedded within Gladwell's writing, but working purely to re-create his formula is a mistake. Mimicry alone rarely results in greatness. It's only by deconstructing the masters and then adding a twist that we produce extraordinary results.

The right question, therefore, is not "How do I write like Malcolm Gladwell?" It's "How do I take Gladwell's formula and make it my own?"

Part II

The
Vision-Ability
Gap

The Vision-Ability Gap

In the late 1870s, not long after the end of the Civil War, millions of dollars vanished from America's banks.

In Baltimore, $250,000 disappeared from the Third National Bank. In upstate New York, Saratoga County National Bank reported half a million dollars missing. And near New York City's West Village, at the Manhattan Savings Institution, a building renowned for its impenetrable security, almost $3 million seemingly evaporated into thin air.

Financial institutions across the country were under attack, and bank executives were panicked. And for good reason. These were not typical bank heists. There were no gangs of menacing robbers pointing guns and threatening tellers. These criminals arrived through the most unusual points of entry, locations few experts considered necessary to safeguard. They came tunneling up from basements, dropping down from ceilings, and ripping through the walls of the businesses next door.

Even more puzzling was their ability to access the vault without the use of explosives. Not one stick of dynamite had been used in any of these burglaries, and most didn't even appear to involve a crowbar.

Investigators were quick to recognize that they were facing a new breed of criminal. As New York City's chief of police, George Washington Walling, would later note in his diary, "As a rule, it is the most intelligent members of the criminal class that drift into this branch of wickedness."

Walling was right. He was witnessing the work of a mastermind. But on one count Walling would later stand corrected: the success of this criminal had less to do with intelligence than with the command of a powerful new skill.

How exactly was this criminal pulling it off? By now his methodology will be familiar: the ability to reverse engineer.

Today, experts regard the man Walling was after, George Leonidas Leslie, as one of the most successful criminals in world history. Over the course of nine years, he spearheaded more than 80 percent of all bank robberies in the United States, earning himself the nickname "king of heists." He is estimated to have overseen more than one hundred bank jobs, building himself a fortune somewhere in the neighborhood of $12 million, at the time when the average American's salary was less than $375 a year.

His approach was simple. Leslie would visit a target bank while playing the role of an ordinary customer seeking to make his first deposit. While arrangements for his new account were being made, Leslie would casually look around, surveying the bank's layout and design.

Next, he would request a safety deposit box. These were located in a more secure section of a bank, providing Leslie with an extensive look at a bank's inner sanctum and bringing him into proximity with the vault. At this juncture, Leslie would casually mention that he was a professional architect and had consulted for a variety of banks around the country. This fabrication gave him the pretext to break free of his role as naive customer, granting him license to walk about freely, remarking on the layout of the vault, pointing out distinguishing features, and matter-of-factly posing questions about the safe—all under the guise of helping a prospective patron.

The idea that this seemingly well-educated, impeccably dressed architect was somehow spearheading a criminal enterprise was laughable—the last thing anyone would have suspected.

Upon returning home, Leslie's work would begin in earnest. He would reach for a pencil, drawing every last detail he could remember. He would map out the size and shape of each room, marking the location of its furniture and any other obstacles that might impede his squad's movements. He would know which tools to bring and how much noise would be generated, having noted the materials used to construct the ceiling, floors, and walls as well as their estimated thickness.

By the time Leslie was done, he had more than a rough sketch. He had a blueprint. Now it was time to identify every potential vulnerability that could be exploited for entry.

How to Plan the Perfect Crime

It would be unfair to attribute all of Leslie's success as a criminal mastermind to reverse engineering. Converting the banks' layout into a blueprint merely constituted the first phase of his plan. Pulling off a perfect bank robbery, Leslie understood, requires a lot more than knowledge. It demands masterful execution, which is a different matter entirely.

This was Leslie's solution: he would construct a full-scale replica of the bank's interior inside a nearby abandoned warehouse. Here he would assemble his gang and unveil his master plan, which included detailed instructions for each of his associates.

Every movement was carefully choreographed, each second meticulously planned.

Next came weeks of practice, which Leslie supervised, timing each trial with a stopwatch. As the group's execution improved, Leslie would ramp up the pressure, introducing new obstacles for the team to navigate. It was not beyond him to blow out the candles midway through, forcing them to practice in pitch dark. This was his way of ensuring that everyone had his directions memorized and were prepared for the unexpected.

So elaborate were Leslie's plans and so thorough his preparations that after his passing, even the most earnest of investigators couldn't resist marveling at his attention to detail. Not only had he drafted blueprints, built replicas, and demanded months of practice in impossible conditions—he had also pinpointed the ideal time to rob a bank:

Friday night. With banks closed over the weekend, it would take employees two and a half days to realize their vault had been cleared. By then, Leslie's team was long gone, their trail ice cold.

With all that extensive planning, most criminals would have been more than a little confident. But Leslie wasn't taking any chances. He insisted that his gang put on costumes, which he procured through his connections at the opera. By day, Leslie's crew were an unsavory pack of hooligans. But come Friday night, they could be found tiptoeing through cobblestoned streets in wigs, capes, and dresses like extras from *The Marriage of Figaro*.

After rehearsals, Leslie would return to his home in Stuyvesant Heights, New York, where he engaged in an entirely different set of practice drills. Ones that enabled him to master safecracking in record time.

While playing the role of customer and touring a bank's facilities, Leslie would identify the precise make and model of the institution's safe. After his visit, he would contact the safe manufacturer directly and, under the guise of needing one for an architectural project he was overseeing, purchase a similar model, which he then proceeded to take apart in the comfort of his own home.

Leslie deconstructed hundreds of safes over the years and developed an expertise in their design and configuration. Eventually, he hit upon a pattern. Most safes, he realized, are alike. On the outside, there is a knob. Turning the knob manipulates a series of metal disks that sit on a spindle inside the door. Bring the metal disks into alignment, and the safe door opens.

Simple enough. The trouble is, deciphering a combination often takes hours and requires calm, uninterrupted focus. Both are in short supply in the middle of a bank heist. Fortunately for Leslie, there was a hack. It involved drilling a small hole into the safe just above the dial, allowing Leslie to physically shift the safe's metal disks into alignment, circumventing the need for a combination.

After he managed to finagle the safe door open, he would putty up the hole and paint it to match the color of the safe's exterior. This ensured that even after a theft was discovered, his technique would continue to remain a mystery.

Unpacking Leslie's elaborate approach offers more than a captivating story. It reveals the extent to which performance is reliant on a lot more than knowledge.

Leslie's bank blueprints provided direction, but executing a successful robbery required a great deal more than that. What those blueprints did not include were instructions on how to break in discreetly, crack the safe in record time, or escape undetected. Those elements emerged through extensive planning, a carefully constructed training regimen, and calculated risk taking.

Reverse engineering offers insight, yes. But how exactly do you turn those insights into mastery? That's what the second half of this book is about.

The Cost of Recognizing Great Work

It's one thing to distill exceptional work into a formula and quite another to reproduce it effectively. And while a proven recipe is undoubtedly useful, it comes with a cost: high expectations.

At first glance, that might seem like a minor inconvenience. In practice, it can be utterly devastating. As the creator of *This American Life*, Ira Glass, observed, when you are developing your skills, there is often a gap between your vision and your ability:

> What nobody tells people who are beginners—and I really wish someone had told this to me—is that all of us who do creative work, we get into it because we have good taste. But there is this gap. For the first couple of years you make stuff, and it's just not that good. It's trying to be good, it has potential, but it's not. But your taste, the thing that got you into the game, is still killer. And your taste is why your work disappoints you. A lot of people never get past this phase. They quit.

The divide Glass is describing—the gap between vision and ability—can be debilitating, especially when you have high standards. Which is a legitimate concern after you've been deconstructing the master in your field. After all, the loftier your vision, the more difficult it is to achieve.

Worse, it's a gap that never truly disappears. Ann Patchett is an extraordinarily accomplished novelist, the winner of too many distinguished literary awards to list in full. To this day, she wrestles with the vision-ability gap each time she starts a new book.

For Patchett, there are three phases to writing: plotting, procrastinating, and producing. The first of these phases is by far the most blissful. When she is generating ideas, Patchett writes:

> The book is my invisible friend, omnipresent, evolving, thrilling. During the months (or years) it takes me to put my ideas together, I don't take notes or make outlines; I'm figuring things out, and all the while the book makes a breeze around my head like an oversized butterfly whose wings were cut from the rose window in Notre Dame. This book I have not yet written one word of is a thing of indescribable beauty, unpredictable in its patterns, piercing in its color, so wild and loyal in its nature that my love for this book, and my faith in it as I track its lazy flight, is the single perfect joy in my life.

It's an intoxicating period, not unlike the morning after a romantic first date or the month between accepting a job offer and starting your first day of work. Patchett's future feels rich and full of promise.

What follows is a period of procrastination. Having published many books, part of Patchett anticipates the grueling journey ahead and resists getting started. She finds herself occupied with productive distractions, consumed with pretend priorities.

Eventually the writing begins, and with it comes stomach-churning, soul-crushing disappointment, which Patchett recounts in gory detail:

> When I can't think of another stall, when putting it off has actually become more painful than doing it, I reach up and pluck the butterfly from the air. I take it from the region of

my head and I press it down against my desk, and there, with my own hand, I kill it. . . . Imagine running over a butterfly with an SUV. Everything that was beautiful about this living thing—all the color, the light and movement—is gone. What I'm left with is the dry husk of my friend, the broken body chipped, dismantled and poorly reassembled. Dead. That's my book.

When Patchett reads this aloud in front of audiences, they assume that she is exaggerating or trying to elicit laughs. She has found it necessary to clarify: she could not be any more serious.

The journey from the head to hand is perilous and lined with bodies. It is the road on which everyone who wants to write—and many of the people who do write—get lost.

On this point Glass and Patchett agree: the price of having a clear vision is not simply disappointment with your own work. It's also a risk factor for quitting. The stronger your radar for excellence, the harder it becomes to stomach mediocrity. And that's a problem, especially when deconstructing the work of masters will invariably raise your standards.

A Brief History of Good Taste

But perhaps that's the wrong way to interpret the vision-ability gap. After all, skill can be taught, but vision and taste are decidedly harder to develop.

Where exactly does good taste come from? There is no shortage of evidence that human beings are born with genetic preferences for specific experiences, though clearly, good taste involves something more nuanced and complex than mere preference. At the very least, it involves a sensitivity to the elements that make a particular object pleasing, an awareness that enables certain individuals to better discern the exceptional from the mundane.

Not everyone agrees that good taste is grounded in genetics.

Some argue it is better explained by economics. According to the late French sociologist Pierre Bourdieu, it is society's upper crust that determines what the world considers tasteful. By embracing particular objects and experiences, the wealthy create social norms for the broader public. The lower classes then adopt these preferences, secretly (and unconsciously) hoping that emulating the rich will make them appear respectable.

Then there are those who believe that taste is a reaction to one's life experiences. It's a response to one's personal history. Taste, according to this view, is an attempt to satisfy psychological needs that have been thwarted over a life span.

Seen through this lens, taste is revealing. The objects and experiences to which we are most attracted are not arbitrary, nor are they objectively pleasing. They tell us something profound about ourselves. Specifically, they expose the psychological desires we crave at the deepest levels.

British philosopher Alain de Botton relishes this perspective and argues that it explains a great deal. For one thing, de Botton suggests, it clarifies why some cultures are drawn to lavish, opulent decors (he cites the Russians and Saudis as examples) while others prefer clean, simple design (such as those popular in Scandinavian countries). Both are a reaction to historical conditions. The Russians and Saudis endured decades of economic deprivation, and since extravagant interiors represent the opposite of poverty, they favor ostentatious decor. (A similar case has been made for the enthusiastic display of gold chains, rings, and teeth that are fashionable among newly successful rappers.) Scandinavians, on the other hand, were raised in relative financial security and do not share a desire for visual reminders of wealth. Instead, they favor calm, peaceful interiors as an antidote to the overstimulation of everyday life.

The precise origin of taste aside, one thing is for certain: developing an awareness for works that move you is an essential precursor for producing extraordinary work.

Novelist Jonathan Safran Foer puts it this way:

What distinguishes, I think, great writers from people who are not great writers, or are not writers at all, [is] taste . . . Not taste in the sense of knowing what is good in an objective way—because there's nothing objective to point you, there's nothing to refer to out in the world—but knowing what it is that you yourself respond to and then making the leap of faith that if you respond strongly to something, there will be people in the world who also respond strongly.

It's a critical observation and suggests something important. Instead of catastrophizing our inability to perform quickly at a high level, we'd be wiser to celebrate the fact that we can sense when improvements are needed.

That instinct is indispensable to achieving greatness.

The Case for Hating More (and the Road Ahead)

In the 1950s, science fiction writer Theodore Sturgeon had heard enough. For years, he sat by as literary critics tore his genre to shreds. The publishing world's tastemakers were dismissive of science fiction and refused to pay it serious attention. Except when they did, which was often worse. Their animosity was evident, and Sturgeon could just tell: they thought science fiction was juvenile, second-rate trash.

Sturgeon became convinced that the critics would not magically see the errors of their ways. So he authored a piece of criticism of his own, which in 1958 became something of a literary sensation.

Sturgeon's argument was pithy, surprising, and memorable. Instead of disputing the critics' point, he agreed with their perspective, catching them off guard. "The existence of immense quantities of trash in science fiction is admitted and it is regrettable; but it is no more unnatural than the existence of trash anywhere." Which is to say, yes, a lot of published science fiction is disappointing, but so is the work of authors in every other category. Science fiction writing is therefore no better or worse than that of other literary genres. To emphasize his point, he issued a provocative declaration: "Ninety percent of *everything* is crud."

Sturgeon's contention, which has been immortalized as "Sturgeon's Law," can be extrapolated to suggest that within any field, 90 percent of what is produced is garbage. That is, 90 percent of art is forgettable, 90 percent of internet content is underwhelming, and 90 percent of restaurants fail to hit the mark.

Clearly, 90 percent represents a somewhat arbitrary and extreme estimate with which not everyone will agree. But Sturgeon's Law does provide a useful figure in one respect: as a benchmark for determining whether or not your taste is adequately dialed in, particularly when evaluating work in a field you wish to master. If half of everything you encounter seems absolutely spectacular, chances are, you are not yet sufficiently attuned to what it is that you truly love.

Which is not to say that the vision-ability gap shouldn't sting. If you're lucky, it will. Harnessed correctly, the desire to perform masterfully and meet your inner standard will provide the motivational fuel for improvement.

The challenge, of course, is knowing how to bridge the divide so that the distance between where you are today and where you need to be feels inspiring, not deflating.

And how exactly do you do that? In the coming chapters we're going to examine a wide range of practical, evidence-based strategies for attaining high performance. Throughout the journey, three groups will command the lion's share of our attention: elite athletes, leaders of booming businesses, and creative superstars.

From athletes we'll discover how to harness the full benefits of practice, master new skills, and execute under stressful conditions. From business leaders we'll learn how to monitor the right metrics and take intelligent risks without putting everything on the line. And from creative superstars we'll learn how to test new ideas and train the people around us to deliver more useful feedback.

It all starts with the first step to elevating your performance at any task. What is it? That's the topic of the next chapter, "The Scoreboard Principle."

The Scoreboard Principle

The phone rings just after lunch. It's your mother. She's just been to the doctor and you can tell from her voice. She's terrified. Eventually, she loops you in. Her blood pressure has spiked, clocking in at dangerously high levels. Medication can do only so much. She's going to need to lose weight quickly and keep it off for good.

"I'll be right there," you tell her, grabbing your coat.

At the house, she breaks down, saying she needs you. She doesn't have the willpower to do this alone. Can you please, please help?

The first thing you do is raid the cabinets. Blueberry muffins, butter-soaked popcorn, white bread. You stuff them all inside a garbage bag. The refrigerator is next. You can't believe your eyes: sliced salami, way too many ice creams, a decadent cheesecake. You fill a second bag. Then a third.

A few trips to the trash shed later, and you are on your phone, searching for the nearest gym. That's when it hits you. A gym is good, but a personal trainer would be better. You book a session, call back, book a few more.

Change of diet, burst of exercise. You're feeling good about this, confident. You give your mom a hug, kiss her on the forehead. "It's going to be okay," you promise her.

A month later, and you're at the doctor's office, sitting next to your mom. The doctor tells you that a few pounds have come off and her blood pressure is showing some improvement. It's slow, but the progress is clearly there.

You look over at your mom. She should feel proud, at least a little relieved. But you can tell immediately that she feels neither of these things. She is petrified. So you say, "We've adjusted her diet. She's exercising three times a week. Is there anything more we can do?"

"There is one thing," the doctor reveals. It's a treatment that shows remarkable promise in clinical trials. Early results indicate that it accelerates weight loss, lowers stress, and prevents people from putting the pounds back on.

Best of all, there are zero side effects.

You're almost reluctant to ask. "How much does it cost?"

The doctor smiles. "Not a penny," she answers, pulling out her desk drawer. "It's this."

How to Build a Business Empire
Using a Single Metric

So, what did the doctor recommend? It's not a medical procedure or an experimental drug, nor is it a new diet or exercise regimen. It's a simple practice that doubles as the secret weapon of a large number of high-performing businesses.

One company that has prospered using this approach is the luxury hotel chain the Ritz-Carlton. If you're not familiar with the Ritz-Carlton, here is everything you need to know: in 2019, the Ritz-Carlton scored perfect marks in every category measured by JD Power and Associates, earning it an annual award for the best luxury hotel for the fifth year in a row.

What makes the Ritz-Carlton so remarkable? The striking combination of classical architecture with modern decor certainly plays a role. But visitors often cite another factor when asked why they enjoyed their stay: the exceptional customer service.

Now, you may be wondering, what kind of customer service could possibly justify the chain's thousand-dollar-a-night price tag? I wondered the same thing myself, and not too long ago I had the opportunity to find out. In 2018, I visited a Ritz-Carlton in the Cayman

Islands with my family. There are lots of charming—yet relatively minor—service flourishes I can tell you about. But the moment that sticks out years later occurred on the final day of our stay.

The bellhop arrived to collect our bags, but we weren't nearly ready. Clothes were everywhere. We would just need ten minutes, we offered apologetically, hoping that he would wait. But instead of loitering outside or offering to come back a little later, he did something we didn't anticipate. He began packing our bags himself and even called in an associate to pull out the furniture to see if my kids had forgotten any toys (they had).

As it turns out, my family's experience isn't unique. Search the internet for "Ritz-Carlton customer stories," and you'll learn that the hotel prepares surprise rose-petal baths on customers' birthdays, leaves chocolate wrenches in rooms requesting repairs, and mails children the stuffed animals they've left behind, along with a photo album of their toy in various hotel locations, including the pool, spa, and gym, enjoying their extended vacation.

How exactly did the Ritz-Carlton become so good at customer service? By relentlessly tracking performance metrics. Each property's management team monitors a slew of figures, from check-in wait times to advance bookings to employee satisfaction. But there's one metric the Ritz Carlton staff monitors obsessively. It's not the hotel's financials, nor is it its customer satisfaction ratings.

Twenty-four hours after guests leave a Ritz-Carlton property, they receive an email asking them how likely they are to recommend the hotel to friends and colleagues (a metric market researchers refer to as a "net promoter" score). This, the Ritz-Carlton has discovered, is the holy grail. Score well on this item, and you haven't just executed a successful stay. You have created a raving fan. Ritz-Carlton employees are taught that exceptional customer service does more than leave customers satisfied—it causes them to gush about the hotel to those in their social circle. And how in the world do you motivate such exuberance? By going beyond a customer's "explicit requests" and addressing their "unexpressed needs."

Responding to explicit requests involves taking questions at face value and fielding them accordingly.

What time is check-in?
Four p.m.

Does the hotel have a coffee shop?
Yes, it does.

I can't find my goggles. Have you seen them anywhere?
I'm sorry. I have not.

All of these responses are perfectly adequate and factually correct. But as any Ritz-Carlton employee will tell you, they neglect valuable opportunities.

Addressing unexpressed needs involves thinking about why a question was posed in the first place. What underlying challenge is the guest hoping to solve? Listening to questions through this lens prompts Ritz-Carlton employees to respond more empathically in ways that set them apart from employees of other hotel chains.

What time is check-in?
Four p.m. Is your flight arriving early? If you'd like, I can help arrange for an early check-in.

Does the hotel have a coffee shop?
Yes, it does. Would you like me to text you the menu?

I can't find my goggles. Have you seen them anywhere?
I have not seen them, Sir. Would you like me to get you a new pair?

By tackling unexpressed needs, Ritz-Carlton employees are able to dazzle their guests, contributing to both memorable service and sky-high net promoter scores.*

And the results are noteworthy. Not just because they consistently

---

* They also produce an impressive number of notable admirers, including Steve Jobs. Before launching Apple's iconic stores, Jobs instructed his team to study the Ritz-Carlton.

land the Ritz-Carlton at the top of luxury hotel rankings but because they demonstrate the extent to which lasering in on a specific measure can generate extraordinary outcomes.

Something powerful happens when we link behaviors to metrics. This chapter is devoted to answering the question "Why?"

The (Countless) Upsides of Keeping Score

The Ritz-Carlton is hardly alone when it comes to focusing on metrics. Businesses today are awash in data. With just the click of a mouse, executives can now eye hourly revenue and customer demand, marketing managers can track website visitors and conversions, and human resources leaders can monitor job applications and employee retention.

There's a reason business leaders have grown enamored with key performance indicators (KPIs), and it's not just because they provide a better handle on their achievements. It's because measurement begets improvement. The moment a metric is introduced, we instinctively pay it more attention and pursue its optimization. Identifying the right metrics can therefore make all the difference between consistent growth and eventual bankruptcy.

Businesses aren't the only ones that stand to benefit from the power of metrics. The same effects can be leveraged by individuals who wish to shape their own behaviors. In fact, a compelling case can be made that metrics represent the single most valuable and underutilized contributor to self-improvement in any domain.

Just look at dieting. What's that extraordinary treatment the physician in the opening anecdote might suggest your mother try? A food diary. In a 1,700-person clinical trial conducted by healthcare experts at Kaiser Permanente, simply asking dieters to record the precise foods they consumed at each meal led them to double their weight loss compared to those who ate the same diet and didn't track their food consumption.

Why does tracking have such a profound effect? Because it prompts dieters to reflect on their food choices and gives them an unvarnished look at their calorie consumption. But it's not just reflecting back on past choices that's useful—it's also the effect tracking has on future decisions.

I've observed a similar effect on time-strapped professionals. One of the first exercises I invite my coaching clients to do involves tracking their time over the course of several workdays, so we can get an objective look at how they spend their week. Afterward, we sit down together and review the findings. The results are always revealing. Invariably, we spot commitments that no longer serve their priorities and activities that take up more time than they should.

But there's a sneaky flaw in this "objective" exercise: the very process of keeping a time log influences the choices we make. That's because it's one thing to squander thirty minutes watching YouTube videos when that decision stays between you and your browser history. But it's a choice you weigh a lot more carefully when you have to report it on a time sheet. Knowing that you—or you and your performance coach—will analyze your behavior later makes immediate rewards a little less appetizing and helps you reach wiser long-term decisions.

The right measure can also expose wasted effort. Once you start collecting performance metrics, anything that doesn't contribute to a desired outcome becomes impossible to ignore. Among my coaching clients, a number have transitioned from working within large organizations to starting small businesses. One shift these clients can't help but notice is an evolution in their attitude toward meetings. They go from mildly disliking large, drawn-out meetings to experiencing physical revulsion at the prospect of spending hours talking with colleagues.

Why the change? Entrepreneurs are keenly attuned to the metrics driving their business. The price of ignoring these metrics is financial ruin. And while well-run meetings have their place, extended, meandering discussions rarely contribute to innovation, execution, and profitability in a meaningful way.

In contrast, how many employees keep track of the metrics driving their career? To be sure, most organizational cultures make it impossible to shun meetings, no matter how well aware a worker might be that they are not a productive use of time. Yet the question remains: Would meetings be so common if all employees had real-time metrics reflecting the outcomes they need to achieve to secure their next promotion?

Tracking is especially useful when it draws our attention to valuable actions we tend to avoid. Activities like reconnecting with old clients, developing new marketing initiatives, or whatever it is that you tend to neglect that prevents you from progressing in your career. Turning a desired action into a metric makes you more likely to follow through. It's because metrics introduce an emotional dimension.

As venture capitalist Ben Horowitz noted in his book *The Hard Thing About Hard Things*, "metrics are incentives." When we see our numbers surge, progress becomes more tangible, sparking satisfaction and pride. In contrast, seeing our metrics plummet generates disappointment, frustration, even shame. These emotional jolts are not trivial. They lend our actions psychic weight, leading us to work harder in pursuit of a higher score.

Simply put, metrics motivate. They lead to better decisions, greater consistency, fewer distractions, and emotional investment. This is the scoreboard principle: measurement begets improvement. Which is why the first step to improving at anything, whether it be losing weight, acquiring a new skill, or mastering a formula you've reverse engineered, begins with relentlessly keeping score.

Why Your Brain Loves Numbers

If there is one domain that expertly harnesses the power of metrics, demonstrating just how influential they can be as a motivating force, it's video games.

Video game developers showcase scores for good reason, even on games that have nothing to do with sports. Experience has taught them that adding a performance metric makes games infinitely more entertaining. It also generates competition—both between opposing players and among players aiming to set a new personal best.

A good friend of mine, Greg Erway, is presently the world record holder in the classic 1980s arcade game Tapper. To earn this title, Greg managed to keep a single game going for more than sixteen hours without pausing to consume a bite of food or visiting the bathroom once. And what did Greg receive in return for this effort? Did he collect a fat check from a corporate sponsor? Carry home a massive trophy? Earn the affection of an army of adoring fans? Not at all. What Greg did get was the distinction of knowing that he had accumulated a higher number of points on a video game than anyone else.

Clearly, Greg's enthusiasm for video games dwarfs that of most people. But his story illustrates the extreme lengths to which people will go just to achieve a metric they consider meaningful.

Today, the use of real-time performance metrics is no longer limited to the world of video games. App developers have grown all too aware of the motivating power of metrics and commonly leverage scores and the prospect of more points to influence a wide variety of behaviors. Gamification is everywhere, and you'd be hard pressed to find an app that *doesn't* feature scores, even when those scores have no obvious rationale for existing. Instead, points are shrewdly doled out to seduce and manipulate users into playing longer games, making return visits, and springing for in-app purchases.

Recent lab experiments reveal that even when scores are completely detached from people's behavior, growing point totals motivate greater effort and higher performance. Researchers have a name for this phenomenon: *numerical nudging*. It refers to the fact that, as the experimenters put it, even "inherently meaningless numbers" are enough to "strategically alter behaviors."

How, then, can we explain the power of metrics to influence behavior? What is it about numbers that makes them such a compelling motivating force? And why are there times when human beings are seemingly mesmerized by statistics?

Psychological needs provide one explanation. Decades of research suggest that all humans—regardless of their age, gender, or culture—are born with three basic psychological needs: the need for belonging, autonomy, and competence. It's the last of the three that growing scores appeal to—the basic human desire for learning, skill acquisition, and mastery. By signaling progress and illustrating achievement, metrics satisfy our instinctive drive for growth.

Others believe that our fascination with numbers runs deeper and represents a once vital survival mechanism run amok.

Andreas Nieder, a physiology professor who specializes in brain science, has spent decades researching how numbers are processed by a wide variety of species, including humans. According to Nieder, all animals are born with a "numbers instinct"—a deeply rooted impulse to seek out numerical information that is essential to their survival and reproduction.

In his book, *A Brain for Numbers: The Biology of the Number Instinct*, Nieder provides a mountain of examples for how numbers promote evolutionary success. Consider the value of counting. At a very basic level, having the ability to distinguish a large quantity of food from a small quantity ensured that our ancient ancestors devoted more attention to rewards that maximized their chances of survival.

Attending to numbers offers other crucial advantages, especially in social settings. The same mathematical inclination that told our ancestors which food source to pursue also provided an instant read on the power and influence of foreign groups. By approximating the size of a newly encountered tribe, they gained strategic information about which tribes they could conquer and which to avoid.

Estimating numbers also helps when it comes to safeguarding reproductive partners. Knowing how many rivals you are competing with tells you when it is necessary to keep a watchful eye on your partner and when it is relatively safe to leave your mate unattended.

For all of these reasons, humans born with a number instinct achieved greater survival and reproductive success. Either you paid obsessive attention to metrics and gleaned a strategic advantage, or you ignored them at your peril.

Vanity Metrics

The fact that centuries of evolution have programmed us to fixate on numerical information presents us with both an opportunity and a curse.

Let's look at the dangers first, of which there are many. Never before have human beings been inundated with so many metrics. Some are valuable; most are not. Over the course of a single workday, the average employee encounters a torrent of numerical information, including unread emails, marketing figures, stock prices, follower counts, and app notifications waiting to reveal their sleep/exercise/mood score. In the past, a craving for numerical insight helped our species survive. Today, it contributes to distraction in the best of circumstances. At its worst, it can lead to full-blown compulsion.

In his book *The Lean Startup*, Silicon Valley veteran and startup expert Eric Ries describes a troubling phenomenon that routinely throws promising new businesses off the rails: an obsession with vanity metrics. Vanity metrics are figures that are easy to amplify and generally excite nonexperts but do not reflect a thriving business. For example, to most nonexperts, if a business generates $100 million in annual revenue, that's impressive. A more seasoned professional would inquire about the company's overhead. If it turns out that the business's operating costs are also in the neighborhood of $100 million a year, the facade of a thriving business crumbles.

Startups, Ries noted, face an avalanche of vanity metric traps. Among the more common culprits: obsessing over total website visitors (instead of focusing on website conversions or sales), fattening up user numbers (instead of increasing paying customers), and maximizing user growth (when active or repeat users are far more valuable). From Ries's perspective, optimizing the wrong metric isn't just wasted effort, it can obliterate a business. By enticing founders with seductive, superficial goals and diverting their attention away from activities that legitimately contribute to a sustainable business, vanity metrics pose a crippling danger.

A similar case can be made for ambitious professionals looking to establish a meaningful career. Socially desirable, but ultimately meaningless, metrics are everywhere. Depending on your goals, they may include the number of people who liked your latest status update, the size of your LinkedIn community, or even the number of zeros at the end of your paycheck. Any metric that seizes your attention but doesn't contribute to your health, well-being, or career is ultimately a distraction. The more attention we devote to vanity metrics, the less attention we have for activities that matter.

Which brings us to the opportunity, one that few people outside the domain of sports fully leverage. Our fascination with metrics suggests that anything we consistently measure receives enhanced attention. And as we've seen, enhanced attention naturally inspires improvement.

The opportunity lies in measuring the right actions and crafting a scoreboard that directs your attention to the right metrics—especially skills that bridge the gap between your ultimate vision and current ability.

So where do you start?

How Athletes Use Metrics to Unlock Opportunities

In 2016, Roger Federer's tennis career was on the verge of extinction.

For nearly two decades, Federer's performance had been nothing short of spectacular. He had won more than a thousand matches, collected seventeen Grand Slam trophies, and towered comfortably atop the Association of Tennis Professionals (ATP) player rankings for a mind-boggling span of 237 straight weeks.

But then, almost inexplicably, his game began to languish. The decline was subtle. One day, an uncharacteristic double fault. The next, a flurry of unforced errors. Straight-set wins had become a little less frequent, and before too long, early-round victories were no longer automatic.

Federer had recently turned thirty-five, and commentators were openly debating a tender subject: Was it time for Roger to hang up his tennis shoes? The facts were not on his side. It had been four long years since Federer's last Grand Slam victory—his only major tournament victory in seven years. Andre Agassi was thirty-two when he won his last major tournament, Pete Sampras thirty-one. On this, everyone could agree: Federer had enjoyed a phenomenal run. But surely, at thirty-five, his expiration date was on the horizon.

Then the unimaginable happened. Federer was in the bathroom, drawing a bath for his twins. He turned a little too quickly. There was a pop, short and distinctive. A few hours later, he was lying in a hospital bed, the swelling in his left knee obscene. An emergency MRI was scheduled. The results were grim. Federer had torn his meniscus, the rubbery cartilage nestled between the shinbone and thighbone. He would need emergency arthroscopic surgery, followed by weeks of intense rehab. It wasn't at all clear when he would be ready to take to the court again.

The days after the surgery were some of the most difficult in Federer's life. He had never experienced a serious injury before, let alone undergone surgery. The prospect of a forced retirement loomed heavily in the background. "[I] was actually quite emotional," he admitted years later, "looking down at my foot and understanding that maybe this leg or this knee will never be the same."

If you happen to be even a casual observer of tennis, you know that this was not the end of Federer's distinguished career. If anything, it ignited what would become a historic and unprecedented second act.

After a brief, ill-advised attempt to return to the court too quickly, Federer gave himself six full months to recover. During that time, he did more than rehab and rest. He analyzed his game from top to bottom, working closely with his coaching staff to identify precisely what he needed to do better.

At first blush, Federer's losses were difficult to explain. Statistically, his strengths were enormous. Fifty percent of his serves were unreturnable. If an opponent did somehow manage to return his serve, Federer would dominate those points as well, winning more than twice as many volley points as his competitors. On average, for every four points Roger Federer earned on a tennis court, his opponent was able to salvage just one.

One element of Federer's game, however, was decidedly less than stellar: his backhand. On this, the metrics spoke volumes. Not only was Federer hitting fewer backhand winners than his opponents, but the moment an opponent forced him into hitting his backhand slice, his chances of winning the point plummeted below 50 percent. And the better the opponent, the more he exploited Federer's vulnerability. Against top-ranked rivals, Federer's backhand was costing him upward of ten points per match.

When Federer returned to tennis in January 2017, expectations were modest. News coverage dismissed him as "a senior statesman," a representative of tennis's "old guard." Federer stunned them all. No one anticipated his advancing far in the Australian Open, much less winning the entire tournament by beating an opponent he had never before defeated in a Grand Slam final: his career-long nemesis, Rafael Nadal.

Federer's 2017 Australian Open victory wasn't simply a one-off. It marked the start of a rousing resurgence. Later that year, Federer would take Wimbledon without losing a single set. The following January, he would successfully defend his Australian Open title, setting a new world record for Grand Slam tournaments won by a male player.

What was it that changed about Roger Federer's game? Once again, the answer is revealed in the metrics.

When you look at his performance in that 2017 Australian Open Final against Nadal, two things jump out. The first is the number of backhand winners Federer hits. Remember, Federer's weakness is his backhand. The more of these you make him hit, the better your chances of winning. Yet somehow Federer pulls off fourteen backhand winners against Nadal, a 350 percent improvement over the last time they played on the same court. Federer has transformed his biggest vulnerability into a major strength.

And how has Federer managed this? He has made three key adjustments to his tennis game. The first is that he now takes his backhand earlier, right off the bounce, so that he can return the ball lower and closer to the net. The second is that he swings with noticeably more power and delivers the ball with faster speed than in the past. And finally, he is putting less spin on the ball and hitting it flatter, further quickening its pace and leaving his opponent with less time to react.

We know all this because we have an astonishing amount of analytics on tennis matches. And because professional sports associations collect mountains of data on every match played, players like Roger Federer are able to pinpoint precisely which elements of their game require improvement.

Which stands in stark contrast to the vast majority of professions. At most workplaces, few people monitor their own behavior with any regularity. And that disconnect between routine actions and long-term outcomes has consequences. If you ask the average executive how their performance on today's conference call compares to their performance last year, they will be hard-pressed to answer. What percentage of the day was spent answering email? No one knows. How have this week's client presentations compared to years prior? For most workers, it's a mystery.

And yet there is strong reason to believe that performance metrics can be even more valuable at work than in sports. It's because in sports, objectives are blindingly obvious. To win a match, Roger Federer needs to do one thing and one thing only: score points. At work, our objectives are a moving target. They tend to vary from day to day, and in some professions, from hour to hour. That variety keeps work interesting but makes it all too easy to get pulled off track or mistake pointless busywork for meaningful productivity.

There is no scoreboard to tell us how we are doing at work. But what if there were? What if the same analysts who deconstruct Roger Federer's game into constituent parts did the same for your performance at the office? What strengths would they find? What vulnerabilities would they reveal? And what if, like Federer, you could use those numerical insights to transform your hidden weakness into a signature strength?

How to Design Your Scoreboard

Federer's unlikely comeback at the age of thirty-five doesn't just offer a striking example of the way metrics can yield game-changing insights. It also reveals the types of metrics that are most useful.

The metrics Federer's team used to turn his game around did something crucial: they broke down long, complex matches into distinct categories of behavior. That allowed Federer's team to assess each element of his game individually. By isolating key components—including his serves, forehands, backhands, overheads, net points—they were able to uncover his unique weakness and formulate a plan to remedy it.

A similar approach is warranted when measuring our own performance in any domain we wish to master. To leverage metrics effectively, we need more than global feedback on performance. We need data that measure our key behaviors and tell us which we are executing well and which we have the potential to improve.

What should you measure? The precise elements worth monitoring will depend on the nature of the task, your level of skill, and your ultimate goals. With that in mind, here are three approaches worth considering.

The first involves breaking down a single activity into multiple subskills. In the same way that a tennis match consists of different types of shots, most intellectual activities can be broken down into several distinct categories of skill. Suppose, for example, that your job involves pitching your firm to new prospects and you want to develop metrics to track your performance. A number of subskills come into play when you present at meetings, including: memorization, delivery, body language, presence, and poise. Recording your pitch and scoring these elements individually will provide you with a clear sense of where your performance is strong and where it needs improvement.

The second approach is useful for tasks where success has less to do with combining disparate skills than hitting on particular features. Writing reports, articles, or client emails offers a useful illustration. In all three cases, effective writing is the main skill. And yet we can still develop metrics that help us assess the quality of a composition.

Let's say you are drafting an outreach email to a client who has yet to sign an important contract. You need this contract finalized quickly. You're hoping to prompt your client to sign, but you want to do so in a way that doesn't come across as pushy or desperate. In fact, if at all possible, you'd like your email to strengthen your relationship. Fortunately, you've collected a handful of well-written emails and reverse outlined them to identify a number of important features.

You've deduced that that your email should include:

- A non-work-related opening, preferably on a topic you've bonded over in the past

- A brief mention of the action you need the respondent to take
- A rationale explaining why taking action quickly will benefit the respondent
- New information your respondent is likely to find valuable, such as an article or insight that illustrates that you are working toward shared goals
- A closing that expresses enthusiasm for the relationship or for hearing back from the respondent

Needless to say, these particular features won't feel appropriate for every email or every respondent. Let's just assume for now that these are the ingredients that you consider essential for a well-executed "Where's that thing you promised me?" email.

The next step involves transforming each element on your list into a scored item. Here's one way to do it. After composing your email, evaluate your draft by scoring your performance. Ask yourself: On a scale of 1 (not well) to 7 (extremely well), how well does this email execute:

- A non-work-related opening, preferably on a topic you've bonded over in the past
- A brief mention of the action you need the respondent to take
- A rationale explaining why taking action quickly will benefit the respondent
- New information your respondent is likely to find valuable, such as an article or insight that illustrates that you are working toward shared goals
- A closing that expresses enthusiasm for the relationship or for hearing back from the respondent

By turning features into metrics, you create a measure that offers you immediate feedback on your performance and draws your attention to elements of your work that can be improved.

A third approach for crafting metrics that track your performance is more holistic than the first two. It involves looking beyond a particular task and evaluating the totality of your performance over the course of a specified time frame.

Executive coach Marshall Goldsmith swears by this technique. A prolific writer and coaching pioneer, he insists that all his clients identify an ideal version of themselves and work backward, listing the specific behaviors their best self would execute on a regular basis. Then he has them rate themselves on each behavior daily. Goldsmith even uses this method on himself. Every evening, a little before bedtime, his assistant calls and reads off a list of questions. Having another person do the asking, he has found, provides accountability and ensures that he follows through.

Goldsmith tracks thirty-six items that range from work-related tasks (minutes spent writing, client check-ins) to health and hygiene (minutes spent exercising, taking vitamins) to showing kindness and empathy to others (complimenting or doing something nice for Lyda, his wife).

Goldsmith's daily questions provide a modern spin on a practice made famous by legendary innovator and American revolutionary Benjamin Franklin. Franklin wasn't always the distinguished figure many of us think of today. Back in his early twenties, he was widely known as a heavy drinker and notorious gossip, a man whose behavior was fueled less by reason and rationality than by an insatiable sex drive. Franklin was all too aware of his personal deficiencies. To counteract his shortcomings, he developed a list of virtues that he hoped to instill into his character through the use of self-report.

A sample of Franklin's daily tracker appears in his 1791 autobiography. Given what we now know of his spotty reputation, it's easy to grasp why certain virtues appear on his list: they represent the inverse of habits he aimed to extinguish. At the very top of his list is temperance (no heavy drinking), followed by silence (minimize senseless gossip) and later chastity (avoid promiscuity).

Franklin's list encompassed thirteen virtues. Every evening, he would pull out his journal and review the list, marking off virtues he had failed to carry out that day.

Goldsmith and Franklin draw upon the same methodology to pursue drastically different goals. Goldsmith's measure is designed to optimize his performance as an executive coach and spouse, while Franklin's virtues were selected with the intention of reshaping his personal character.*

That doesn't just demonstrate the flexibility of a daily tracker approach. It highlights a crucial benefit of developing a list of target intentions in the first place. It's a process that compels you to step back, reflect deeply, and identify the achievements you consider essential.

In sports, the outcomes that define success are unambiguous. To win, players must accumulate points, baskets, runs, or touchdowns. Life doesn't work that way. In the real world, there are infinite paths to success. And the first step to winning is becoming clear on the points you're trying to score in the first place.

Using Your Scoreboard to Level Up

No matter which of these methods you use as your scoreboard—measuring subskills, features, or daily habits—certain advantages will be apparent right away.

There is the added clarity you experience from having a concrete set of predefined goals. There's the elevated sense of control that comes from limiting your attention to a modest set of outcomes. Tracking your performance also makes you more aware of your decisions, prompting you to make better choices.

But then there are advantages that are less obvious—like the opportunity for immediate feedback. Most working professionals receive

---

* There is also a level of precision in Goldsmith's measures that Franklin's lack. Goldsmith doesn't track fuzzy goals like "order" and "industry," both of which feature prominently on Franklin's list. He monitors the exact number of minutes invested in important tasks. That specificity is useful. Behavioral science research indicates that the more explicit and unambiguous our intention, the more likely we are to follow through.

remarkably limited feedback on a regular basis. And to the extent that we do receive feedback, it tends to arrive after extensive delay (like annual performance reviews) or when we've done something wrong.

That's an odd state of affairs, given what we know about skill development. If there is one finding that the science of expertise considers sacrosanct, it's that immediate feedback is vital to improvement. And the more rapid the feedback, the quicker we learn. That's because objective data don't just help us assess the quality of our performance—they contain important clues about the adjustments we need to make to be successful.

By selecting a set of metrics and self-scoring our performance, we gain immediate feedback without having to wait for input from others. And that's important. Because whether you are working to deliver a compelling pitch, craft an effective email, or execute a formula you've reverse engineered, receiving regular feedback on your performance is a vital ingredient for achieving mastery.

Another nonobvious advantage of having a predetermined set of metrics is that it empowers you to think more strategically. Once you are clear on the metrics that define success, you can use those metrics to do more than rate your performance retroactively. You can apply them in advance when deciding which activities are worth pursuing in the first place.

Chef Daniel Humm, a partner at one of Manhattan's most celebrated restaurants, Eleven Madison Park, applies this approach when constructing his menu. Most restaurants are content with a menu that features dishes the chef believes are tasty. Not Eleven Madison Park. Humm has a set of criteria that determines whether a dish is even worth making. In order for a dish to appear on Eleven Madison Park's menu, it must be delicious, creative, intentional, and beautiful. Only then does Humm consider it worth developing.

Humm's four fundamentals—delicious, creative, intentional, and beautiful—serve as performance metrics when applied retroactively to a dish that already exists, but they can also serve as a filter for evaluating whether a dish is promising enough to pursue. The same holds true for any creative endeavor.

When I first learned of Humm's approach, I was struck by its similarity to the way I develop articles for media outlets. As a writer, I run my ideas through a filter to determine whether they are worthy of an eight-hundred-word piece. Specifically, a prospective idea must tick off four boxes for me to consider it worth tackling. The topic must: (1) relate to work, (2) feature science-based insights, (3) include actionable takeaways, and (4) make the reader feel smarter for having read it. Any idea that fails to meet these fundamentals is quickly abandoned. It's a process that ensures that I both produce valuable content and avoid hours of wasted effort.*

A final nonobvious advantage to using metrics is that they help illuminate the hidden patterns that underlie success by exposing leading indicators.

A leading indicator is a metric that predicts an important outcome in advance, while the outcome can still be influenced. In contrast, a lagging indicator reflects the final result, after the outcome has been determined.

To illustrate the difference between the two, imagine that you quit your day job to pursue your dream of selling handmade artisan candles. Your goal is to match your current annual salary within the first year. A number of factors will determine whether or not you succeed in twelve months. They include the number of candles you are able to produce in an average week, the popularity of your e-commerce site, and the frequency with which you secure booths at live events, like street festivals and farmers' markets. Individually, none of these factors can tell you whether or not you will eventually earn enough to match your current salary. What they can do is help you track the drivers of profitability before the year is through.

In this example, your annual salary is the lagging indicator; it's an outcome you're trying to achieve. In contrast, production speed, website traffic, and event attendance are leading indicators;

---

* I also use these attributes as metrics on the rating sheet I use when reviewing written articles. In this way, they serve double duty—both as a filter before I start, confirming that I'm on the right path, and as a performance metric afterward, ensuring that I have executed effectively.

day-to-day activities that you believe will bring about that desired result.

At first glance, the difference between leading and lagging indicators might seem like esoteric business jargon. It's not. In fact, it's a distinction that represents one of the most compelling reasons for collecting metrics in the first place.

By gathering data on our behavior and the outcomes we hope to achieve, we start to identify important leading indicators—or drivers—of success. These insights can be game-changing, not just to organizations but to anyone hoping to optimize his or her performance. Once you know which leading indicators predict your success, you can start to focus on them intently.

Earlier we looked at metrics exposing the hidden vulnerabilities in Roger Federer's tennis game. Those numbers don't just reveal weaknesses, they also point to some remarkable opportunities. Here is one Federer's team is likely to have noticed. When Federer is serving, the first point of a game turns out to be strangely meaningful. The data suggest that when Federer scores first, the chances of him winning the game skyrocket to a mind-boggling 97 percent.

Like Federer, we all have leading indicators in our daily lives that are just waiting to be discovered.

Let's suppose your goal is to build a side business in the evening and on weekends while maintaining your day job. To make your dream a reality, you wisely develop a set of metrics to track each day: the number of minutes per day invested in building your business, as well as a variety of daily habits like sleep, exercise, and nutrition.

Just what might you uncover after collecting a month's worth of data? A great deal. For example, you might find that you have a lot more energy for working on your business on days when you've slept for seven or more hours, jogged for fifteen minutes before breakfast, and avoided consuming more than 800 calories for lunch. All three data points represent leading indicators of a successful day that can be deliberately shaped through careful planning.

Productivity expert Cal Newport has identified his own leading indicator: hours of unbroken concentration. Newport tallies these hours manually on a piece of paper because he finds that one of the strongest drivers of his personal performance is the ability to work free of distractions. He admits that there's one other benefit to keeping his tally visible: "the embarrassment of a small tally motivates a more intense commitment to finding time to focus."

Ultimately, the search for leading indicators is the quest for manageable antecedents of success. The better you are at pinpointing controllable behaviors that drive a desired outcome, the better your chances of elevating your performance and achieving your objectives.

And it all starts with a single activity: tracking metrics.

How *Not* to Measure Success

What does it feel like to start your own business?

Ask any group of entrepreneurs, and you'll quickly discover that emotions run the gamut. For some, it's a proud moment signifying enormous personal achievement. For others, it's an event marked by crippling uncertainty and stomach-churning fear.

One word you rarely hear used to describe the experience is forgettable.

But for David Douglas, it was more than forgettable—it came as a complete shock. When Douglas first learned about his landscaping business in 2013, he had zero recollection of starting anything of the kind. Then, when he discovered that he also had a painting and design company to his name, he knew for sure. Something was amiss.

Douglas is one of the first known victims of the Wells Fargo account fraud scandal, a colossal corporate debacle fueled by an obsession with metrics. It came about when leadership at the California-based financial institution began pressuring its staff to deliver on a single metric at the expense of all others. That metric? The number of products sold to each customer.

In the late 1990s, the company's analysts discovered that the more accounts a customer had, the more profitable they tended to be. That insight transformed corporate strategy. No longer would

Wells Fargo grow exclusively by acquiring new customers. Instead, it would turn its focus to selling existing customers more products.

So, what happens when an entire organization becomes consumed with optimizing a single metric? In the case of Wells Fargo, the answer is it succeeds—and in the process loses sight of both its financial goals and moral compass.

To ensure that employees across the board were focused on selling more products, Wells Fargo developed precise quotas. Staffers were instructed to sell at least four banking products to 80 percent of their clients. That was the floor, the minimum requirement for staying employed. The actual target was much higher. Management even developed a slogan to make the metric memorable. No longer was speaking to a customer called "advising a client." It was now referred to as "going for gr-eight."

On top of unforgiving sales goals, employee performance was tracked incessantly. Every day—at 11:00 a.m., 1:00 p.m., 3:00 p.m., and 5:00 p.m.—district managers across the country would get on a conference call to compare sales figures. Top earners were lavished with praise. Those at the bottom were subject to threats and ridicule.

Over time, managers learned to do anything they could to avoid humiliation, and the pressure trickled down. Soon, some employees found themselves working unpaid hours to reach their quota. Others began pleading with family members, neighbors, and friends to open accounts. In at least one instance, a Wells Fargo employee was found opening numerous accounts for homeless people in an attempt to meet the numbers.

It didn't take long for the pressure to take its toll. Not only did Wells Fargo alienate customers with aggressive sales tactics, it completely demoralized its workforce along the way. Employees could routinely be found crying at their desks, vomiting in bathrooms, and bolting out of meetings to head off panic attacks. One staff member admitted to drinking hand sanitizer before calls to steady herself. "We were constantly told we would end up working for McDonald's," a former branch manager told the *Los Angeles Times*. She, too, began working unpaid weekends.

Eventually, some workers realized the situation was untenable and took matters into their own hands by creating fraudulent accounts. Which is where customers like David Douglas come in. His sham businesses were the invention of Wells Fargo employees who were so consumed with meeting their quotas, they were willing to damage Douglass's credit rating and saddle him with unjustified bank fees.

So far in this chapter, we've looked at all the benefits that come with developing a scoreboard and using it to track our performance. But it would be wrong to suggest that metrics are an unmitigated good. At times, numbers can lead us astray, as they did for Wells Fargo.*

Psychologists have a term for the hysteria that swept through the offices of Wells Fargo: *surrogation*. It occurs when people become so consumed with hitting a number that they forget the outcome that number is intended to promote.

The metric becomes a substitute, an end in itself.

Once you learn about surrogation, you start to realize that it's everywhere. Surrogation is the reason car dealerships are willing to give you a better price on the last day of the month. Surrogation is the reason baseball hitters with a strong average elect to sit out the final game of the season. Surrogation is the reason many of us pace in circles just so we can bask in the glory of having our pedometer declare that we have walked ten thousand steps.

In many ways, surrogation is a natural consequence of metrics. It's because numbers are such a powerful motivating force that, in

---

* The remarkable thing about the Wells Fargo scandal isn't just how perfectly it encapsulates the dangers of overemphasizing a single metric. It's that the metric Wells Fargo pursued wasn't particularly lucrative. The vast majority of fraudulent accounts opened by Wells Fargo employees didn't generate a penny. Those that did brought in a paltry $2.4 million—less than 1 percent of the company's annual revenue. How does that figure compare to the fines and lawsuits that its employees' actions will cost the firm? That total is projected to eclipse several billion dollars, or roughly one thousand times the revenue generated.

many cases, they induce tunnel vision—even when we are measuring ourselves.

Three Secrets of Personal Scoreboards That Work

Losing track of the big picture represents just one potential pitfall of tracking metrics. Listing every possible misstep could fill an entire book. So instead, let's turn our attention to a few best practices for avoiding counterproductive metrics and designing the best possible scoreboard.

The first best practice is the most obvious: **collect multiple metrics.** Wells Fargo made the fatal error of singling out one metric. Anytime you reduce your focus to a single number (sales, likes, meeting requests), you increase the likelihood of optimizing for that number at the expense of other crucial factors.

The second best practice is to **aim for balance** in the types of metrics you collect. One example of balance is tracking a combination of *behaviors* and *outcomes*. For some, there is a temptation to focus only on behaviors because behaviors are controllable, while outcomes, in many cases, are not. That's a mistake. The only way to find lead indicators is to record both actions and outcomes and work backward, uncovering hidden drivers.

Another example of balance concerns time frame. The ideal scoreboard reflects both short-term and long-term outcomes. This is especially vital for goals that take a long period of time to complete. It's easy to get discouraged when a project takes weeks or even years to bring to fruition. Measuring short-term outcomes makes progress easier to appreciate, keeping us motivated and making extended projects feel more achievable.

This is why you see sales teams with lengthy sales cycles measure more than closed deals. They also track the number of new prospects, request for proposals (RFPs) received, and proposals submitted—all of which reflect short-term metrics that contribute to the number of deals a sales team eventually produces. Similarly, many authors don't look at the number of published articles or books as a measure of their performance. They also monitor their daily word count.

By the same token, it can also be all too easy to overlook long-term outcomes at the expense of short-term results. The New York Stock Exchange has witnessed countless companies sacrifice decades of success at the altar of favorable quarterly earnings. In far too many cases, going public introduces unrelenting pressures on companies to produce short-term results, rendering long-term investments harder to justify.

A third example of balance comes about when we gather both desirable and undesirable metrics. It's not enough to track positive behaviors and outcomes. The ideal scoreboard tracks both the measures we hope to boost as well as those we need to minimize.

Undesirable metrics are especially valuable when they reflect more than just the inverse of an intended outcome. Used correctly, they reveal new information on specific aspects of performance that could be improved. In high-end restaurants, for example, many chefs track uneaten food left on customers' plates after each course. Doing so helps them determine which elements of a dish were less successful. By tracking what didn't work, they gain new insight into what they can do better.

Another important function of undesirable metrics is that they can be used as guardrails, alerting us when desirable metrics are having too much sway. Former Intel CEO Andy Grove, a metrics pioneer whose approach to quantifying performance influenced a generation of Silicon Valley leaders, believed that every metric has the potential to backfire. Grove is credited with introducing a crucial imperative: "For every metric, there should be another 'paired' metric that addresses the adverse consequences of the first metric."

What Grove is saying is that metrics are powerful motivators. Therefore, if you're going to set up a scoreboard, you need to ask yourself: What if I'm too successful on this measure? By anticipating the negative consequences of a desirable metric, you can develop a second, paired metric that prevents you from losing sight of the bigger picture.

Wells Fargo would have benefited from heeding Grove's advice. Looking back, it's easy to see how the financial giant could have eluded legal and financial calamity by incorporating this one tweak.

Had Wells Fargo simply paired the desirable metric they sought to increase (the average number of customers' accounts) with an undesirable metric it needed to minimize (e.g., the number of customers feeling pressured by a Wells Fargo salesperson), they could have easily detected that its aggressive approach was causing significant damage.

A final best practice for creating an effective scoreboard that reliably improves performance is to **evolve your metrics** from time to time instead of mindlessly following an outdated formula.

As we refine our skills, the measures worth monitoring will invariably change. Some metrics will no longer benefit from tracking, while other new behaviors and outcomes will suddenly be worth adding. Instead of viewing our scoreboard as a fixed benchmark, we are better off using it as a malleable tool that adapts to meet our evolving skills and objectives.

Invariably, the biggest benefits of using a scoreboard come at the outset, when we first start tracking and reflecting on our behaviors and outcomes. Evolving a scoreboard not only ensures that the metrics we track align with our current goals, it also serves to introduce a level of novelty that renews our interest and engagement.

How often should you refresh your metrics? The answer will vary, depending on you, the particular task you are working to master, and the rate at which your industry evolves. A good rule of thumb, however, is to reflect on whether your metrics are serving you at the beginning of each quarter.

However often you choose to refresh your targets, chances are your performance will improve through the use of metrics. The simple act of selecting measures, collecting data, and reflecting on the results is bound to lead to improvement.

Mastery begins with metrics. But it doesn't end there. Because even the most insightful metrics are only part of the equation. Next, you need opportunities to stretch your skills on a regular basis. How you create those opportunities is the subject of our next chapter.

How to Take the Risk
Out of Risk Taking

Among the many delights of reading a popular nonfiction book is the irresistible thrill of discovering a bizarre and surprising piece of trivia. So, let's cut to the chase. Here are three deliciously esoteric facts, all on the topic of food:

- Fact #1: The reason doughnuts have a hole in the middle is to eliminate the uncooked center.
- Fact #2: Sandwiches were the accidental invention of a gambler. Historians credit their creation to a member of the British nobility, the Earl of Sandwich, who in 1762 asked to be served sliced roast beef between two slices of bread, enabling him to eat with one hand and gamble with the other.
- Fact #3: Serving ice cream in waffle cones was unheard of before a quick-thinking ice cream vendor at the 1904 St. Louis World's Fair ran out of bowls and desperately needed a solution. Fortunately for him, in the next booth over stood a Syrian cook selling a thin, crisp pastry, which he graciously agreed to roll up into cones.

Little did they know that their spontaneous collaboration would unleash a worldwide food craze.

Now let me ask you this: How likely are you to remember these facts a year from now?

A number of factors are likely to influence your prediction. Perhaps the most obvious is the general reliability of your memory. Then, of course, there's your interest in the topic of food, your current level of alertness, and the degree to which you find these particular factoids surprising or worth sharing with someone you know.

One element you probably won't consider when estimating your likelihood of recalling these facts: the font in which they are printed.

If you're like most people, the notion that something as incidental as font might affect your memory a full year from now will probably strike you as absurd. And yet research suggests that it can be surprisingly impactful. Why? Because it increases the amount of mental effort we put toward understanding a block of text.

In 2010, Princeton psychologist Daniel Oppenheimer and his team brought students into the lab and had them learn about a fictional species. Their participants received one of two booklets. The first was printed in a large, easy-to-read font. The other featured a smaller, grayer font.

Easy to read

Hard to read

Both groups were allotted the same amount of time—ninety seconds—to read the material and then told to do an unrelated task so that the information would no longer be top of mind. When Oppenheimer's team tested the students' memory fifteen minutes later, the results were striking. The group given the easy-to-read font made more than twice the number of errors as those forced to decipher the hard-to-read text.

Oppenheimer later replicated this finding in real-life settings, recruiting high school teachers who taught the same course multiple times during the same semester. The teachers were asked to hand one class clear, legible notes, and the other the same notes jostled up and down while being photocopied, deliberately making them blurry and therefore challenging to read. Once again, the students who had to concentrate harder while processing the material performed better, this time across a wide variety of subjects that included AP English, physics, history, and chemistry.

The results of these classroom experiments led Oppenheimer to wonder about learning in other everyday situations, particularly meetings and presentations. Today, most of us rely on laptops and tablets to take notes quickly and rarely resort to pen and paper. And yet we learn better when we're forced to think. Could there be a downside to the convenience of note taking on a device? To find out, Oppenheimer conducted a new study and found that we're far better at absorbing information we've written by hand. It's because writing is slower than typing. That limitation forces us to think harder and requires us to decide what information is essential and what we can safely exclude.

Taken together, Oppenheimer's research makes a compelling case that increased effort leads to deeper learning. Education expert Robert A. Bjork has a term for this phenomenon: *desirable difficulty*. Over the past five decades, Bjork has conducted a mountain of studies illuminating the factors that contribute to sustained learning. His findings are unmistakable: we learn best when we're challenged in ways that stretch the limits of our current abilities.

The notion that desirable difficulties facilitate growth extends well beyond the domain of education. Bodybuilders, for example, develop their physique by methodically targeting distinct muscle groups and pushing them to exhaustion. Strain serves as an essential catalyst—one that unleashes a cascade of biological reactions that results in increased mass, stamina, and strength.

A similar observation applies to sports. World-class athletes don't acquire new skills by clinging to their comfort zone. They do so by practicing at the upper limits of their abilities, combining daring experimentation with a healthy willingness to fail.

As I write this, the International Gymnastics Federation is facing enormous pressure to revamp its scoring guidelines. The reason is simple: Simone Biles. For years, the four-time Olympic gold medal winner had been performing at a different level than her competitors. Then came her record-setting triple-twisting double somersault in the 2019 US Gymnastics Championships—the first witnessed in human history. The move is so hard to execute that the highest available score under the current rules fails to fully capture its difficulty.

Clearly, Biles is a gifted athlete. Yet her remarkable achievements would be impossible if not for her voracious appetite for challenge and willingness to embrace risk. She continues to acquire new skills not by relying on talent but by testing the upper bounds of her ability.

That anecdote about Simone Biles might lead you to suspect that you know where this is going—that in this chapter I'm about to encourage you to toughen up, find your courage, and take more risks. You could not be more wrong.

What Successful Businesses Know About Failure

To summarize: growth requires strain. A moderate degree of difficulty is essential to both mental and physical development.

Teachers know it. Bodybuilders know it. Athletes know it.

Yet what's the one place where stretching our limits and experimenting with new techniques is most challenging? The workplace. Paradoxically, the one domain in which skill building is arguably most essential is the same domain in which learning is also hardest to achieve.

Why is learning at work so hard?

For one thing, it's because the cost of workplace failure tends to be substantial. Most managers show little tolerance for mistakes, no matter how well intentioned, and penalize those who make them. Unlike the fields of sports, music, and education, where there exists a profound appreciation that learning occurs through experimentation and feedback, the world of work is consumed with instant, reliable results.

When it comes to failure, the workplace is unforgiving. Every day is game day. There are no opportunities for practice.

A second reason skill-building at work is difficult is that the opportunities for taking risks are surprisingly limited. Businesses, after all, are optimized for efficiency, not employee growth. One way organizations achieve efficiency is by requiring their employees to perform the same task again and again. The more often employees repeat tasks, the faster they get and the more efficient the organization becomes.

While efficiency has its advantages, facilitating learning is not one. As the example of Simone Biles illustrates, we don't learn through simple repetition. We learn by attempting something difficult that lies just outside our comfort zone, observing the outcome, and making adjustments. That's how learning happens. And when we are denied the opportunity to take intelligent risks, the chances of our acquiring new skills shrinks.

Then there's a third barrier: even if we do somehow manage to endure the possibility of failure and identify an intelligent risk worth taking, there's still one other crucial impediment to learning in the workplace: the absence of consistent, detailed, and immediate feedback. Simone Biles knows instantly whether a daring new jump is successful. She doesn't need to wait for an annual performance review, hire an executive coach, or initiate an awkward conversation with her manager. That access to ongoing feedback is priceless. It empowers Biles to learn rapidly from her experiences and make informed adjustments in a way that is simply impossible for most workers.

Which is why, no matter how committed organizational leaders might be to the idea of helping employees grow, the realities of the modern workplace make it remarkably difficult for them to do so.

There is something deeply ironic about the fact that risk taking and feedback are so hard to come by in the workplace. After all, successful organizations take on enormous risks and adapt to market feedback all the time. The best companies don't play it safe. Like Simone Biles, they are constantly working to grow by taking on new challenges. They gamble on new products, enter untested new markets, and invest in research and development without any guarantee of a return. They take these risks because they know that doing so is the only reliable path to thriving in business.

Just how are these organizations able to jeopardize so much risk? By figuring out something crucial: how to take the risk out of risk taking. Using a set of strategic, nimble, and inexpensive practices, many of the most innovative organizations and entrepreneurs are able to reap the benefits of risk taking without putting everything on the line.

Over the coming pages, we're going to learn exactly how they do it. We're about to unpack four key methods that businesses use to minimize risk while generating compelling real-world feedback that helps them calibrate their approach. Along the way, I'm going to show you how you can apply their techniques to take on more challenges, conquer desirable difficulties, and shrink the gap between your current ability and ultimate vision without fearing the occasional failure.

The Staggering Power of Test Audiences

In the early 1990s, General Electric was on the verge of leveraging what, on paper, seemed to be the perfect marriage of supply and demand.

On the supply side: GE's warehouse of electrocardiogram (EKG) machines, essential tools for detecting heart disease. On the demand side: the world's largest producer of heart disease patients, India. Coronary heart disease represents the leading threat to human mortality, and at the time, nearly two-thirds of heart disease patients resided in India.

The business equation could not have been more perfect. Except for one baffling complication: GE's machines weren't selling.

At GE headquarters, the questions mounted: What was going on here? All over the globe, sales were rising, yet somehow in India, the one location most in need of EKG machines, the needle was grounded near zero. Was it the marketing? The product? Some alternative approach to treating heart disease?

Mystified, GE's research team did some digging. What they discovered transformed the way GE, as well as a wide range of other global conglomerates, develops products today.

As it turned out, there were several barriers to selling GE's machines—not least of which was the price tag of $20,000. In India, $20,000 is a fortune, enough for a medical facility to hire a team of full-time employees. Most Indian hospitals simply couldn't afford what might be considered pocket change by an American urgent care clinic.

But another, more significant issue existed. Indian physicians were concerned about the weight of the machine. At first, this piece of feedback struck GE as odd. Sure, the standard EKG machine was heavy, weighing nearly sixty-five pounds. But the machines were designed to sit in an office. What exactly were these Indian doctors planning to do with them?

Which is precisely when it hit them: unlike American physicians, whose patients visit a medical office, Indian doctors spend a substantial portion of their time traveling, seeing rural patients with limited means of transportation. To Indian doctors, the effectiveness of GE's technology was academic. What they needed was a device they could both afford and easily transport from village to village without risking injury.

A few years later, GE presented its solution: a seven-pound, battery-operated EKG machine that came complete with a handle, so that it could be carried around like a suitcase. It retailed for a fraction of the price of the original—just $500—and enabled GE to finally break through to the Indian market in a major way. What GE wasn't expecting is that their portable device didn't just sell in India. It sold everywhere, including the United States, where it was enthusiastically adopted by first responders and sports medicine teams, which often needed to administer immediate treatment outside medical clinics.

GE's EKG machine experience taught it a vital lesson: that the accepted model of developing products for the United States and later hoping to sell them in emerging markets is risky. It's all too easy to miss the mark, as GE did with its $20,000 stationary machine.

There was a smarter alternative—one that involves turning the standard practice on its ear. They called it *reverse innovation*. By creating products specifically designed for the developing world, where requirements are tougher and testing is inexpensive, it could generate solutions that are also likely to resonate with industrialized markets.

Today, reverse innovation is an approach to product development that's spread beyond GE to Coca-Cola, Microsoft, Nestlé, Procter & Gamble, PepsiCo, Renault, John Deere, and Levi Strauss. By testing new ideas in emerging markets, companies are able to collect rapid, inexpensive feedback from a population that is often more difficult to appeal to than those they eventually plan to target.

And it's not just large corporations using this approach—it's also entertainers, speakers, and politicians. About a decade ago, I visited a New York City comedy club renowned for surprise appearances by established comedians, when *Parks and Recreation* actor Aziz Ansari took the stage. Ansari grabbed the mic and pulled a batch of handwritten jokes from his jacket pocket, placing them on a wooden stool. Over the next fifteen minutes, he proceeded to read off his notes, starring the jokes that received a strong response. A few years later, I came across many of those same jokes in his book, *Modern Romance*.

Ansari's use of comedy clubs as testing grounds for new material is a well-established practice among comedians. In his book *Little Bets*, Peter Sims recounts Chris Rock's routine of touring small New Jersey comedy clubs in advance of a major performance. Much like a corporation testing a new product, Rock uses audience feedback to help him calibrate his material before a high-stakes performance.

Opportunities for pretesting material in front of low-stakes audiences exist in every industry, not just comedy. Long before Zig Ziglar became one of the world's first recognized motivational gurus, he was a struggling door-to-door cookware salesperson in South Carolina longing to break into the speaker circuit. To gain experience in front of large audiences and calibrate his keynote, he accepted every speaking invitation he could muster, even when it meant presenting to comically small groups. Ziglar treated those early events as his comedy clubs and bragged about having delivered over three thousand free speeches before being paid a cent. Rotary Clubs, Lions Clubs, chambers of commerce, university business programs, and churches, he discovered, are delighted to welcome expert speakers—especially when the presentation is free.

Political candidates use a similar approach to hone their platforms and perfect their speeches on the stump. The vast majority of their appearances take place in front of modest crowds at senior centers and diners and VFW halls, especially early on in a candidacy. Through these frequent, low-stakes speeches, politicians discover winning phrases and resonant themes that get voters nodding along.

In each of these examples, the key to improvement involves gathering feedback from a tiny segment of a population, minimizing risk, and using the input to make ongoing adjustments. For speakers and entertainers, live appearances are clearly a must. But thanks to the internet, the rest of us don't even need to leave the house.

When Scott Adams first began illustrating a comic strip in 1989, the storyline featured a dorky engineer and his sarcastic dog. Occasionally, the engineer might venture out to work, but the plot would always return to the odd couple and their madcap adventures at home. A few years into the comic's syndication, Adams began including his email address in the margins of the strip for those inclined to share their feedback. Through those reader emails Adams discovered that some of his comics drew an outsized response: those taking place in the office. That insight led him to adapt his approach by focusing his comic exclusively on the workplace, which rocketed *Dilbert* to stratospheric heights.

By including an email address, Adams was able to open up the lines of communication with his audience, resulting in crucial feedback that led to a more successful comic. Today, gauging fan reaction has never been simpler. Even more important, it's never been easier to pilot material with a *subsection* of fans and gather preliminary feedback before rolling out a final version.

That's precisely the way comedian and *Daily Show* cocreator Lizz Winstead uses Twitter. Winstead shares anecdotes and cracks jokes on the social media platform multiple times a day. She's not just building her following; she's also pretesting material. The tweets that attract the most likes and retweets are the ones she expands on in her comedy. Winstead uses Twitter the way Ansari uses comedy clubs, Ziglar used churches, and politicians use spaghetti dinners: to gather low-risk feedback and adjust accordingly.

Using the internet to gather feedback isn't limited to those with an established fan base. Today, there is no shortage of specialty outlets looking for original content, giving creators the opportunity to gauge the reaction of niche audiences.

Years after *Dilbert* took off, another fledgling cartoonist named Jeff Kinney was debating giving up on his ambitions for syndication. Kinney had struggled for years to break into newspapers and been summarily rejected. On a lark, he submitted a sample of his work to a niche kids' education website, FunBrain, to determine if his cartoon would resonate with a younger audience. The reaction to Kinney's depiction of middle school wasn't just positive—it generated a booming readership, giving him the confidence to head to Comic-Con in search of a publisher. Less than a year later, the cartoons Kinney submitted online were turned into a book series called *Diary of a Wimpy Kid*, which has sold more than 200 million copies and been translated into fifty-four languages.

A crucial benefit of testing material through online media outlets is that they often pair novice writers with experienced editors who can provide preliminary feedback long before a work is published. Best-selling author Atul Gawande credits the intense editing he received from his online editors with turning him into a writer. In the late 1990s, Gawande was working as a surgical resident at Harvard when a friend begged him to produce one or two articles for his fledgling website. The new publication, called *Slate*, was an unknown quantity and struggling to recruit contributors. Would Gawande help out for a short while? Despite being a "terrible writer," Gawande was willing to give it a shot. Looking back, he now says, it was this experience of receiving ongoing, consistent feedback that inspired him to pursue a second career in writing.

It goes without saying that not everyone has the time, resources, or inclination to publish their work online. There's also no guarantee that the feedback an online piece generates will be sufficiently instructive to help its creator make adjustments. It's for this reason that a wave of entrepreneurs now pre-test their material and gain immediate feedback using paid advertising.

Author Tim Ferriss provides perhaps the most striking example of the way this approach can be used intelligently. In his early thirties, Ferriss wrote an unprecedented and ambitious first book: part coming-of-age memoir, part guidebook to business automation, part freedom manifesto. Naming it was proving tricky. His initial attempt, *Drug Dealing for Fun and Profit*, albeit memorable, was generating more than a little pushback from booksellers. WalMart even took the unusual step of preemptively refusing to place it on its bookshelves, which is when Ferriss realized he needed a new title.

After generating a list of options, Ferriss was stuck. Any of these could work, he realized. But which one title is best?

Unlike cartoonist Scott Adams or comedian Lizz Winstead, the unpublished Ferriss didn't have a sizable audience he could leverage. So he did the next best thing: he set up a Google AdWords campaign, testing to see which title generated the most clicks. The entire experiment cost him about $200, and in less than a week, he had found a clear winner: *The 4-Hour Workweek*. He also managed to evade a few definite clunkers (e.g., *Broadband and White Sand*, *Millionaire Chameleons*) that would have made his book's eventual success challenging, if not altogether impossible.

Ferriss's methodology has wide-ranging applications that extend far beyond the world of books. Online platforms like Google and Facebook now empower anyone with a modest budget to reach a highly targeted audience and gain rapid feedback on a concept's appeal.

And because in most cases an online audience is unfamiliar with a creator, winning their attention and praise is significantly harder than engaging an established fan base. Like selling products in an emerging market, it's a higher bar to clear, suggesting that when a concept does start to gain traction, it is all the more likely to resonate with existing fans.

Testing headlines is just the tip of the iceberg. Paid ads can also be used to invite viewers to engage with websites, watch videos, or attend live presentations. The opportunities for gathering immediate, low-risk feedback from a tiny subsection of an audience have never been greater.

We are living in a golden age of feedback. Test audiences are everywhere. The question isn't whether to test, it's why aren't you testing more?

Why You Need a Pseudonym

It was just before midnight, and the police looked panicked.

Of all the cities where lawless pandemonium threatened to erupt, sleepy, middle-class Worcester, Massachusetts, was nowhere near the top of the list. And yet, there they were. Worcester's finest. All seventeen of its on-duty police officers, struggling mightily to contain a rowdy mob of nearly four thousand, as the rain poured down from above.

A van pulled up, igniting the crowd into a frenzy. It was the band. The one everyone had come to see. The one about to take the stage inside Sir Morgan's Cove, Worcester's tiny, dilapidated rock club. They called themselves The Cockroaches.

Except by now, word had gotten out. Everyone who was anyone in Worcester was already in the know. "The Cockroaches" was just an alias—a decoy used by one of the most famous bands in the world. There were no Cockroaches. Mick Jagger and the Rolling Stones were about to perform in front of three hundred obscenely lucky fans.

The year was 1981, and the Rolling Stones' ruse had finally caught up with them. They had been doing this for years. After an extended hiatus or before the launch of a major tour, they would use a pseudonym to book shows, giving them the opportunity to practice in front of a live audience without the pressure of having to deliver a perfect performance.

Operating under a pseudonym, like the Rolling Stones, is a second approach to minimizing the risk in risk taking. It also turns out to be surprisingly common in the world of business.

Consider The Gap, a clothing retailer headquartered in San Francisco. The Gap uses subbrands to target different audiences at distinct price points. Instead of risking the possibility of confusing shoppers, it uses Old Navy to appeal to value shoppers, Banana Republic to sell to a more affluent audience, and Athleta to attract activewear buyers. The Gap creates and acquires new brands even when it can sensibly roll out its new merchandise under an existing brand, in part because it has learned that marketing multiple brands grants it flexibility to take risks and more easily adjust when those risks fail to pay off. Everyone has heard of Old Navy, Banana Republic, and Athleta. Those are the successes. Few are likely to remember Forth & Towne, Piperlime, and the Gap's other failed attempts to break through to consumers. Those subbrands were quietly abandoned not long after their launch.

Subbranding is just one method companies use to operate under a pseudonym. Then there are private labels. Walk into any supermarket and you'll find a sea of options from a variety of brands. A large portion of them are actually created by the retailer. Except they don't go by the store's name. They go by Kirkland at Costco, Great Value at Walmart, and Insignia at Best Buy.

Target manages a staggering thirty-six private labels, ranging from Archer Farms and Good & Gather for groceries, to Merona and Cherokee for clothes, to Fieldcrest for bathroom products. Like the Gap, having a roster of brands allows Target to minimize risk and gamble on multiple identities without jeopardizing the overall brand. Another advantage to producing multiple private labels: stocking them creates the appearance of a store with a wide product selection, when in fact, it's primarily the label that is changing.

And it's not just retailers that invent new brands—established brands often disguise their identity, especially online, where it's become difficult for them to sell their merchandise at premium prices. On Amazon.com, you'll now find items developed by thriving brands like GNC, Equal, and Tuft & Needle selling under different brand names at rock-bottom prices. It's a strategy that enables them to gather quick feedback on new products without cannibalizing their existing line of consumer offerings.

In each of these cases, pseudonyms allow companies to experiment with new products and identities without assuming huge risk. But there's another benefit to leveraging pseudonyms. They can also be used to reintroduce existing products, placing them in a new light, without the baggage of a brand's existing identity.

That's what happened in 2018 when a group of Instagram influencers visited the opening of a Santa Monica pop-up boutique named Palessi. Inside, they encountered contemporary artwork, plush sofas, and an exclusive selection of luxury boots and high-heeled shoes elegantly arranged on glass backlit displays. Selfies were snapped, videos recorded, thousand-dollar purchases made.

It wasn't until much later that the fashionistas discovered that they had been duped. There was no Palessi boutique because there is no Palessi brand. Every shoe in the store had actually originated from Payless, the struggling discount shoe retailer barely one year removed from bankruptcy. Palessi was the invention of Payless's marketing agency, which recorded a soon-to-be viral video showing so-called fashion experts willing to shell out upward of $600 for a pair of Payless shoes that retailed for less than $35. So long, of course, as they were sold under a pseudonym.

Creating an offshoot brand to test new ideas is common practice in business, and it's an approach that's equally useful in the arts.

Ten years into a resounding career as one of England's most accomplished mystery writers, Agatha Christie became consumed with the idea of writing a romance novel. Her publisher did not share her enthusiasm. Christie had a devoted readership, and there was reasonable concern that a switch in genre, no matter how temporary, would dismantle her following. But she was determined and ultimately released her work under the name of Mary Westmacott. It was a wise move. All told, Christie published six romance novels over the course of her career. None achieved a fraction of the acclaim lavished on the mysteries that had made her famous.

More recently, J. K. Rowling borrowed a page out of Christie's playbook following the conclusion of her record-breaking Harry Potter series. Rowling's follow-up work, a violent, decidedly not-for-children crime series, was published not under her name but under the pseudonym Robert Galbraith. Using the Galbraith name empowered Rowling to venture into a new genre without risk to her reputation, and—importantly—enabled her to gauge readers' and critics' responses before disclosing her involvement. Had the reception been icy, it's quite possible we would never have learned Galbraith's real identity. In fact, it's entirely possible that it wasn't even Rowling's first publication under a fictional name.

The desire to experiment with a new genre was also the driving factor behind singer David Johansen's decision to adopt a pseudonym. As front man of the edgy 1970s punk band the New York Dolls, Johansen had a reputation to protect. So when he felt the urge to blend lounge and calypso in the late 1980s, adopting an alter ego seemed prudent. What he wasn't expecting was that his second career as the flashy, fun-loving Buster Poindexter would win him more fans than his actual identity ever had. Following the enormous popularity of "Hot Hot Hot," Johansen grew tired of performing as Poindexter, calling his inescapable earworm of a single "the bane of my existence." Not long after, he abandoned the Poindexter identity and reunited the New York Dolls.

Johansen's pseudonym granted him the freedom to do more than experiment—it gave him the luxury of discarding it the moment it stopped being fun.

Sell First, Build Later

Nick Swinmurn's life was going nowhere when a billion-dollar lightning bolt struck.

The former film student turned minor-league baseball ticket attendant was at the mall, hunting for boots and having no luck. The trouble was he knew precisely what he wanted: a pair of brown Airwalk Desert Chukka boots. Lots of stores had them—just not the ones he wanted. One store carried the wrong color, another the wrong size. Hours went by. Frustration mounted. Which is when it occurred to him: there *has* to be a better way to shop for shoes.

The year was 1999. Swinmurn was living in the San Francisco Bay area, so the next step seemed obvious: he started a website. It was called Shoesite.com.

Swinmurn's nascent business plan had one blip: he didn't have any shoes to sell. Nor did he have the budget to build up his inventory. His business résumé was blank, and he had never even met an investor.

So he walked into his local shoe store, Footwear Etc., and offered a win-win proposition. "I'll take some pictures, put your shoes online, and if people buy them, I'll buy them from you at full price." The manager happily agreed. Within days, sales started rolling in. And when they did, Swinmurn would personally drive to the mall, pay with his own money, and place the shoes in the mail.

A year later, after raising $150,000 from a few friends, some family, and his chiropractor, Swinmurn renamed the business after the Spanish word for "shoes": *zapatos*. Then he tweaked a few letters until he had Zappos, a name that seemed "fun and different." Roughly ten years later, Zappos would sell to Amazon for a staggering $1.2 billion in stock.

In retrospect, it's tempting to dismiss Swinmurn's success as the product of good fortune. Yes, as a resident of the Bay Area he was immersed in startup culture, and sure, 1999 was the ideal time to jump onto the internet bandwagon, and of course, looking back, it seems mystifying that no one else anticipated that shoppers would eventually be willing to purchase shoes online. But that account of Zappos' rise fails to do justice to the brilliant strategy Swinmurn used to bring his vision to life.

Swinmurn didn't build a massive warehouse and stock it with shoes. Doing so would have required enormous resources, which he did not possess. What did he do instead? He sold photos of shoes that he could secure after consumer demand was established. By selling a prototype, Swinmurn managed to greatly diminish the risk involved in starting a retail business. He did so by selling first and procuring second.

Swinmurn is not the first to leverage this approach. Preselling products that don't technically exist turns out to have a long and storied history in the world of business.

Years before he was summoned to face the firing squad in Apple's conference room, Bill Gates was a middling Harvard sophomore resigned to becoming a lawyer. In December 1974, the new issue of *Popular Electronics* made its way to his dorm room, featuring the world's first personal computer on its cover. It was called the Altair 8800. Gates had spent much of his free time in high school coding and became convinced that he could develop software that allowed other programs to run on top of what, at the time, was fairly primitive technology.

The obvious thing for Gates to have done was to plunge forward and develop his software, hoping he could sell it after it was complete. But doing so would have been seriously risky. For all Gates knew, the New Mexico company that was now selling the Altair already had software waiting in the wings.* Like Swinmurn, Gates sought assurance that he was on the right path. So instead of investing weeks constructing a program and neglecting his coursework, he got creative.

The first thing Gates did was compose a letter to the Altair's manufacturer, claiming that his team had already built software for their computer, which he and his associates were prepared to lease. When his letter didn't generate a response, Gates picked up the phone and called the manufacturer's CEO, offering to deliver a live presentation of his software. When would be a good time?

Only after Gates had confirmation that the CEO was willing to meet did he and his programming partner, Paul Allen, begin developing BASIC, a programming language that served as the foundation for Microsoft and later set the stage for Gates's short-lived collaboration with Apple.

Today, we are accustomed to the strategy both Swinmurn and Gates used, with startups winning million-dollar investments on the basis of little more than a pitch deck. We eagerly pull out our credit

---

* It didn't. In fact, it too was selling a product that did not technically exist. *Popular Electronics* had composed its cover story using photographs and specs provided by the Altair 8800's manufacturer, Micro Instrumentation and Telemetry Systems (MITS). MITS had precisely one working model of the Altair 8800, which (tragically) got lost in the mail. Even the photograph on the magazine's cover was a sham. It featured the Altair 8800's exterior but was an empty shell, devoid of any computer technology.

cards after encountering a charming sales pitch and a digital rendering on Kickstarter. We barely flinch when Elon Musk generates $14 billion in preorders for a car that has never been built, when all it took was a few tweets.

These examples illustrate something crucial about intelligent innovation. When we are developing our skills, our focus naturally tilts toward improving our execution. We want to write the perfect script, develop the perfect website, compose the perfect speech. There are times, however, when we would be better off postponing the pursuit of excellence in favor of first confirming that our approach is one that others crave.

It does us no good to create the perfect version of something no one wants. One way to avoid that trap, and in the process mitigate risk, is by vaulting ahead to the next step. For many professionals, that next step involves selling an idea to a customer, client, or manager. Starting with sales is essential to helping businesses and creators alike steer clear of doomed projects, assess potential more quickly, and, critically, take lots more risks.

Discovering the next step can be as easy as reflecting on the question: If I executed this successfully, what would I do next? The answer can range from creating a sales page like Nick Swinmurn, to setting up a meeting like Bill Gates, to approaching someone you know with a daring proposal.

Legendary talent agent Irving "Swifty" Lazar built a business empire using this latter approach. In the second half of the twentieth century, Lazar was among the most influential agents in the world, as renowned in the hills of Hollywood as he was in the publishing houses of New York City. Lazar's stable of clients reads like a stroll down the Walk of Fame: Humphrey Bogart, Diana Ross, Gene Kelly, Cary Grant, Cher, Madonna, Noël Coward, Vladimir Nabokov, Ernest Hemingway.

You'd think that to attract so many stars, Lazar must have had a massive agency with lawyers, negotiators, and scouts. He didn't. It was him and an assistant—that was it.

What was his secret? He started with the sale.

Lazar pitched everyone, even actors and authors he'd never met. Once he got a bite from a movie studio or publishing house, he would work backward and approach the celebrity he had pitched, informing them that he had a deal ready to go. As novelist Irwin Shaw once observed, "Every writer has two agents—his own and Irving Lazar."

While Lazar's unconventional approach to dealmaking features a degree of ethical flexibility that would make many people uncomfortable, the underlying principle is at once undeniably useful and easier than ever to employ. Confirming interest in our ideas before investing in their execution can take the form of a pitch letter for the writer, a wait-list for the entrepreneur, a prototype for the inventor.

Ultimately, the value in selling first and producing later isn't just that it minimizes risk and provides early feedback. It empowers creative thinkers to take more swings, multiplying their chances of hitting on winning ideas.

To Grow, Think like a Venture Capitalist

What comes to mind when you read the words *venture capital*?

Chances are, it's some variation of money, investors, and startups. Here's one association that probably didn't make your list: fishing. And yet hundreds of years ago, it was fishing that ignited the approach to investing that defines today's VC industry.

Back in the nineteenth century, whaling—the hunting of whales for their meat, bones, and oil—was big business. A successful voyage could yield a profit of thousands of dollars (amounting to millions in today's currency), making whaling an attractive career. Each year, hundreds of crews sought their fortune on the Atlantic Ocean.

Before too long, the rise in competition severely diminished supply. Now, to succeed, whalers found themselves journeying further and further offshore. The extended voyage thrust crews into dire conditions. They risked running out of food, losing their sanity, and, more often than captains cared to disclose, getting lost at sea.

As the dangers of whaling mounted, a new type of investment emerged. Along came brokers with relationships among both the moneyed elites and experienced captains who were eager to embark on future expeditions. Serving as intermediaries between the two groups, whaling agents helped the wealthy finance voyages while spreading their investments across an assortment of ships. In so doing, they helped investors mitigate against the possibility that an entire investment would perish along with any single ship.

To this day, VCs are built on the idea that diversifying investments minimizes risk. And it's not just investment firms that leverage this strategy—it's also the game plan driving the world's most successful conglomerates. We take for granted that Disney, a company founded to produce cartoons, now operates theme parks, vacation properties, cruise lines, residential communities, streaming services, and manages Pixar, Marvel, and ESPN. Or that Warren Buffett's company, Berkshire Hathaway, which originally produced textiles, now operates the world's largest real estate firm and owns Duracell, GEICO, Fruit of the Loom, and Dairy Queen. Even Buzz-Feed, which began as a website devoted to curating and producing viral content, now develops television shows, cookbooks, events, and merchandise.

Profitable companies rarely stick to one product or a single industry. They diversify. And with that diversification comes lower risk. Like those intrepid whaling ships navigating the hazardous Atlantic Ocean, a single product or offering can, for a variety of reasons, sink. But the chances of an entire portfolio of investments, spread across a broad array of products, industries, and customers, simultaneously going bust are significantly lower.

This same principle of reducing risk applies to you. In much the same way as spreading financial resources across a range of offerings mitigates risk, so, too, does investing in a range of professional opportunities.

The career decisions of Lynda Weinman offer a useful illustration. In the mid-1990s, Weinman had carved out a niche for herself in Hollywood. As a special-effects animator for the multimillion-dollar franchises *Star Wars*, *RoboCop*, and *Bill and Ted's Excellent Adventure*, she was in high demand. An early-adopting Apple enthusiast, Weinman had taught herself computer graphics and started fielding requests from colleagues wondering if she could share her expertise. So she took on some teaching on the side and discovered that she enjoyed it. When she couldn't find a computer graphics textbook simple and intuitive enough to recommend, she wrote one and gave it a simple and intuitive title: *Designing Web Graphics*. The book was a success, prompting more teaching requests than she could handle. Weinman improvised by holding weeklong intensives and weekend seminars. Some of her events were recorded and sold on VHS cassettes. She even set up a website to distribute worksheets and notes to her students, calling it Lynda.com. In April 2015, barely two decades after Weinman taught her first class, her website was purchased by LinkedIn for $1.5 billion.

What's notable about Weinman's story is that unlike Zappo's Nick Swinmurn, she did not set out to construct a lucrative business empire. She did so by following her interests, developing new skills, and relentlessly diversifying the ways in which she served her audience. She went from teaching traditional classes to writing textbooks, to holding weeklong intensives, to making VHS recordings, to creating internet-based subscription offerings—all at a time when it was unheard of for professional educators to build a portfolio and diversify their offerings.

In Weinman's case, diversification didn't just keep her solvent or enable her to take more risks. It positioned her to capitalize on the rapid ascent of online education.

Portfolio careers like Weinman's, where individuals find multiple ways of leveraging their skills by serving a variety of patrons—not just a single employer—make individual risks vastly easier to tolerate. The more diversified your career, the less stressful any one business relationship becomes.

Building a portfolio career might seem simpler when you are a freelancer or business owner. After all, both roles allow you to choose the types of clients, projects, and industries you wish to serve. But that doesn't mean diversifying is impossible for employees working within organizations. On the contrary, in many ways, it makes it easier.

One way having a day job makes diversification easier is that it provides ongoing opportunities for experimentation. Those experiments can take the form of proposing a novel approach on an upcoming project, spearheading innovative collaborations with other departments, or testing out new client offerings. All of these experiments have the potential to grow employees' skill sets and elevate their value by expanding the definition of their role.

Another way having a day job makes diversification easier is by empowering salaried employees to take smarter risks outside the office. In 2014, researchers at the University of Wisconsin examined the success rates of entrepreneurs, comparing those who quit their job to run a new business against those who played it safe and kept their day job while quietly developing their business on the side. Surprisingly, full-time commitment to a business venture did not turn out to be the winning strategy. Cautious employees were significantly more likely to succeed. Why? Because they possessed the financial stability to reach more patient, strategic decisions—a luxury not available to those whose livelihood was constantly on the line.

A base salary provides security—financial reassurance that no matter how poorly things go on a side venture, failure is salvageable. Which, in a way, is the unifying principle connecting the four business strategies we've explored together in this chapter. Whether we experiment with a small subsection of our audience, or perform under a pseudonym, or presell our ideas in advance, or diversify our portfolio, risk taking is dramatically easier once the cost of failure shrinks.

We're often told that growth requires courage—that the only way to improve is to somehow find the gumption to stomach more risks and embrace situations that make us uncomfortable. But as we've discovered in this chapter, that's not the only path to personal development. Tackling difficult challenges and putting everything on the line are simply not the same thing.

No, when it comes to developing our skills and growing our abilities, the wise approach isn't taking more risks. As Nick Swinmurn, Bill Gates, Warren Buffett, and the many other luminaries we met over the course of this chapter will tell you: far wiser to find intelligent opportunities that render risk taking entirely less risky.

Practicing in
Three Dimensions

Picture this: You are only minutes away from delivering the most important pitch of your life. Your team has been working furiously, slaving away for weeks, preparing you for this presentation. They know, just as you do, that the stakes are monumental.

Win this account, and your agency will catapult to the top of your industry. Lose, and you'll have no choice but to retreat, scale back, let people go. Your company's morale will be decimated, your leadership questioned. Everything you've worked for, everything you've built, comes down to a thirty-minute pitch.

The morning of the presentation flies by in a disorienting blur. Maybe you've eaten breakfast, maybe not. For the life of you, you can't remember whether you said good-bye to your children before leaving the house. It is entirely possible that you are now on your sixth cup of coffee.

But the moment you enter the boardroom, the doors click, and everyone turns to you, something happens. Your vision sharpens. Your breathing slows. Seemingly out of nowhere, the exact right words are magically leaving your lips.

When, just two slides into your presentation, your laptop is seized by the spinning rainbow wheel of death, you march on, unfazed, presenting masterfully without the benefit of slides. When impossible questions are raised, you see them coming a mile away and dispatch one after the other with confidence and charm. Near the end of the presentation, when you are asked how you might handle a potential crisis on the company's horizon, you pull out copies of a memo you've prepared to address that very possibility, complete with strategic objectives, talking points, and a PR campaign.

Afterward, your new clients will rave about your performance. They call you "brilliant," "masterful," "a rock star." Privately, their CEO will playfully ask if you can see the future. You will laugh modestly and reassure her that you are, in fact, only human. And no human can see the future. Or can they?

On the surface, the question seems patently absurd. Until, that is, you consider the behavior of star athletes.

Professional tennis players like Serena Williams regularly face serves exceeding 120 miles an hour. That's barely enough time to blink an eye, let alone lift, aim, and swing a racquet. And yet somehow she manages to not only make contact but also hit returns with such precision and power that her opponents are left gawking. How does she do it? The same way New York Mets slugger Pete Alonso blasted an astonishing fifty-three home runs in 2019. If you analyze video of any of his moon shots, you'll notice something peculiar: his swing starts *before* the ball leaves the pitcher's fingertips. A similar phenomenon occurs in hockey, where goalies like New Jersey Devils Hall of Famer Martin Brodeur make gravity-defying saves by leaping before a puck is even struck.

So what do scientists make of all this? How do they explain the ability of athletic superstars to anticipate what will happen next? And perhaps most important: Can their strategies be leveraged off the field and in everyday life?

Let's find out by delving inside the mind of an expert.

How Athletes See the Future

When Tony Romo announced his retirement from professional football in the spring of 2017, the response the league over was a collective shrug.

For nearly a decade, Romo had served as the Dallas Cowboys' starting quarterback, helming a period in the team's history that could only be described as underwhelming. His last few years were particularly forgettable. Mired with injuries to his back and neck, Romo had been relegated to the sidelines for months at a time and had long ago lost his starting job to the younger, more dynamic Dak Prescott.

In the end, to the casual fan, the two most memorable facts about Romo were that he had once inexplicably botched the hold of an easy field goal, costing his team the season, and that in 2007, he had dated Jessica Simpson.

So when, a few months after his football retirement, Romo made his live television debut as an NFL analyst, expectations were understandably low. Romo had exactly zero broadcasting experience and was younger than some of the quarterbacks he was "professionally" analyzing. "Tony is a work in progress," the chairman of CBS Sports admitted, sounding less than confident. No one knew what to expect. Thirty minutes before his first telecast, Romo's producer pulled him aside and tried to center him: "Just be yourself."

By the time the playoffs rolled around that season, Romo's performances had become one of the biggest football stories of the year. He was earning rave reviews everywhere—from producers, players, fans—and not just because of his intoxicating enthusiasm. It was because of Romo's uncanny ability to do something no one in the broadcast booth had ever done before: forecast plays before they occurred.

Starting with his first telecast, Romo would look down at the field and detail precisely what the offense was about to do, well before the snap. Then he would glance out at the opposing team's defensive scheme and call out its strategy with equal precision.

He would do this repeatedly, week after week, astonishing fans with what appeared to be a mystical mind-reading ability. Before too long, the internet erupted with Romo memes, branding him "Romo-stradamus" for his clairvoyant abilities. The *Wall Street Journal* was moved to analyze Romo's predictive abilities, examining the 2,599 calls he had made as a broadcaster. Its conclusion: Romo is right more than 68 percent of the time. For context, they provided a striking comparison: that's a percentage higher than Romo's throwing accuracy as a professional quarterback.

Romo's predictive abilities are undoubtedly impressive. What they are not, however, is superhuman or even unusual. At least not among professional quarterbacks, who receive extensive training on reading and adjusting to opposing teams' formations. Enhanced anticipation is a common feature of expertise, and not just in football. It's a skill researchers have observed across a wide range of domains.

Now, suppose we somehow convinced Tony Romo to join us in the lab for a few imaging scans, allowing us to monitor his brain activity as he broadcasts an NFL game. What insights are we likely to glean? What makes experts like Romo different from, say, a casual football fan?

The first thing we're likely to discover is that when Romo analyzes players on a football field, his brain is *less* active than the average fan's. Surprisingly, experts use less energy than novices when processing information yet get better results.

How can this be? Years of experience have taught experts to quickly distinguish relevant from irrelevant cues, enabling them to home in on just the bits of data that are worth evaluating. Their attention is highly selective, focusing on a small number of essential cues. Unlike the casual fan, Romo isn't distracted by unruly fans or wacky mascots—he knows precisely what to look for and effortlessly ignores everything else.

But it's not just tuning out the irrelevant. It's also squeezing more information out of seemingly benign signals.

In 1978, British psychologists published a clever study illuminating just how much more experts are able to glean by locking in on a few telling clues. In the experiment, two groups of tennis players—experts and novices—were shown film of tennis players serving. On each serve, the film was stopped precisely forty-two milliseconds before the servers made contact with the ball, and participants were asked a question: Where will the serve land after it is struck? Inexperienced players didn't have a clue. But like Tony Romo, expert tennis players were significantly more accurate in their predictions. They were able to tell where the ball was headed by scanning for information a novice player ignores, like the direction of the servers' torso, the bend of their elbow, and the angle of their racquet.

A second reason experts like Tony Romo expend less brainpower is that they consider fewer options. Experience has taught them which events are likely to occur in a given context and which are not. As the Zen monk Shunryū Suzuki noted, "In the beginner's mind there are many possibilities but in the expert's mind there are few." MRI studies of artists, radiologists, and chess grand masters bear this out. Romo's extensive knowledge of football enables him to eliminate plays with a low probability of transpiring, limiting his focus to a small universe of likely options, resulting in both lower cognitive load and sharper predictions.

In addition to seeing less overall activation on Tony Romo's brain scan, the activity that does register is likely to be more widely dispersed throughout his brain. Unlike novices, experts utilize a broader mix of brain regions to analyze information because they're not simply reading their environment. They're reading their environment, interpreting the information, and preparing a response all at the same time. In contrast, novices perform the same tasks but do so consecutively, one at a time.

The third major difference we're likely to find between an expert and a novice is anatomical. Certain features of Tony Romo's brain are likely to be bigger than those of a casual football fan. That discrepancy reflects neuroplasticity—the human brain's capacity for reorganizing itself to better meet demands it frequently encounters. Repeatedly performing the same activity prompts the brain to adapt. It does so both by quickening the connection between participating neurons and by forming additional neurons to take on some of the cognitive load. Over time, those adaptations pile up, contributing to physical differences between the brain of an expert and a novice.

Take London cab drivers, whose job requires them to memorize and recall their city's layout. MRI scans reveal that the longer drivers have been operating a taxi, the larger their hippocampus, a brain region involved in both long-term memory and spatial navigation. Critically, long-term studies show that it's not simply that people with better memories choose to become taxi drivers. It's that the experience of driving a taxi actually changes people's brains.

All those physical manifestations—quieter activation in the brain, more selective attention, fewer options under consideration, greater interplay across different brain regions, and more pronounced anatomical features—are neurological hallmarks of expertise. They reflect the brain's adaptation to the development of a deep and sophisticated knowledge set, one that empowers experts to pinpoint crucial information, anticipate future events, and respond faster than everyone else.

When fans gush over Tony Romo's predictive abilities, there's an assumption that Romo is extraordinarily talented or some type of football savant. And yet archival video of his rookie season paints a vastly different picture.

Back in 2003, Romo was an undrafted third-string quarterback struggling to hold on to his job. There's footage of his practice sessions with the Cowboys' then coach, Bill Parcells. It's not pretty. "Come on, Romo!" Parcells is heard barking, visibly irate. "You should've known presnap what to do there!" It took Romo four years to convince Parcells to let him play. Along the way, video shows Parcells regularly pulling Romo aside and scolding him for taking too long, for not reading, extracting, anticipating. "You gotta get the ball out of your hands. You're gonna get killed. They'll be licking their chops. You'll be like liverwurst on rye!"

So where did Romo's expertise come from? How exactly did he go from the brink of unemployment to one of the most brilliant minds in football?

The short answer is practice. But not the type we typically associate with the term. As you're about to discover in this chapter, most people's conception of practice is far too limited. Research now shows that our performance on both mental and physical tasks improves dramatically when we expand our definition to the way that athletes like Tony Romo have utilized practice for decades.

So far in Part Two of *Decoding Greatness*, we've examined two ingredients for bridging the gap between a bold vision and our current ability: identifying key metrics and creating low-risk stretch opportunities. In this chapter, you're going to gain a set of tools that empower you to extract more knowledge from your experiences, master skills quickly, and anticipate future events before they happen.

How do you predict the future? Ironically, step one is to go back in time.

What the Best Coaches Have in Common with Hollywood Directors

For a brief moment before dialing Steven Spielberg, Robert Zemeckis considers the possibility that he will be fired.

This was long before Zemeckis collected multiple Academy Awards for *Forrest Gump*, *Who Framed Roger Rabbit?*, and *Cast Away*. The year is 1984. He is a virtual nobody, lucky to be directing his fourth film.

The call he is about to place to his executive producer concerns a delicate matter. Zemeckis has screwed up, royally. An actor he's hired isn't remotely working out, and he needs Spielberg's input. He's about to pose a ludicrous question: Would it be possible to replace the movie's lead a month into shooting? This was a decision with dramatic implications. Finding a new actor could take weeks, demoralize the cast, and delay the movie's release by months. Then there's the matter of the current lead's salary, a not-insignificant $3.5 million.

Zemeckis has recordings he wants Spielberg to watch—dailies, as they're called in Hollywood. Each morning, a movie's director, editor, and cinematographer gather to review the previous day's recordings. It's a process that allows them to analyze their work, identify strong performances, and adjust their filming approach in real time. The dailies are what first alerted Zemeckis's team that they had a problem. "There's a hole in the middle of our screen," Zemeckis reluctantly admitted on one of their review sessions. "The lead actor doesn't work."

Spielberg agrees to meet and reserves the Amblin studio screening room so the two can watch the recordings together on the big screen. The lights dim, the projector whirs, the film appears. The scene takes place in a 1950s café. Two customers are sitting at the counter, leaning over in an identical pose with their heads turned left, hands on the back of their hair. The doors to the diner are pulled open. "Hey, McFly?" A group of teenage boys streams inside. Both customers turn to look simultaneously, as if performing a choreographed dance. "What do you think you're doing?"

The camera zooms in on Marty McFly, the teenage hero of *Back to the Future*, as he attempts to make sense of the scene unfolding before him. "Biff?" he whispers in disbelief. Except it's not the charmingly clumsy Michael J. Fox playing Marty. It's the sad-eyed, statuesque heartthrob Eric Stoltz in the lead role.

Zemeckis and Spielberg watch dozens of scenes like this, and it is evident in all of them that something is missing. That something is comedy. Stoltz is a captivating actor and one well suited to drama. But *Back to the Future* is not a drama. On the contrary. It's the kind of film that requires comedy because its plot threatens to unravel the moment you give it too much thought.

In the end, Zemeckis barely has to press. Spielberg has already reached an identical conclusion: Stoltz needs to go. Not only does Spielberg grant his blessing, he proceeds to do Zemeckis's bidding by calling NBC and using his influence to arrange for Michael J. Fox to join the film on top of his daytime duties starring in *Family Ties*.

No one knows for sure how successful *Back to the Future* might have been with Eric Stoltz in the lead, though it's hard to imagine it doing much better than it did with Fox. What we do know is that Zemeckis felt Fox's slapstick was essential to the role, and that watching the dailies enabled him to make a vital adjustment that brought the finished product in line with his initial vision.

The use of film to calibrate performance isn't limited to Hollywood studios. It's just as common in professional sports.

Not long ago, ESPN asked John Harbaugh, head coach of the Baltimore Ravens, to track his time and report back on how he spent a week during the regular season. The resulting article featured a minute-by-minute breakdown of the week Harbaugh spent preparing his team to face the Chicago Bears.

How many hours does Harbaugh spend watching film? A staggering amount: nearly six hours a day. Harbaugh devotes more time to reviewing previous games than any other activity, including running practices, meeting with players, and mapping out his team's game plan—*combined*. As a strategic thinker, he understands that learning from past performance is one of the smartest things you can do to prepare for the future.

Golden State Warriors coach Steve Kerr shares that philosophy. So much so that he's instructed his team to study film during actual games. Halftime in the Warriors' locker room now begins with highlights from the first half. Except the reel doesn't feature exceptional plays, the kind monopolizing *SportsCenter*. Kerr prefers screening plays the Warriors can learn from and capitalize on with a minor adjustment. Throughout the first half, Kerr can be seen motioning to an assistant and mouthing "clip that" after a play takes place that he wants his team to review.

What follows this midgame film session is the third quarter, and no team has dominated the third quarter more emphatically than Kerr's Warriors. In the 2018 NBA playoffs alone, the Warriors outscored their opponents by an astonishing 159 points in the third quarter. That's a margin eight times larger than any other quarter and more than triple the differential of the other three quarters combined. Moreover, it's not an anomaly. When ESPN looked at the Warriors' third-quarter performance over the previous four years, it found that "the Warriors lead the NBA in virtually every category in the third quarter, from points per game to offensive and defensive efficiency."

Directors, athletes, and coaches rely on film to help them learn from the past and make crucial adjustments, ones that can make all the difference between dismal failure and colossal success. Needless to say, they have access to a tool most people lack: objective recordings of performance.

So, what about the rest of us? What do you review when there is no tape?

A Three-Minute Exercise That Turns Experience into Wisdom

Take a look at this matrix:

2.65	8.23	6.87
7.98	4.31	3.25
0.99	2.55	1.23
4.49	5.69	9.03

As you can see, it contains twelve three-digit numbers. Two of these twelve numbers add up to ten. Can you find them? Which two numbers are they?

But wait, hold on. Before you get started, let's make things interesting. Imagine that I gave you a stack of matrices just like the one above and offered to pay you each time you found the solution within twenty seconds.

How many of these brain teasers would you solve then?

That's the exercise Harvard researchers put in front of hundreds of adults. Then, after participants gathered some experience solving a number of matrices, they added another set of instructions.

One group was told to take three minutes and reflect on their performance. Were there any strategies they found particularly effective? Given their experience so far, what could they do to improve their performance on the matrix exercise in the future? This was the self-reflection condition. It involves stepping back and contemplating one's experience as if replaying a mental tape.

A second group was told to pause for three minutes. This was the control condition. It allowed researchers to assess the impact of reflecting on the past against simply taking a break. Following the brief time-out, all the participants were given more matrices to solve.

So, what effect did self-reflection have on performance? When experimenters tallied up the scores, the results were compelling. Self-reflectors outperformed break-takers by a significant margin, solving over 20 percent more puzzles. A brief invitation to think about what they had learned and how they might apply those lessons in the future was all it took to spark considerable improvement.

In later studies, the experimenters replicated this finding and showed that self-reflection aids performance even when no money is on the line. They then tested self-reflection in the real world and found that inviting employees to reflect on the lessons they learned during a training session increased their understanding of the material by a remarkable 23 percent.

The benefits of self-reflection, or *reflective practice*, as it is termed in the field of education, are several.

First, reflective practice prompts us to do something we rarely do over the course of the workday: pause and consider our progress. In so doing, we are briefly jolted awake, freed from the fog of mindless reactivity and routine habits, and made to examine the value of our actions. If things are going well, we can plunge forward with renewed confidence. If, on the other hand, our outcomes prove lacking, we're compelled to seek adjustments.

Reflective practice also facilitates deeper learning by prompting us to search for higher-order principles. In the case of that "Add to 10" brain teaser, it's no wonder self-reflection proved so valuable. All it takes is a brief moment of contemplation to realize that there's a shortcut to solving the problem: subtract each number from ten. (10 minus 4.31 equals 5.69. Is 5.69 on the matrix? If yes, that's the answer. If not, try a different number.) Trying to combine each of the twelve numbers one at a time involves lots more calculations and way more effort.

Similar shortcuts appear when we reflect on our experience at work. We can't help but stumble upon useful lessons that elevate our performance and empower us to better anticipate future events.

A final benefit of reflective practice is that it leads us to compare our recent experiences against our prior beliefs, stimulating to the emergence of insight. In the early 1900s, philosopher and education expert John Dewey wrote extensively about the benefits of reflective practice, which he considered an essential tool for learning and development. Observation alone is not enough for education, Dewey believed. Knowledge only comes about when we reflect on our experiences, revise our beliefs, and test our assumptions.

Dewey's influence continues to play a role in the field of education where, to this day, teachers are urged to reflect after delivering a lesson plan, contemplating questions like "What went well?" "What could have gone better?" and "What should I try differently next time?"

Outside academia, however, the use of reflective exercise is limited. To the extent that self-reflection takes place among working professionals, it tends to be inspired by annual milestones like birthdays or New Year's, a mandatory performance review, or, for those able to afford it, the prompting of a coach.

It's hard to justify taking time out for self-reflection when doing so doesn't immediately help you meet a deadline. For some, turning attention inward can also feel unnatural or awkward. But perhaps the biggest barrier to reflective exercise is that there exists no workplace norm supporting its use. We rarely see prominent leaders pausing to self-reflect in the office, and even if we did, we'd likely dismiss the display as epically narcissistic.

We've been taught that education occurs from the outside in— that learning happens through exposure to new information. But that's only half the equation. Reviewing past events with an eye for insights, patterns, and predictions is how we turn experience into wisdom.

A Beginner's Guide to Reflective Practice

So let's say you're open to trying reflective practice. What's the best way of getting started?

One method that is surprisingly common among top-performing inventors like Thomas Edison, artists like Frida Kahlo, and athletes like Serena Williams, is journaling.

Journaling has a dreadful reputation. Before you dismiss the practice as the domain of lonely, melodramatic teenagers, let's reframe by considering another group entirely: Navy SEALs.

One of the first lessons soldiers like Navy SEALs learn is that in battle, capturing the high ground is critical. It gives you much-needed perspective. Without it, you can easily make fatal errors because you are missing the big picture. The same applies to everyday life, where daily emergencies and endless commitments are a constant threat to achieving larger strategic objectives.

Developing a daily practice to pause, reflect, and strategize can yield substantial benefits that compound over time. We've already seen how reflective practice can foster quicker learning, higher confidence, and deeper knowledge. That's just the beginning. Writing about daily events has also been shown to help us process emotions, quiet anxiety, and diminish stress. By placing our own narrative spin on events, we no longer feel as if events are happening to us. Writing about our lives tips the scales, restoring our sense of control.

Journaling by hand, in particular, forces us to slow down. Because most adults think faster than they write, we're compelled to pause and reflect as we wait for our hand to catch up, examining our thoughts in a way that rarely occurs on a busy day. This simple practice can yield surprisingly profound insights, not unlike when a therapist repeats your words back to you, illuminating a hidden motive or a limiting belief.

Psychologists have identified an array of other benefits to journaling, but instead of providing a comprehensive list, I want to highlight a particular kind of journaling that I have found to be especially useful in promoting self-reflection, learning, and skill development: the five-year journal.

A number of different versions of these journals are sold in bookstores, and they all have one thing in common: they feature five blocks for entries on the same calendar date—one for each consecutive year. Each day, journalers handwrite a few lines in the space provided. Then, one year after starting, something magical happens. They revisit the page of their original entry and, after entering a few observations on the present day, have the opportunity to review the entry they wrote on the same day the previous year.

I give every coaching client I work with a five-year journal because I have found it to be an invaluable tool for discovery and growth. In addition to sparking self-reflection through nightly journaling, rereading entries strengthens memory for past events and helps you detect patterns in both your professional and personal lives.

Among the many lessons I have come to appreciate about myself by keeping a five-year journal:

- Lesson #1: Communal experiences are usually better than I anticipate.
- Lesson #2: The most productive days are ones devoid of emails.
- Lesson #3: I tend to forget about negative interactions and am not very good at maintaining grudges.
- Lesson #4: On days when I neglect cardio training, my sleep suffers.
- Lesson #5: The greater the struggle involved in a project, the bigger the payoff when it succeeds.

That last observation is worth expanding on. We often forget how much effort went into our past successes. Consequently, when new challenges arise, we overestimate their difficulty and underestimate our ability to overcome barriers. A five-year journal serves as a nightly reminder of conquered obstacles, overblown fears, and meaningful achievements.

It also provides a running catalog of our past mistakes, which is equally useful because it prevents us from needlessly repeating them. About a year ago, I was considering hiring a consultant with whom I had worked in the past with mixed results. Just before I was about to give him the go-ahead on a new project, I came across a journal entry that I had written two years prior, which said something to the effect of " ███████ is not to be trusted." We have not worked together since. Without that entry, I would likely have repeated an easily avoidable mistake—and why? Because of Ron Friedman lesson number three.

Research tells us that memory is not the precise, enduring snapshot of events that we like to think it is. Rather, it decays with time, is subject to a host of cognitive biases, and changes slightly each time we recall an event. None of these deficiencies applies to written entries, making journals a far superior tool for learning from the past and improving our predictions of the future.

At the same time, by expanding our time frame from the immediate present to the distant past, five-year journals promote smarter, more thoughtful decision making. One of the essential keys to wisdom is the ability to zoom out and think about the long-term ramifications of a choice, beyond the immediate, short-term gain. The more we reflect on our past experiences, the better positioned we are to reach wise decisions in the present.

Keep in mind not all journaling needs to focus on life in general. You could instead focus on a single skill that you're working to master, like writing, formulating new ideas, or pitching potential clients. Ultimately, the value of a five-year journal is that it automates reflective practice, prompting us to distill the lessons we've gleaned from the past and revisit strategies worth building on in the future.

The Case for Thinking More and Doing Less

In the weeks before the 2016 Olympics in Rio de Janeiro, the very last thing Michael Phelps does each day is go for a swim.

There is a precision to this ritual, the type usually reserved for a religious ceremony. It begins with Phelps stepping wordlessly onto the starting block. He angles his body forward and stretches his arms behind his back, his right hand clasping the left, and quickly lets go, swinging his arms emphatically like a hawk about to take flight.

His dive is explosive, all velocity and no splash. It sends him streaking through the water, his legs undulating rhythmically, thrusting him farther and farther along. He is halfway down the length of the pool before rising for his first breath and notices the steam collecting on his goggles. But then his massive wingspan takes over, propelling him toward the wall where he performs a masterful flip and continues pushing forward, his hips high, his stroke flawless.

By the time Phelps completes his final lap and turns his head toward the scoreboard, there is splashing everywhere. His opponents are too late. The gold is his. He throws both arms in the air and hears the fans erupt: "USA! USA!"

His mom is smiling. Exhilarated, he draws in a deep breath.

And then, he falls asleep.

Phelps was, of course, nowhere near a swimming pool. He was lying comfortably in bed, performing a nightly imagery exercise he'd been doing since the age of twelve, long before earning any of his twenty-eight Olympic medals.

Lindsey Vonn is another Olympic medalist who relied on mental rehearsal to gain an edge before competition. Not only did Vonn visualize herself slaloming downhill, she did so while forcing her lungs to suck air in and push it out, simulating the unnerving, treacherous conditions of a high-speed run.

Brazilian soccer legend Pelé would save his imagery exercises for the locker room. Prior to a big match, Pelé would grab two towels and lie down on a bench, placing the first towel beneath the back of his head and the second over his eyes. He would then visualize himself playing soccer as a child, recapturing the joy of first discovering his love of the game. Then he would call to mind a highlight reel of his many sensational plays on the field, particularly ones that turned around a match or carried his team to victory. These would ignite his confidence, reminding him that he'd done it before and could do it again. Finally, he would turn his attention to the task at hand by keying in on his opponents, going over his strategy, and imagining himself executing it perfectly.

A generation later, Manchester United striker Wayne Rooney was forced to acknowledge using a similar approach when word leaked of a bizarre habit. Days before each match, Rooney would pester his coach for details on the exact colors of uniform, socks, and sneakers the team would wear on game day. When questions arose about his obsession with outfits, Rooney came clean: "I lie in bed the night before the game and visualize myself scoring goals...." For Rooney, having specifics made the imagery feel more real. The more trivial the detail, the more effective the exercise. "You're trying to put yourself in that moment and trying to prepare yourself to have a memory before the game."

There is no shortage of Hall of Fame–caliber athletes who credit their success to mental imagery. Golfer Jack Nicklaus made it a habit, even in practice, of visualizing the trajectory, bounce, and roll of each shot before lifting a club. Hockey great Wayne Gretzky used his imagery routine to practice lasering in on the empty patches of net behind a goalie, picturing them decorated with red lights and ribbons. Heavyweight champion Mike Tyson would imagine himself punching with such devastating force he'd see his fist bursting through the back of an opponent's head.

Why are so many athletes captivated with imagery? The short answer is because it works. And not just in sports. Research indicates that the value of mental rehearsal extends to a wide variety of domains, and can even save lives. Studies show that surgeons who mentally rehearse procedures in advance of entering the operating room commit fewer errors and experience less stress during surgery. Musicians who practice playing a piece in their head before sitting down at the piano learn compositions more quickly. Public speakers who visualize their performance before getting up onstage experience less anxiety, appear less rigid, and deliver more compelling presentations.

So far in this chapter, we've examined the overlooked value of past experience and explored a number of ways top performers use reflective practice to enhance their knowledge. That's the first dimension of practice: mining the past. In this next section, we're going to examine a second underutilized tool for developing our expertise: practicing in the future.

The Surprising Downside of Visualizing Success

In 2016, four years before she shocked Serena Williams by winning the US Open finals, fifteen-year-old Bianca Andreescu wrote herself a $3.5 million check. She had no intention of cashing it. It was an advance on the prize money she'd receive after winning the final Grand Slam of the year, a prop designed to motivate her and help her visualize success.

"I believe we create our reality with our mind," Andreescu told *Good Morning America* the Monday after her historic win. She is hardly alone in this conviction. If anything, some would argue that the only thing she is guilty of is thinking too small.

In the early 1990s, back when he was an unknown, struggling actor, Jim Carrey wrote himself a check for $10 million and dated it three years out, adding the memo "Acting services rendered." He placed it in his wallet and carried it everywhere, believing, like Andreescu, that visualizing success would help shape his reality. Just before the date on his check was set to expire, he revealed on *The Oprah Winfrey Show*, he received an offer to make *Dumb and Dumber*, which brought with it a payday that turned his vision into reality.

Both Andreescu and Carrey's stories are compelling. What they are not, however, is proof. For every tennis champion and Hollywood superstar whose million-dollar visions become a reality, there exist countless hopefuls whose visions never come close to materializing. Their stories receive markedly less attention because failed athletes and washed-up performers rarely appear on prominent talk shows.

A little after *Dumb and Dumber* hit theaters and Jim Carrey was becoming a household name, researchers at UCLA led an experiment designed to quantify the value of visualizing success. The study involved just over a hundred freshmen in an introductory psychology class. A week before the students' midterm exam, the experimenters divided the students into three groups. Those in the first group were instructed to visualize themselves receiving a high grade on the midterm. Those in the second group were also asked to use visualization, with one key difference. Instead of imagining a successful outcome, they were told to visualize the process of studying, including the specifics of where, when, and how they might prepare for the exam. Those in the final group were simply asked to monitor how much time they spent studying over the coming week.

By now, you can probably guess where this is going. Which group performed best on the midterm exam? The group that visualized studying, of course. Visualizing the process led to more studying, lower anxiety, and a higher grade. But that's not all the researchers discovered. They also found that compared to the control group (the students who did no visualization whatsoever and simply tracked their study time during the week), the students who followed the Bianca Andreescu/Jim Carrey method of visualizing success actually did worse. Their scores were the lowest of any group.

Why would visualizing a positive outcome lead to a worse grade? The emotional payoff we experience when we imagine ourselves achieving a desired result diminishes our appetite for doing the work necessary to be successful. We're temporarily sated, even when we're logically aware that the entire experience is a fantasy. Yet that's not the case when our mental simulation is focused on process. Mentally rehearsing the specific actions we need to take in advance reliably elevates our performance.

Five Ways Visualizing Process
Makes You Perform Better

Imagine that tomorrow morning, you'll need to write a ten-page proposal. To prepare, like Michael Phelps, you lie down on your bed, close your eyes, and visualize the following day.

What are the practical benefits of performing this exercise?

The first is that mentally simulating a task helps you **identify obstacles** before you encounter them. You might, for example, remember that you'll need to reference a few books that are currently sitting on your bedside table, or that you are scheduled to have new carpeting installed in your office tomorrow morning, or that you're not entirely sure how to transition from one section of your proposal to another.

A related advantage is that this exercise gives you an **emotional preview** of what you're likely to experience when the time comes for you to start writing. Perhaps the notion of having to produce a lengthy document under a tight deadline causes you to feel overwhelmed. That's useful information. Knowing how you are likely to react enables you to prepare a productive response before you begin.

Now that you are alert to these challenges, you can begin to **front-load decisions** in advance of sitting down to do the work. You may, for example, elect to work from home the following day, so that you can avoid the commotion at your office. You might plan to download a few older proposals as a reminder of how you've produced similar presentations in the past. And to avoid feeling overwhelmed, you may decide to turn on your out-of-office email autoresponder so you can work without interruption and commit to taking stress-reducing walks anytime you need one.

As you go about visualizing yourself sitting at your desk, focusing intently, crafting the various components of your draft, you are likely to shrink your anxiety and **grow your confidence.** Not only is this mental simulation helping you perfect your game plan in advance, it contributes to an expectation of success.

Now, contrast this experience with that of a colleague who neglects to do an imagery exercise and starts thinking about their proposal only after showing up to work. Although you have yet to commit a single word to paper, you are far more likely to be successful the following day.

For athletes like Michael Phelps and those preparing for a physical activity, imagery provides even more benefits. Studies show that when we imagine ourselves performing an action, we **activate the same neural pathways involved in physically doing the behavior.** In other words, when Phelps closes his eyes and pictures himself leaping into a pool, parts of his motor cortex light up as if he is literally diving off the block and plunging into a crisp body of water.

Over time, all that mental activation adds up, contributing to faster processing and deeper mental associations. And it's not just Phelps's brain that benefits. Imagery has also been shown to engage athletes' muscles, as well as their cardiovascular and respiratory systems, without overtaxing their body and risking burnout in the way that additional physical practice might. In fact, one study found that compared to athletes who rely on physical practice alone, athletes using imagery can cut their practice load *in half* without negatively impacting their performance at all.

How to Use Mental Practice

So let's say you're sold on the value of using imagery. How do you do it effectively? A few rules of thumb are worth mentioning.

First, researchers use the term *imagery* (not *visualization*) for a reason. The more senses you involve, the more effective your simulation is likely to be. If you're preparing for an important talk, imagine the chatter of the audience before you begin, the feel of the clicker as you lift it in your hand, the heat of the stage lights warming your forehead. Those details help place you in the moment more effectively than merely visualizing yourself giving a speech.

A second is that you can make your imagery more vivid by alternating between first- and third-person perspectives. Using an internal first-person perspective (e.g., imagine looking out at your audience) will elicit a more visceral response, which is valuable when you want an emotional preview. But at times that experience can feel overwhelming or is no longer as evocative because you've done it multiple times. This is when it's useful to alternate to an external third-person simulation (e.g., imagine yourself sitting in the audience, watching the presentation). Doing so lowers the emotional temperature, helps you envision how an audience might respond to certain elements of your performance, and enables you to see yourself succeeding.

Another useful tip is to occasionally picture yourself faltering or encountering an unexpected hurdle. The key is to keep going and think through exactly how you might navigate that momentary setback and then resume your typical routine. This practice will not only help you anticipate challenges, it will also elevate your confidence by instilling the belief that you can recover from whatever situation happens to arise.

Tennis icon Billie Jean King utilized imagery in precisely this way on her path to securing thirty-nine Grand Slam titles. In an interview on NPR's *Fresh Air* recorded after King's retirement, she revealed her approach to picturing every potential adverse scenario at the US Open and how she might respond, before stepping onto the court: "I always thought about the wind. I thought about the sun. I thought about bad line calls. I thought about rain if we had to wait, things that were probably out of my control, and how would I respond to them."

King's preparation went beyond simulating her play. She also imagined her demeanor between points. "I would think about how I wanted to act. Like they teach in acting, act as if, it's the same thing in sports. Do you stand up straight? Do you have your body language speaking in a confident way? Because 75 percent of the time when you're on the court, you're actually not hitting a ball. And I think that's where the champions come through. So I would visualize all these different possibilities."

A final point worth noting: effective imagery does not require a major outlay of time. Research suggests that the optimal length is no more than twenty minutes, with some studies reporting benefits after as little as three minutes of focused simulation. Given the enormous versatility of mental rehearsal and the fact that it can be performed anywhere, anytime with no equipment, it's hard to comprehend why imagery has yet to receive the attention it deserves outside the domain of sports.

How *Not* to Practice

Every season, between the months of April and September, Aaron Boone and the training staff of the New York Yankees commit coaching malpractice 162 times a year.

Their missteps transpire in full view of fans like clockwork, three hours before the start of each game. If it's 4:00 p.m. and a baseball game is scheduled at Yankee Stadium, chances are Coach Boone and his staff are conducting batting practice, a ritual professional baseball teams have relied on to prepare for games dating back to the nineteenth century.

There's just one problem: batting practice is an exercise so far removed from the science of top performance that it isn't just ineffective. It actively makes hitters worse.

To appreciate why batting practice is counterproductive, it helps to recall why anyone bothers to practice in the first place. What makes practice useful? One obvious answer is that it's a method of improving performance. Another is that it's a tool for acquiring new skills.

Batting practice promotes neither.

If you've ever arrived early for a baseball game or watched a home run derby on television, the scene will be familiar to you. Players take turns stepping into the batter's box and smashing the ball as hard as they can, just as they would in a real game. Except it's not a professional pitcher throwing at them. Pitches during batting practice are delivered by a coach, who stands behind an L-shaped screen with protective netting and deliberately tosses the ball at a fraction of the speed a batter can expect to encounter during an actual game. To make matters worse, no attempt is made to reproduce the confusing spins that make professional pitching so bewildering to hit, or to vary pitch type. Hitters are simply invited to take massive cuts at lazy, straight-line pitches over and over again, while fans watch in awe as baseballs rain onto the upper deck.

The fact that hitters are about as unlikely to encounter soft-toss pitching during a real game as they are to be struck in the face by a hot dog is not a consideration. Every team takes batting practice—not just the Yankees. And yet practicing at a reduced level of difficulty has serious consequences, a number of which are counterproductive.

As any baseball player will tell you, to succeed as a hitter, you need outstanding timing. Making contact requires you to anticipate precisely when and where a ninety-mile-per-hour pitch will arrive within striking distance. Slow pitching throws that calculation off.

Baseball hitters also need to quickly decipher pitch type by reading a pitcher's body language. Batting practice doesn't help with that because there is no pitch variation—there's only one mind-numbingly predictable toss. Finally, succeeding at batting practice incentivizes players to swing at angles that can backfire because they're optimizing for straight-line, spinless pitches they rarely see in games.

So far in this chapter we've examined two underappreciated dimensions of practice: reflective practice, which involves unpacking the past, and imagery, which involves simulating the future. The third dimension of practice—practicing in the present—is both the most obvious and the easiest to get wrong.

Russian-born pianist Vladimir Horowitz once said, "The difference between the ordinary and extraordinary is practice." It's an appealing notion. If only it were so simple.

Why Your Brain Prevents You from Learning (and What to Do About It)

As baseball's misguided batting practice routine demonstrates, not all practice is beneficial. On the contrary, in many cases, it can sabotage the very skill you're working to improve. And not just when you commit the fairly obvious blunder of practicing at reduced levels of difficulty. Often your development stalls even when you rehearse in conditions entirely representative of real-life settings.

In part, it's because our brain is working against us.

One of the benefits of extensive training is that certain actions start to occur quickly and automatically over time. We no longer have to think deeply about what to do next the way we did when we first started. One quintessential example is reading. Another is driving. The first time I drove a car, I squeezed the steering wheel so hard that my fingers were sore for hours. More than twenty years later, it often seems like I pay more attention choosing which podcast to play than I do to the actual driving.

Psychologists call this *automaticity*. It refers to our ability to perform complex skills while paying them very little attention. It's a consequence of expertise.

For the most part, automaticity is a godsend. It helps us outsource a slew of important routines throughout the day, such as brushing our teeth, getting dressed, and making breakfast. With our attention freed up, we're able to focus on more challenging tasks, like reflecting on the implications of an interesting article we just read or plotting how we might navigate a delicate matter at work.

Automaticity works by converting the conscious into the unconscious. Neurologists can map its progression in the brain using MRI scans. At first, complex behaviors require the attention of the brain's evolved frontal region called the cerebral cortex. But then, as we grow more familiar with certain actions, they become the domain of lower, subcortical regions, including the basal ganglia and the cerebellum. Expertise frees up the more sophisticated cerebral cortex, allowing us to focus less on our actions and allow our minds to wander.

Now, you might think that automaticity is an unmitigated good. After all, what possible downside could there be to performing actions effortlessly while thinking about something else? But as it turns out, automaticity can make improvement harder to achieve. The less attention we pay to our actions, the harder it becomes for us to elevate our performance or acquire new skills.

And herein lies a paradox. Experience begets automaticity. And automaticity stifles learning. How, then, do you improve on a task you already perform reasonably well?

The answer comes to us from the work of the late cognitive psychologist K. Anders Ericsson. Ericsson, a distinguished researcher, was best known for a 1993 study of violinists that became the basis for the "10,000-hour rule"—the popular notion that mastering a skill requires focused, feedback-rich practice over a lengthy period of time.*

Drawing on decades of research into the lives of top performers,

---

* Despite the popularity of the "10,000-hour rule," Ericsson didn't believe there is anything especially significant about surpassing 10,000 hours of practice. Far more important, he felt, is the quality of your practice.

Ericsson identified the precise features of practice that contribute most to skill building and expertise.

The most effective practice, Ericsson found, **tackles perceived weaknesses,** or elements of an activity that you find especially difficult to execute. Another key is to **break down complex tasks** and isolate specific aspects, focusing on them one at a time. Ideally, **feedback is immediate,** enabling you to make incremental adjustments and try again, thereby ensuring that the time you invest practicing translates into gradual improvement and growth.

That's a far cry from the way most people practice—to the extent that they practice at all.

Visit your local driving range, and you'll see golfers ripping shot after shot off a tee. Blasting drive shots is fun, cathartic, and largely ineffective. Rarely will you find players hitting out of bunkers, practicing uphill putts, or testing their ability to read the contours of difficult greens—despite the fact that mastering any of these elements would do far more to elevate their game and improve their scores.

Working on our weaknesses is unpleasant, stressful, and hard. But it's a process that does something crucial for skill development: it breaks the spell of automaticity.

By facing up to our shortcomings and tackling them head-on, we can't help but pay close attention to the links between our actions and the underwhelming outcomes they produce. The discomfort we feel drives us to search for novel solutions and experiment with different paths, making performance breakthroughs more likely.

Experts don't achieve mastery through mere repetition. They do so by targeting weaknesses, pursuing stretch goals, and relentlessly pushing the bounds of their abilities. It's the only way to improve at a task you already perform reasonably well and elude the grasp of automaticity.

There's one other thing experts know: it's not enough to reproduce game-time conditions when game-time conditions feel routine. Often, the only way to jolt an experienced mind awake is to force it to do something that feels entirely new.

Keeping Practice Fresh,
Rewarding, and Productive

The first time Dan Knights launched himself out of a moving airplane twelve thousand feet above the ground, he was hoping for more than safe landing.

Knights is a "speedcuber," a title reserved for Rubik's Cube aficionados capable of unscrambling the classic brain teaser in shockingly little time. Except he's not just any speedcuber—he's a world champion. Back in 2003, Knights entered *The Guinness Book of World Records* by solving a Rubik's Cube faster than anyone had thought possible: an astonishing twenty seconds. And how did he achieve that milestone? By adopting an intense practice regimen that included "speedcubing" while leaning out of a speeding car, solving a cube blindfolded, and, once those conditions were no longer sufficiently challenging, skydiving and solving a cube in free fall without activating his parachute until he was done.

Now, you may be wondering: Why would any of that be helpful?

Knights's extreme workouts reflect a technique researchers call *pressure acclimatization training*. It involves practicing under extreme conditions that trigger even more anxiety than a performer is likely to experience in real-life settings. Practicing in pressure-filled situations provides performers the valuable experience of managing their fears, tuning out unexpected distractions, and executing under duress.

Dialing up the pressure is one path to ensuring that practice continues to stimulate learning long after we become familiar with a skill. And while hurling yourself out of a plane to practice in mid-air might strike most people as excessive, the underlying principle is one that is worth taking seriously: ramping up the difficulty is essential to effective practice.

Fortunately, there are plenty of ways to make practice challenging without putting your life on the line. One simple approach is to seek out novelty. A crucial mistake to avoid anytime you're working to develop a skill is to follow the same practice regimen for more than a few days. Predictability fosters boredom, and boredom is the enemy of focus, memory, and learning.

Novelty, on the other hand, is an attention magnet. Our brains are naturally drawn to new features in our surroundings. It's an instinct we inherited from our ancestors, for whom noticing environmental changes was a matter of life and death. You can leverage the allure of novelty by introducing regular variations into your practice regimen. That may include changes in the drills you perform, the locations in which you choose to do them in, or the people you invite to practice alongside you.

Even mixing up the order in which you practice can help keep the experience fresh and, surprisingly, facilitate faster learning. We tend to assume that mastering a skill requires practicing the same action over and over, making slight adjustments each time, until eventually we land on the perfect execution. But that's not what the research shows. As it turns out, we are far more apt to learn when we avoid endless repetition and instead alternate among tasks.

Among the first studies to unearth this unexpected insight compared the performance of basketball shooters after three days of practice. The first group practiced shooting the same shot, twelve feet away from the basket, for three straight sessions. The second group practiced a variety of shots that included the same twelve footer, as well as eight and fifteen footers. At the end of the week, the experimenters invited both groups to the gym and recorded which could hit twelve footers most consistently. The results weren't even close. The group practicing a variety of shots was nearly 40 percent better.

Initially, this finding seems hard to explain. After all, two-thirds of the shots taken by the mixed-practice group weren't even tested. How in the world did they do better? It's because toggling between tasks forces us to think about the appropriate response each time, instead of mindlessly repeating the same action. It also teaches us to notice subtle differences in our execution, which fosters deeper understanding.

The most effective practice regimens avoid extended repetition, even if that means spending less time working on a target skill. Instead they harness the power of novelty and shake things up by blending an assortment of tasks, which results in sharper learning and stronger performance.

A second method of ensuring that practice remains challenging is introducing new hardships.

Years before he helped the New York Knicks win two NBA championships and served three terms in the US Senate, Bill Bradley was a lanky Missouri high school student desperate to level up his basketball game. But he had two weaknesses that were impossible to ignore: lackluster speed and inconsistent dribbling.

An ambitious teenager might have resolved to visit the track a few times a week and perhaps devote ten extra minutes to dribbling before practice. Not Bradley. He instinctively recognized that neither exercise would push him hard enough. His solution: he inserted ten-pound weights inside his sneakers, positioned chairs throughout his school's gym, and taped cardboard rectangles to the lower half of his glasses, blocking his view of the ball. Seven days a week, Bradley's practice regimen consisted of him whizzing down the court, swerving between obstacles, his legs hoisting the weight of a much larger man, while keeping his eyes level on imagined defenders without glancing down at the floor.

Bradley's obstacle course now seems like child's play when compared to the circus-like workouts of today's athletic superstars. Stephen Curry's practice regimen includes dribbling up and down the court while attempting to catch a tennis ball, flinging shots all the way from the locker room tunnel, and putting on virtual reality glasses that fire disorienting strobe lights, preventing him from seeing the court and requiring him to make do with incomplete information.

Former Olympian Michael Phelps's practice regimen highlights the benefit of not just seeking out new challenges but strategically selecting ones that prepare you for nightmare scenarios, no matter how unlikely they may appear. At the 2012 Beijing Olympics, Phelps plunged into the pool at the start of the 200-meter butterfly and opened his eyes to find his goggles filling with water. Alarmed, he kept swimming, barely making out the walls in time to avoid bashing his head. With two laps to go, the force of the water became too great, and Phelps could no longer see a thing.

Incredibly, Phelps was prepared for this very instance. His coach had insisted that he devote a portion of his practice to racing in the dark. All those laps in a pitch-black pool had led Phelps to an insight: when visibility was lacking, he could track his position by counting strokes. Not only did Phelps complete that Olympic 200-meter butterfly by counting strokes, he also somehow managed to increase his speed and set a new world record in the process.

The final approach to ensuring that practice continues to foster learning is by far the most surprising. It involves abandoning your standard practice regimen altogether and turning your attention to an entirely new task.

When Heisman Trophy winner Herschel Walker joined the Dallas Cowboys in 1986, fans expected plenty of acrobatic jumps and elusive spins on the football field. What they most certainly did not anticipate was seeing many of those same moves on display during Walker's off-season performances with the Fort Worth Ballet.

Walker was not the only football player to study dance. Nor was he even the first NFL player to perform onstage with a professional ballet company. Ballet, football players know, is an extraordinarily demanding exercise requiring agility, balance, and concentration— all highly desirable skills that contribute mightily to success on the field.

For football players like Walker, ballet represents one example of cross-training—the practice of mastering a related activity in an adjacent field. Cross-training offers a slew of benefits, including keeping players fit, introducing transferable techniques, and strengthening underused muscle groups. It also offers athletes an activity they can practice all year round, while mitigating the risk of boredom or burnout.

Which isn't to say that all football players secretly swap their uniform for a leotard in the off-season. Some box to promote balance, speed, and stamina. Others prefer jujitsu and karate training to develop quicker movements, better hand release techniques, and greater concentration. Many stay sharp by playing the Madden NFL video game series, which enables them to develop their pattern recognition skills while resting their bodies.

Cross-training is an approach with the potential to benefit

performers in any field, given the right choice of activity. When he's not writing novels, Haruki Murakami runs and swims because both activities promote endurance, a skill he believes is essential to producing lengthy literary works. During his reign as host of *The Daily Show,* Jon Stewart made time for one hobby outside work: solving crossword puzzles. It's an activity that sharpens verbal skills and strengthens obscure associations—both vital ingredients to writing jokes.

Over the past decade, the number for business leaders enrolling in improv classes has spiked sharply, though not because of a sudden appreciation for sketch comedy. Instead, there's a growing recognition that the deep listening and mindful presence required to excel as a leader are far better developed on the stage than in the office boardroom.

For a busy professional, the idea of adding cross-training to a calendar already bursting with commitments can feel intimidating. Which is why rather than viewing cross-training as yet another requirement we need to somehow squeeze in, we're better off applying its lessons to selecting our hobbies. By identifying elements of our performance that we hope to improve and asking ourselves what other (fun) activities require similar skills, we can make more strategic decisions about which tasks are worth mastering outside the office.

That can mean singing karaoke for the salesperson terrified of presenting to an audience, drawing illustrations for the writer hoping to improve his attention to detail, and playing video games for the surgeon eager to improve her fine motor skills.

Ultimately, what makes cross-training so valuable is that it provides fresh opportunities for novelty, challenge, and growth—which, as we've seen, are both essential for learning and increasingly hard to come by as your skills develop. And yet when we look at the practice routines of those at the very top of their field—the Peles, and Michael Phelpses, and Billie Jean Kings—one thing stands out: a tireless pursuit of adversity, past, present, and future.

It's because they know that progress without difficulty is impossible and that mastery isn't a destination. It's a way of life.

How to Talk to Experts

L ate in the fall of 2001, the hottest ticket in Hollywood was not a glitzy movie premiere or an exclusive award ceremony. It was a private ten-day acting seminar led by the man *Time* magazine had declared Actor of the Century: Marlon Brando.

All the big names were in attendance: Leonardo DiCaprio, Sean Penn, Whoopi Goldberg, Robin Williams. Every few minutes, a new limo glided up to the curb, another celebrity streaming in.

They were there to learn from a legend. This was one of the most accomplished thespians of a generation, the Godfather himself, the trailblazer who had popularized Method Acting, now prepared to reveal the secrets of his craft. Actor Edward James Olmos recalled the thrill of the invitation and the momentous anticipation that filled the room as the symposium was about to begin. "Brando had never taught an acting class before," he later told the press. ". . . This was going to be his legacy to the acting community."

Brando had hired a camera crew for the occasion. He planned to have the footage edited and sold to film schools and acting programs. He even brought on a director to oversee production.

When the moment arrived, Brando gave the signal. The cameras began rolling. Class was in session.

What happened next is something no one in the room will ever forget.

The *Hollywood Reporter* recounted the event this way:

When the doors flung open, the 78-year-old Brando appeared wearing a blond wig, blue mascara, a black gown with an orange scarf and a bodice stuffed with gigantic falsies. Waving a single rose in one hand, he sashayed through the warehouse, plunked his 300-pound frame onto a thronelike chair on a makeshift stage and began fussily applying lipstick.

"I am furious! Furious!" Brando told the group in a matronly English accent, launching into an improvised monologue that ended, 10 minutes later, with the actor turning around, lifting his gown and mooning the crowd.

This was just the beginning. Over the course of the ten-day program, Brando had his audience observe improvisational scenes featuring Samoan wrestlers and a troupe of little people, invited a homeless person off the street and tried to teach him the basics of acting, and asked his students to remove their clothes in full view of their classmates.

Eventually, Brando's students were invited to perform a variety of improv exercises, which he offered to critique. Brando was merciless in his feedback. When he didn't like what he saw, he didn't wait until a scene ended. He burst onstage and thundered his dismay, barking out, "Lies! Lies!"

At first, many in the audience assumed that Brando had thought things through, that there was a method to his madness. Here is the way Edward James Olmos rationalized Brando's unconventional entrance: "He was stressing a basic fundamental of acting. Which is that you must be willing to show your ass and fail. If you're not willing to do that, you might as well get the fuck out of here."

All of which may have been true. Except it didn't stop Brando's students from growing increasingly disillusioned. Three days into the program, several students staged a walkout, declaring the seminar "a circus." The number of attendees continued to dwindle as the course progressed. Even the director quit.

Though the particulars of Brando's disastrous acting program are unquestionably bizarre, the lesson is hardly unique: experts rarely make great instructors.

We tend to assume that high performers are keenly aware of the skills that set them apart and possess the ability to impart that knowledge to anyone they choose.

Neither of those assumptions is true. If they were, the most celebrated coaches in sports would be retired superstars, like basketball's Magic Johnson and Isiah Thomas. Both NBA champions tried their hand at coaching and proved to be bitter disappointments. In hockey, Wayne Gretzky registered four failed seasons as head coach of the Phoenix Coyotes before abandoning the sport altogether for a far more successful career in winemaking. In baseball, the winningest coach over the last century was not its best hitter, Ty Cobb, but Tony La Russa, an unremarkable journeyman whose career batting average was an appalling .199—a full 50 percentage points lower than the average player's.

And it's not just sports. In academics, university professors have two primary responsibilities: to produce high-quality research and to educate students. Many parents make the reasonable assumption that the best researchers—the kind whose noteworthy publications win them jobs at prominent universities—are also the most effective teachers. There is little evidence to support this conclusion. On the contrary, studies suggest that selecting an instructor on the basis of his research credentials is about as useful as choosing a doctor on the basis of his favorite ice cream flavor.

A comprehensive analysis published in the *Review of Educational Research* assessed the performance of more than half a million professors by looking at the quantity and impact of their research, as well as their students' evaluations. The conclusion? The relationship between a professor's research output and teaching performance is essentially zero.*

---

* More alarmingly, there is also evidence that students have better educational experiences in classes taught by part-time faculty than tenured professors (most of whom secured their jobs by excelling in research).

To be fair, it should come as no surprise that domain expertise and teaching performance do not go hand in hand. Doing and explaining are different skills.

Many of us tie our shoelaces on a daily basis. Despite that experience, the idea of writing a step-by-step manual on shoelace tying is an intimidating proposition. To author a compelling guide, you'd need to possess writing know-how, a sophisticated vocabulary, and an understanding of the way people learn complex motor skills. Tying your shoelaces every morning teaches you none of these.

Except it's not *just* a lack of training. Studies reveal that expertise actively hinders our ability to explain. As it turns out, the better we perform a task, the worse we get at communicating how we managed to do it.

Which raises an obvious question: Why?

When Knowledge Makes You Dumber

Jimmy Fallon looks rattled.

Hands covering his face, he begins talking to himself. "Oh no, oh no, oh no." He buries his head on the couch and turns sideways claiming the fetal position.

His partner, *Wonder Woman* Gal Gadot, is unfazed. "Listen, it's going to be okay," she offers encouragingly. She kneels down beside him, pats him on the back. "We're going to do great. We're going to do great. Don't break on me right now."

Fallon is acting, of course. He's pretending to be distraught over his team's chances of winning a game of charades. It's a scene that encapsulates everything that makes *The Tonight Show* so endearing: silly competitions, colossal celebrities, Fallon's hijinks.

By the time the game begins, Fallon is all business. Gadot reads her clue. The countdown starts.

Her first gesture involves forming a fist and positioning it just below her chin.

"Song!" Fallon says.

Gadot nods, adding "Mm-hmm," even though she's not allowed to speak.

She holds up three fingers. "Three words," says Fallon. Right again.

Gadot's next move is considerably harder to interpret. It involves bringing both hands to her pelvis, squatting down, and thrusting both arms downward in a long, sweeping motion.

Fallon is visibly uncomfortable. He places a cushion on his lap, raises his eyebrows at the audience, and mouths, "Whoa."

Gadot repeats the gesture to applause, but Fallon is mystified. He looks everywhere: his producers, the audience, the other players. Eventually he hazards a guess. "'Birth of a Nation'? 'Baby Got Back'? 'Push It'?"

Mercifully, the buzzer sounds. Gadot looks devastated. "Ahh! It was that bad?" she asks, demoralized. "I thought I'd help you guess it."

The answer, she eventually reveals, was the Bruce Springsteen classic "Born to Run."

"Oh, 'Born to Run,' of course!" Fallon says, adding "I'm so mad. That was fantastic. That was my fault."

Fallon, of course, is being far too generous. His inability to interpret Gadot's gestures has nothing to do with the quality of either player's performance. It reflects a phenomenon called the *curse of knowledge*, which can be summarized as follows: knowing something makes it impossible to imagine not knowing it.

To appreciate why clues Gadot felt were straightforward and obvious sailed clear over Fallon's head, consider a Stanford experiment that involved a simple game, not unlike the kind featured on *The Tonight Show*. Within the study, eighty students were grouped into pairs of two. Each team member was assigned a role: they were either "tappers" or "listeners." Tappers were asked to review a list of highly recognizable songs (for example, "Twinkle, Twinkle, Little Star," "Silent Night," "Rock Around the Clock") and select three they knew well enough to tap to their partner by beating their hand against the desk. Listeners had one task: to watch the performance and name that tune.

Before the game began, the researchers asked the tappers a simple question: How many of the songs they were about to perform did they think the listeners would recognize? The tappers were optimistic, estimating a 50 percent success rate. The reality was much different. By the time the experiment ended and all forty pairs had completed their turn, the actual number was a paltry 2.5 percent.

Both Gal Gadot and Stanford's tappers wildly overestimated the value of their clues, and the curse of knowledge tells us why: knowing the answer changes the way we think. It makes a naive perspective unimaginable.

Why are we so bad at simulating not knowing? Psychologists believe it's because our brains evolved to gobble up new information, not banish what we've already learned. No matter how hard we might try or how motivated we might be to relate to those who don't share our experiences, we're simply not built to ignore useful information. Which makes sense. In the evolutionary past, keeping valuable intelligence top of mind and wielding it at every opportunity kept us alive.

While the curse of knowledge may have served a crucial survival function thousands of years ago, today it wreaks all sorts of havoc beyond simply muddying our performance on inconsequential parlor games.

The fact that we are incapable of imagining the thought process of those who don't share our knowledge explains why business owners often make dreadful marketers. For one thing, they are too close to their offerings to appreciate the way an ordinary customer conceives of their problems. Then there's the fact that they are aware of their competitors, which often leads them to overemphasize differentiating features that a typical customer considers irrelevant.

The curse of knowledge also leads many qualified professionals, particularly those embarking on new roles, to undervalue their skills. A common experience among new consultants, for example, is the happy discovery that they actually know a lot more than they initially assumed. It's not because they've spontaneously sprouted new abilities. It's because they're comparing themselves to experts they worked with or studied in the past. Their clients don't share that experience. They're too consumed with their own industry to be nearly as knowledgeable and are often delighted with insights that a new consultant may (naively) dismiss as obvious.

Why Experts Can't Help Giving Lousy Instructions

But perhaps the biggest challenge posed by the curse of knowledge is the enormous wrench it throws into our ability to learn from experts. Not only are experts incapable of putting themselves in our inexperienced shoes, there's also evidence that they can't help but underestimate how long skill acquisition actually takes.

Ask Novak Djokovic how many hours you should set aside to learn how to hit a 120-mile-per-hour ace, and the answer you receive is likely to be a fraction of the required time. Why? Because the idea of *not* knowing how to hit a 120-mile-per-hour ace is as foreign to Djokovic as not knowing how to read is to you and me.

Worse, having Djokovic coach you isn't guaranteed to help. Most of the actions Djokovic executes when he is serving are performed unconsciously. Years of experience have enabled him to compress his thinking and automate his movements without any reflection, freeing him up to focus on other crucial factors.

On the court, that's an advantage. In the classroom, it's a disaster.

It's a hurdle that educational psychologist Richard Clark has spent decades exploring. Clark relies on a painstaking technique called *cognitive task analysis* that involves extended interviews with experts, using questions designed to elicit a step-by-step account of everything they do. Next, he reviews video of the experts in action and determines how many of their behaviors they mentioned in their breakdown. Clark has analyzed experts in a host of fields, from tennis pros to intensive care nurses to federal judges. His conclusion? Experts leave out a staggering 70 percent of the steps required to succeed, because they rarely think about them. Most of their actions unfold unconsciously.

Interestingly, when experts do pay close attention to behaviors that typically occur automatically, their performance often crumbles. We have a name for this phenomenon in sports: choking. It's what happens when experts are placed under inordinate stress and responds by directing their attention inward, monitoring each step of a complex set of actions, instead of allowing their performance to flow automatically.

Here's what choking might look like for Djokovic. Instead of simply walking up to the service line and pounding a down-the-line ace, in the heat of a Wimbledon fifth-set tie break, with millions of people looking on, Djokovic might suddenly find himself counting the number of times he bounces the ball, second-guessing the positioning of his grip, and reminding himself to keep his shoulders square while swinging the racquet. That's a lot of information to process, and it's likely to upend Djokovic's play. It's why choking tends to result in failure.

It's worth clarifying that it's not the intense pressure that causes players to wilt—it's the overthinking.

In 2008, researchers from the University of Michigan and University of St Andrews invited golfers of varying skills to an experiment. They started by having all the golfers putt on an indoor green and measured their performance. Unsurprisingly, the experienced golfers vastly outperformed the novices.

Next, they had the golfers describe their actions by writing a short essay. "Record every detail that you can remember," read the instructions, "regardless of how insignificant they may strike you."

The goal here was to illuminate what happens when golfers are made to reflect on their actions—when they are forced to make the unconscious conscious. After this brief writing exercise, the golfers were once more given the opportunity to putt, and their performance was measured again.

So, what did the experimenters find? Verbalizing the process had disastrous ramifications for the experienced golfers. And no wonder. The pros had already mastered a complex set of intricate tasks. The last thing in the world they want to do is deconstruct an automatic process.

The novice golfers, however, had a markedly different reaction. They benefited from the reflection exercise. When there's no automatic process to disrupt, executing a list of steps is precisely how novices learn a new skill.

Which brings us to a final barrier to learning from experts: they can't help communicating in ways that novices find overwhelming. Years of experience have taught them to shrink extraordinarily complicated ideas into time-saving abstractions. They also toss around specialized jargon that feels second nature to them and sounds like gobbledygook to everyone else. If you've ever felt baffled during a conversation with a mechanic, physician, or Home Depot sales associate, chances are it was their expertise that was getting in the way.

Simply put, experts think differently. They apply shortcuts they're not aware of, avoid contemplating their behaviors, and can't begin to imagine not knowing the things they know. Ask them to deconstruct the actions leading to their success, and they somehow neglect to mention 70 percent of them. And the 30 percent they do report? It's conveyed using language that most people find anywhere from challenging to incomprehensible.

How, then, can we learn from those who know best?

What to Ask an Expert

You're at the gate, surrounded by business travelers, winter coats, and carry-ons, when the announcement comes. Your flight has been delayed. Technical malfunction. The airline is searching for an alternative plane, a new crew. It's unclear when you'll be departing. Stay tuned for further instructions.

Your initial reaction is alarm. You've got a connecting flight to catch, an early morning meeting. Just as you're about to search Orbitz for other airlines, you notice the arrival of a new face, someone you think you recognize. You can't place it at first, but then it dawns on you: it's *her*. The one with the podcast and best-selling books and upcoming Netflix special. She's *the* expert in your industry—the one everyone agrees is at the top of your field. And here she is. At your gate.

You might be intimidated if she didn't look so flustered. Not only is your flight AWOL, but there are no seats available and far too many passengers for such a small terminal. Even standing room is at a premium. You do your best not to stare but can't help noticing that she is scanning the walls, searching for an outlet. Yours is the last one, and just as she's approaching, you decide to take a risk.

"Would you like to use this?" you ask, removing the charger cable from your phone.

"Are you sure?" she asks, to which you quickly nod. "That's very generous. Thank you. My phone just died."

Just then, the man sitting next to you stands up and runs off, reminding you that you really should be searching for another flight. And just as you're about to start, she takes his seat and offers you a smile.

And then it hits you. She has no phone. The flight's delayed. There is nothing else to do but talk. People would gladly pay thousands of dollars for a private conversation with this expert. And here you are, the opportunity of a lifetime dropped into your lap.

So what should you ask? What questions can you pose to prompt an expert to share valuable insights? And what, if anything, can you do to help mitigate the curse of knowledge from muddying the discussion?

When talking to experts, three categories of questions are worth considering: *journey questions*, *process questions*, and *discovery questions*.

Journey questions are designed to achieve two objectives: unearth the experts' road map for success and remind them of their experience as a novice. Understanding an expert's path from amateur to professional is likely to give you a strong sense for how you can re-create the process yourself (assuming, of course, that your field hasn't changed too drastically). Asking experts to reflect on the start of their career is also likely to help them relate more effectively to a novice mind-set, prompting them to offer more helpful suggestions.

Questions focused on an expert's journey can include:

- What did you read/watch/study to learn your craft?
- What mistakes did you make at the beginning?
- What do you wish you had spent less time on that ended up not being very important?
- What metrics have you learned you need to keep an eye on?

Process questions get at the nitty-gritty of execution. They're designed to illuminate the experts' approach by drilling down on the specific steps they apply to bring their work to life. These answers are especially valuable for reverse engineering because they pull back the curtain to reveal how a complex work is developed.

Keep in mind that broad questions about an expert's approach will likely result in partial information. As we've seen, in the mind of an expert, many actions occur automatically, with limited forethought or contemplation. For this reason, it's important to avoid asking general questions and err on the side of asking for specifics.

Questions focused on an expert's process can include:

- I'm curious about your process. What do you do first? What's next? And after that?
- Where do you get your ideas and strategies?
- How do you go about planning?
- What's your daily routine when you're in [planning/creating/marketing, etc.] mode?

Finally, **discovery questions** focus experts on their initial expectations and invite them to compare those naive beliefs with what they know today. By directing experts' attention to unexpected revelations, you get them thinking about useful insights they didn't possess at the very beginning, back when they were in your shoes.

Questions focused on an expert's discoveries may include:

- Looking back, what was most surprising to you?
- What do you wish you had known when you first started?
- What factors turned out to be crucial to success that you weren't expecting?
- If you had to do it today, what would you do differently?

It's worth keeping in mind that the answers you collect will differ from expert to expert, and that's okay. You're not looking for a single breakthrough that guarantees success, because that doesn't exist. You're simply uncovering the factors a particular expert believes make the biggest difference.

What Focus Group Moderators Know
About Uncovering Secrets

Having the right questions is just the beginning. Even more important is posing them in a way that gets experts to open up and following up with responses that unveil even more useful information.

Let's start with the first of these two requirements: getting experts to open up.

One set of specialists who have mastered the art of getting people to divulge sensitive information within short periods of time are focus group moderators. Many of their techniques can easily be applied in conversations with experts.

Among the many tactics moderators use to extract useful information, first and foremost is embracing a mind-set of *naive curiosity*. If you've ever been in a focus group, you know that moderators are not worried about others' impressions of their knowledge. They routinely ask basic questions and resist making assumptions because doing so puts participants at ease and yields fuller responses.

There's a quote you may have heard that goes "If you're the smartest person in the room, you're in the wrong room." Moderators are never the smartest people in the room because they know that impressing others is the last thing you want to do when you're trying to get them to open up. By subduing their ego and making themselves vulnerable, moderators are able to learn more.

Focus group moderators also strategically sort their questions, and not by placing the most important items first. They prioritize questions that are easy to answer and make respondents feel comfortable. For this reason, many surveys begin by asking you your gender (an easy, noninvasive item) and don't ask about your household income (a complicated, highly personal item) until the end. Researchers know that you are more willing to divulge sensitive information after a period of answering innocuous questions.

But where moderators really earn their paycheck is by being exceptional listeners. One of the things you discover while moderating groups is that the quality of information you elicit often has less to do with the initial question than it does with your ability to nod, stay quiet, and wait for a respondent to elaborate. Effective listening is essential to demonstrating that you value a speaker's contribution, which prompts them to say more.

Professional moderators often come prepared with a list of phrases they can deploy to get respondents to elaborate on or clarify something they've said. Having a list of prewritten statements makes it easy for moderators to interject respectfully when they need more information.

Elaborators can take the form of "That's interesting—what makes you say that?" or simply "Say more about that." Given that experts are prone to speaking in jargon and abstractions, having a few go-to **clarifiers** handy is likely to prove especially valuable. There are phrases like "Can you say that another way?" and reporter Kate Murphy's recommended clarifier: "Wait. Back up. I don't understand."

Keep in mind that with experts even the most effective elaborators and clarifiers are not guaranteed to help. It's because experts aren't just more knowledgeable. The information they possess is also compressed in ways that make it difficult to communicate. We therefore need to do more than just ask and listen—we also need to translate, converting the language of expertise into lessons a novice can readily grasp.

One approach to demystifying experts involves asking for **examples.** Experts are prone to using abstractions, complex ideas that beginners find vague. The opposite of abstractions is specifics.

When it comes to learning, studies show that starting with examples—as opposed to abstract, theoretical lessons—leads to faster comprehension and fewer errors. It's because examples are concrete, which both makes them easier to comprehend and prompts listeners to generate their own explanations, contributing to a deeper level of understanding.

Another technique you can use to translate is to look for **analogies.** Analogies explain the unfamiliar in terms of the familiar. If a friend tells you he's starting an online aviation marketplace connecting people, pilots, and planes, you're likely to have one or two questions. But the moment he says, "It's Uber for planes," it's as if a veil has lifted. By linking an idea that seems complex or vague to a knowledge structure you already possess, clarity is achieved.

Finding the right analogy is essential to understanding experts— just don't count on them to have one handy. As subject matter experts, they don't need to use everyday concepts to grasp ideas inside their field. For a novice, however, bridging the unfamiliar with the familiar can make all the difference. It's therefore worthwhile asking the expert if they can provide a simple analogy or metaphor, or suggest one yourself and confirm that it's a good fit. Even if the analogy you pose isn't a precise match, hearing why it doesn't track will likely further your understanding.

When examples and analogies aren't enough, you can ask for a **demonstration.** "Can you show me what you mean?" is often all it takes to prompt an expert to transition from telling to showing. Like examples, demonstrations make the abstract concrete and lead us to generate our own explanations. A demonstration might not always be practical or convenient, but that doesn't mean the question isn't worth posing. Experts often have access to resources that novices are not familiar with (like libraries of video recordings, transcripts, or screen captures) that are easily shared and reflect the ideas they're trying to communicate.

Another technique worth using is one that therapists often wield to help clients feel heard. It's called a **repeat back,** and it involves paraphrasing what you've heard to confirm your understanding. Saying "Let me see if I have this right" and then restating a complex idea using different words does two things. One, it leads us to process information more deeply. And two, it reveals gaps in our comprehension. If repeat backs feel unnatural to you, use them sparingly, saving them for critical ideas. You might be surprised at how well they work at prompting others to find a clearer way of communicating.

Toward the end of your discussion, you may choose to insert two questions, both commonly used by investigative reporters: "Is there anything I didn't ask that I should have?" and "Who else would you recommend I speak with to learn more?" The latter allows you to turn a single expert interview into several conversations, especially if your expert is kind enough to offer introductions. And that's important—and not just because it weaves you into a community of knowledgeable practitioners. It also helps you develop a fuller picture of what expertise in your domain looks like.

Earlier we learned that most experts leave out a staggering number of steps when asked to verbalize their process. Seventy percent of their actions somehow go missing. There is, however, one solution researchers found that tempers the experts' amnesia: interviewing multiple experts.

Once the number of interviewed experts jumps from one to three, the percentage of missing actions shrinks to a manageable 10 percent.

The upshot: in most cases, no single expert can teach you everything you need to know. Like creativity, mastery is achieved through combining ideas. The more experts you study, the clearer the road map gets.

Why Most Feedback Is Surprisingly Harmful

Pop quiz: Who's the greatest writer of all time?

William Shakespeare is one common answer. Literary scholars praise his sophisticated plots, exquisite wordplay, and enduring influence.

But what do Amazon's readers think?

Here's one recent review, left by a customer who purchased a sweeping collection entitled *William Shakespeare: Complete Works*:

> What language is this written in? It would be nice if the publisher would let us know that this collection is written in a language nobody has spoken in centuries. Might as well be in Klingon. Waste of money.

Russian novelist Leo Tolstoy doesn't fare much better. Here's a Goodreads.com review of his literary classic *War and Peace* that garnered thirty-four likes:

> This book is [a] bloated old piece of crap. How this even got published in the first place is beyond me, much less how it has been considered a "classic" for years. . . .
>   I wish I had never picked this up. I am an angrier, more cynical person for it. If Tolstoy wasn't already dead, I would wish him so.

And lest you think it's simply older writers whose classical works fail to resonate with modern audiences, a cursory glance at the reviews of more recent books by Jonathan Franzen ("Overrated, Overwrought, Overhyped"), Gabriel García Márquez ("One Hundred Hours of Boredom"), and Toni Morrison ("Beloved - Not!") suggests otherwise.

We live in a world bursting with feedback. Never before have creative professionals had access to more information about the way their work is perceived. In their book on the evolution of computing and design, *User Friendly*, Cliff Kuang and Robert Fabricant note that while it's tempting to think that the internet's main contribution is connecting people in remote locations, its larger influence may be turning feedback into a central feature of business transactions and, more broadly, human relationships. Not only are we now invited to rate sellers, products, and service providers after even the smallest of transactions, the internet has trained us to "like" our friends, "endorse" our colleagues, and (most strikingly) resist purchasing anything lacking positive reviews.

On the one hand, the explosion of feedback over the past decade provides clear advantages. It enables customers to make more informed purchase decisions, roots out subpar products and unethical merchants, and empowers businesses to evolve by adapting to customers' demands. It also provides creative professionals with a flood of data points they can use to fine-tune their performance.

And yet, as the customer reviews of many literary classics illustrate, not all feedback is valid, insightful, or instructive.

In the first half of this chapter, we explored the unexpected challenges to learning from experts and discovered strategies for navigating those barriers. This second half is about drawing insight from the feedback of nonprofessionals and members of the general public in ways that help us further narrow the gap between our vision and ability.

Let's begin by examining why much of the feedback we're exposed to tends to have limited value. Receiving useful feedback turns out to be surprisingly challenging, even when those providing input are genuinely trying to help.

In person, the desire to maintain a positive relationship often prevents friends, colleagues, and family from serving as honest brokers. Online, the more provocative the review, the more likely it is to attract attention. The reward structure is one that incentivizes reviewers to focus on looking smart, not being helpful, which is easiest to achieve by being critical. Add to that the fact that reviewers don't see the reaction of the person they are critiquing, and it becomes easy to understand why so many online reviews are inflammatory and callous, consisting of feedback that no reasonable person would ever consider delivering face-to-face.

But there's a bigger issue with feedback, including feedback that's accurate, objective, and sincere. A comprehensive analysis published in *Psychological Bulletin* analyzed more than six hundred feedback studies and concluded that while feedback often improves performance, it's by no means guaranteed to help. In fact, in a stunning number of instances—over one-third—feedback actively *damaged* performance.

We need the feedback of others to improve. Yet the feedback we routinely receive often ranges from sugarcoated to hypercritical and carries with it the disastrous potential of undermining our work.

So how do we train those around us to do it better?

How to Train Your Friends to Provide Useful Feedback

Before Quentin Tarantino directed his first film, *Reservoir Dogs*, the high school dropout stayed afloat by taking part-time jobs and sleeping on friends' couches.

Tarantino was a ravenous cinephile, determined to make it in Hollywood, and devoted his evenings to writing screenplays. A few years into his quixotic journey, he managed to snag a handful of minor acting roles, most notably appearing as an Elvis impersonator in an episode of *The Golden Girls*.

Still, Tarantino sensed that acting would take him only so far. If anything, it was his writing that would help him break through. Tarantino labored tirelessly over his film scripts. He was painfully aware of just how much was at stake. At twenty-three, there was only so long he could keep bouncing from job to job, couch to couch, praying for his big break.

So when a studio executive agreed to review his script for *True Romance*, Tarantino was ecstatic. Who knew? Maybe this was it. At the very least, he'd get some sense of whether he was on the right track.

Here is the response Tarantino's agent received:

How dare you send me this fucking piece of shit. You must be out of your fucking mind. You want to know how I feel about it? Here's your fucking piece of shit back. Fuck you.

Now let me ask you a question: What's wrong with this feedback?

Sure, it's not the reaction Tarantino was hoping for. And yes, it is on the harsh side. But it is, unquestionably, feedback. The studio executive doesn't like the script. End of story. Move on.

And yet, clearly, it is not what we have in mind when we ask for feedback, is it?

Jerry Seinfeld knows exactly what this feedback is missing — and it has nothing to do with the fact that it's unexpected or insulting. It's lacking a central feature of useful feedback: specificity.

"I always think about people that write books," Seinfeld explained in a 2018 *New York Times Magazine* interview. "What a horrible feeling it must be to have poured your soul into a book over a number of years and somebody comes up to you and goes, 'I loved your book,' and they walk away and you have no idea what worked and what didn't. That, to me, is hell. That's my definition of hell."

When comedians like Seinfeld perform live, the feedback they receive is loaded with specificity. It tells them precisely what's resonating and what's not because each punchline elicits its own reaction. Seinfeld scrutinizes the feedback he receives religiously, like a chef sampling a dish or an NFL coach analyzing film. He even claims that if you were to play him a recording of his act with all the jokes removed, he could still identify the precise bits by listening to the audience's laughter: "The timbre of it, the shape of it, the length of it—there's so much information in a laugh."

When feedback is specific, it speaks to a particular element of a complex work. In so doing, it temporarily ignores the totality of a performance in favor of isolating a single component. It's the difference between telling Tarantino that his script is a "piece of shit" and explaining that his protagonists are not relatable.

It's the precision that makes the feedback instructive.

Reading a written work out loud is one way of eliciting feedback that reveals an audience's reaction, and it's one that authors like David Sedaris now use before publishing a piece. Sedaris takes unfinished essays on the road and reads them in front of live audiences, jotting down notes on their reactions. It's a useful exercise for works designed to provoke strong emotional reactions.

Another method of securing specific feedback is to be intentional with the questions you pose. Instead of asking "What do you think?" or "Can you give me some feedback?," which often results in vague responses along a positive-to-negative continuum, take time to pinpoint the precise notes your work needs to hit in order to be successful and ask about them. For example, if you are drafting an important proposal, instead of asking a colleague for feedback in general, you could ask how engaging he or she found your opening paragraph or whether the timeline feels sufficiently ambitious.* The more specific the feedback, the better positioned you are to make use of your audience's response.

Which brings us to a second feature of useful feedback: it prioritizes improvement over assessment. The best feedback does more than tell us whether or not we've succeeded. It helps us uncover opportunities for getting better.

One mistake people often make when seeking feedback is asking questions designed to elicit praise. "Do you like it?" It's a question that screams for reassurance and validation. No matter how comforting it might feel to hear others applaud our work, compliments don't help us improve, especially when we've pressured people into making them.

Sometimes the desire to be liked and the desire to get better are competing goals, and it's important to recognize that tension. That same desire to be liked can also compromise our audience's willingness to share critical feedback. Which is why instead of making it easy for others to compliment us, we are better off making it easy for them to find opportunities for improvement.

Ironically, one approach to soliciting better feedback is to avoid asking for feedback altogether. Instead, ask for advice.

In 2019, a team of Harvard Business School psychologists ran a series of studies investigating the best approach to collecting input. Compared to asking for feedback, asking for advice resulted in fuller assessments of what worked and what didn't, and led to more suggestions for improvement—in some cases over 50 percent more ideas.

Why the dramatic difference? Feedback, the researchers believe, prompts reviewers to compare a performer's current effort against how well they've done in the past. Advice, on the other hand, orients reviewers to the possibilities that lie in a performer's future.

---

* In chapter 4, we looked at creating a list of important metrics and rating our own performance. Once you develop those items, another approach to gathering specific feedback becomes available: you can simply convert the items you developed for yourself into open-ended questions and pose them to your audience.

Focusing on the future leads reviewers to consider opportunities for improvement, resulting in a richer, more fruitful critique.

Another approach to generating higher-quality feedback involves posing questions that target your weaknesses head-on. Comedian and playwright Mike Birbiglia has colleagues review his script and then asks, "When were you bored?" It's a question that is easier for reviewers to answer than "What didn't you like?," yet for Birbiglia, it serves a similar purpose in pinpointing elements that warrant revision.

Just as important: Birbiglia's question focuses reviewers on the script, not the performer. It's easier for friends and colleagues to critique a document than it is for them to critique Birbiglia. It's why a question like "What's one thing that would make this presentation more compelling?" is better than "What's one thing I could do better?" The latter implies you're doing something wrong, which is risky for a reviewer to admit. Most people prefer lying to damaging a relationship.

Two other features of useful feedback are worth noting: audience and timing.

The audience you solicit feedback from, whose critique you take seriously, should be a select group. When looking for feedback, we can easily settle for audiences of convenience—people we can reach quickly, without much effort. That's a mistake. For feedback to be useful, it needs to come from people whose views are representative of your target audience—the group with whom you ultimately aim to resonate.

That advice might seem obvious, yet it's a trap that a surprising number of intelligent people fall for on a regular basis. Aspiring writers often invest years perfecting a novel or script, and whom do they turn to for feedback? Their friends and family, ignoring the fact that they could not find a more biased audience if they tried. At the office, we often commit a similar error. Most workers are far more likely to solicit feedback on a new business idea from a colleague or spouse, when running it by an existing client would yield far better information.

Twitter now provides political leaders with a constant stream of voter feedback on news events in real time. On paper, that's a positive development. In reality, it's contributed to greater polarization on both sides of the aisle. Twitter users—particularly those with the free time and inclination to publicize their views—are not representative of the average voter. By calibrating their views to the feedback of a nonrepresentative audience, Twitter-reading politicians risk becoming less representative of the general public.

The takeaway is simple: when it comes to feedback, *quantity* is not the same as *quality*. We're better off avoiding high-quantity, low-quality feedback, no matter how convenient or tempting it may be. Getting feedback from the wrong audience is worse than getting no feedback at all.

Which brings us to the issue of timing. In sports, feedback is ongoing and immediate. When NBA player LeBron James shoots a jumper, he quickly learns whether or not he's succeeded. When his shot is off, its trajectory yields clues revealing what he should do differently on his next attempt. That constant stream of experiment and feedback is a large part of what makes sports so exhilarating.

Knowledge work is different. Whether you're drafting a proposal or developing a website, incessant feedback is both impractical and distracting. (Imagine receiving feedback after typing every letter.) A number of recent studies have discovered that when it comes to complex mental tasks, frequent feedback is not simply unhelpful, it actively undermines our performance and stifles our learning. It's because executing challenging activities requires our undivided attention. Ongoing feedback breaks our concentration, preventing us from sustaining our focus.

Constant feedback is likely to be especially damaging for work involving creativity. Creative ideas thrive under conditions that feel safe and require time to mature, congeal, and evolve. Being on the receiving end of endless evaluations long before we're ready makes it harder for us to play with ideas, take risks, and attempt the unconventional.

The upshot? Feedback is valuable, but only to a point. Too much feedback leaves us feeling vulnerable, frenzied, and overwhelmed.

There are, however, two occasions when feedback tends to be especially helpful for knowledge work: early and late.

Early feedback aligns well with a practice market researchers call *concept testing*. It's input that reveals whether an idea is generally headed in the right direction and worth pursuing. Before the yogurt company Chobani began pairing yogurt with chocolate and nuts, it ran the idea by a segment of customers to gauge their reaction. Consumers loved the pairing—especially those who ate their breakfast away from home. That research confirmed that Flip yogurts were worth developing and informed the clever one-piece packaging, which was designed to appeal to eaters on the go.

Late feedback is designed to achieve a different purpose: to help fine-tune execution. An outside perspective can once again be useful after we've taken an assignment as far as we can take it, when we feel too close to a project to evaluate it objectively.

Internationally acclaimed novelist Salman Rushdie believes that avoiding feedback in the middle stages of writing is crucial: "I think young writers these days are so trained in that collective act of reading each other's work and discussing it and producing the work through this workshop process. . . . That's fine as a learning process. It's not great, in my view, when you're actually writing."

Rushdie does, however, welcome late-stage feedback and actively seeks it out from trusted readers. "[In later drafts,] I become very interested in what other people have to say . . . And I do things as a result of the feedback—especially if 2 or 3 people read it and agree that the same thing is a problem."

Rushdie's approach to shunning reader input for much of the creative process runs counter to conventional wisdom. We're often told that the secret to improvement is feedback and that the more feedback we receive, the faster we'll improve. Except that's not true. More feedback isn't always better. As we've discovered in this chapter, the majority of feedback is worse than useless—it's harmful.

To improve, we need feedback that meets a particular set of criteria. We need it to be specific, improvement-focused, reflective of the audience we are trying to reach, and properly timed. The good news is that all four elements are simple to achieve, so long as we stay mindful of the difference between quality and quantity feedback, and commit to asking the right people the right questions at the right times.

How Top Performers Convert Feedback into Growth

There's one thing we haven't talked about. It's the giant elephant in the room—the crippling weakness all ambitious performers suffer from and no one willingly admits. It's the other reason we turn to our friends and family for feedback, loathe performance reviews, and, at times, invest weeks (if not years) "perfecting" projects in isolation before reluctantly seeking outside input.

We're petrified of negative feedback.

It's not an unreasonable impulse. Hearing that our best efforts are falling short is a painful, unsettling experience. In part, it's because of the way the human brain experiences failure.

Encountering criticism triggers the release of cortisol, a stress hormone that elevates our anxiety, disrupts our focus, and prevents us from listening attentively. Feeling threatened, we assume a defensive posture, characterized by fight (respond defensively) or flight (end the conversation), neither of which comes remotely close to sparking self-reflection or stimulating growth.

Often, the emotional fallout is made worse by the stories we tell ourselves about our setbacks. Negative feedback is never simply about a lackluster performance on a task. It's about what that failing represents—what it reveals about our talent, ability, and potential.

For all these reasons, learning from negative feedback doesn't come naturally for most people. Yet doing so is a critical skill—one that enables top performers to grow from their misfires, remain confident in the face of disappointment, and harness the insights they receive to elevate their game.

So what's their secret? How do we overcome our natural aversion to criticism? What does the research suggest we do to grow from negative feedback?

Before we get to the solutions, let's make this concrete by considering an example. Suppose you're getting ready to deliver an important presentation in front of everyone at your company. You're nervous, so you invest a lot of time preparing. Then, a week before the big day, you corral three trusted colleagues into the conference room and ask them to observe your talk.

Their reaction is not as positive as you expected. Dismayed, you grab a pad to take notes, chiding yourself to maintain your composure. Now, let's pause here for a moment. And let's assume that your colleagues' critique is generally on point. What can you do to leverage their feedback without feeling defensive, deflated, or overwhelmed?

The first strategy is to **translate negative feedback into corrective actions.** In other words, identify changes you can apply to address the feedback. The moment you convert a critique into options, it feels less like a rebuke and more like an opportunity.

For instance, suppose you pose Mike Birbiglia's improvement-focused question to your audience, asking "When were you bored?" The consensus, you learn, is that your opening and conclusions were compelling but the middle of your presentation dragged. Naturally, that feedback initially stings. But the moment you pinpoint potential fixes, like adding an anecdote, posing a question, or cutting three slides, your attitude shifts. You become grateful for the improvement the feedback inspired.

Neurological research bears this out. Most of the time, making a mistake activates an area of the brain called the anterior insula, which is central to the experience of pain, sadness, and fear. In contrast, learning that we've succeeded activates the brain's reward system, which is rooted in the ventral striatum. The ventral striatum is active when we think about winning an important new client, scoring a promotion, or going on an exciting date.

In 2015, researchers at the University of Southern California made a fascinating discovery. Not all mistakes activate the painful anterior insula. Sometimes they activate the pleasurable ventral striatum. What determines which area lights up? It turns out that when mistakes are combined with new learning, we experience them as rewarding. The wisdom we gain allows us to see new opportunities for avoiding mistakes and succeeding in the future.

Turning negative feedback into corrective action is rewarding for another reason: it makes failure feel temporary. Just because your presentation isn't cutting it right now doesn't mean it's doomed to stay that way forever. Implementing any one of the changes you've identified is likely to produce different results.

A second strategy is to take a break, step back, and **introduce psychological distance** between you and your work. When we are immersed in an activity, our focus naturally narrows. We experience tunnel vision, which makes us both defensive and resistant to suggestions that involve additional work. Taking time to reflect on big-picture objectives, beyond the immediate task, promotes long-term thinking and makes us more receptive to criticism.

It's important to remember that responding to feedback quickly and responding to feedback intelligently are not the same thing. Research suggests that taking time to sulk and contemplate our disappointment can actually benefit us in ways few people anticipate. Although we don't typically associate brooding with top performance, it's in those agonizing moments of raw self-reflection that we discover important insights about ourselves and deepen our motivational reservoir for achieving success.

Adopting a long-term perspective reminds us that we still have time to improve, that not getting this one task right doesn't define who we are. That extended time frame relieves the immediate pressure to prove our competence in the moment and makes us more willing to sacrifice discomfort for long-term growth.

A final strategy is to **reinterpret the experience of struggle.** In Western cultures, struggle is considered a negative experience. It suggests that you're "not getting it," an idea that poses all sorts of threats to our sense of competence, intelligence, and self-worth. But people in Eastern cultures view struggle differently. For them, struggle isn't an indication of inability—it's a sign that you're learning. Everyone is expected to struggle, regardless how smart or gifted they may be, because that's how intellectual advancement comes about.

Viewing struggle as a natural and desirable part of growth is a perspective that is associated with a wide range of benefits: a willingness to persevere in the face of difficulty, a healthy appetite for new challenges, and importantly, greater openness to outside feedback.

Eastern cultures aren't the only ones with a welcoming attitude toward struggle. It's also the prevalent attitude among comedians, who consider the ability to withstand a disastrous performance (known affectionately as "bombing," "dying," or "eating it hard") a career-enhancing rite of passage.

Many comedians, including John Oliver, view the number of times they've suffered through poor performances as a point of pride. "I've bombed so many times, I literally cannot remember the worst," he said on a *Late Night with Jimmy Fallon* segment devoted to chronicling the many failures of superstar comedians. "I've re-pressed the humiliations—I've had so much that they've all just be-come a blur of public disgrace."

Amy Schumer credits her willingness to endure weeks of bru-tal sets night after night with igniting her transition from amateur stand-up to professional comedian. "Five of us toured and I died on stage every night. I would cry on the tour bus, and then go out and do it again the next night—sometimes two shows a night. . . . By the end, I was pretty desensitized. I'd just been in so much pain every night that I stopped caring—and once that happened, it became more about my experience onstage."

Aziz Ansari doesn't just welcome struggle—on nights when his set earns massive applause, he's strangely crestfallen. Here's how he explained the experience to NPR's Terry Gross on *Fresh Air*: "You get to a point where you almost get mad at yourself when you do really well because you think—oh, that means I'm not taking enough risks. And if I do a set where I just completely tank, that means I really went for something and tried something difficult. If I'm just killing all the time, I'm just worried too much about having a good time and doing a good show in that moment. But you really are pushing yourself if you do something and it goes horrible."

At first blush, Ansari's appetite for adversity and negative feed-back seems bizarre, if not outright masochistic. Yet one group shares this craving for criticism: experts.

Research conducted at Columbia University and the University of Chicago reveals that while beginners prefer receiving positive over negative feedback, experts don't hold that preference. Those with experience and a track record of success are more interested in negative feedback because they recognize that it contains vital clues to improvement. While positive feedback is certainly flattering, it can't help you get better. At best, it simply encourages you to do more of the same.

It's a fascinating perspective and one that places an entirely different lens on the value of criticism. To paraphrase Ansari, it doesn't mean you don't have what it takes. It simply means you tried something daring and found the limits of your ability. And while receiving negative feedback may not be pleasant in the moment, after a certain level of experience, it's a positive sign. One that tells you that you are continuing to stretch, learn, and grow.

Author and essayist Chuck Klosterman has spent decades interviewing top performers in music, sports, and pop culture. Here's what that experience has taught him about the relationship between feedback and success: "If you want to avoid criticism, it's better to be good than it is to be great."

We would all do well to take that observation to heart. If you're looking to achieve a moderate level of success, positive feedback can help you get there. But if you're aiming to surge to the top of your field, shatter expectations, and establish a legacy, negative feedback isn't simply something you need to tolerate. It's a promising indicator that you're on the right track.

Conclusion

Stumbling on Greatness

When Vincent van Gogh was growing up, the last thing in the world anyone close to him could have anticipated was that he would become a famous artist.

Who could blame them? Not even historians can point to a single childhood episode suggesting that he had the slightest interest in art, let alone possessed an enormous hidden talent. What they did know about young Vincent was that he was moody, driven, and obsessed with the most peculiar objects.

While his siblings entertained themselves with marbles and dolls, van Gogh would wordlessly slip out of the house and embark on lengthy expeditions. He'd return home hours later, armed with wildflowers, beetles, and abandoned bird nests. These, he would smuggle upstairs to the attic, where he would catalog his discoveries and update his burgeoning collection.

Alarmed by their son's erratic behavior, van Gogh's parents sent him off to boarding school, where Vincent was lucky enough to be placed in the class of one of Europe's best art instructors. Engaging and charming, he inspired many students. Van Gogh was not one of them.

The following year, van Gogh dropped out of school entirely. He was fifteen years old. After an extended period of moping, he proceeded to fail at a number of professions: bookstore clerk, tutor,

preacher. It wasn't until the age of twenty-seven that he began de-
voting entire days to drawing and painting. A few months later, he
declared himself an artist.

Today, van Gogh is recognized as one of the most influential artists in world history. That's not just an impressive achievement—it's
one that is staggeringly difficult to explain.*

Consider the following facts: van Gogh was not born with unmistakable talent, nor did he display particular promise when he
brazenly declared himself a professional. He received virtually no
instructional training over the course of his career and only labored
as an artist for a grand total of ten years.

Just how did he get so good?

We know a lot about Vincent van Gogh's professional development—arguably more than any artist who ever lived. It's because
throughout his thirty-seven years on the planet, he wrote an extraordinary number of candid letters to relatives and friends. After his
tragic death, his letters were collected by the wife of his brother
Theo. All told, there are more than eight hundred letters, each offering a compelling and unvarnished window into van Gogh's processes, struggles, and turbulent emotional universe.

So, what was van Gogh's secret? How did he manage to develop
his skills without the benefit of a teacher? And how exactly did he
transform himself from abject novice to revered master in such a
remarkably brief period of time?

The short answer is that he leveraged many of the techniques
we've discovered in *Decoding Greatness*.

The first thing van Gogh did when setting out to become an
artist was identify models he could deconstruct, analyze, and reproduce. He mastered figures by replicating the dynamic paintings of

---

* Though mental illness undoubtedly influenced van Gogh's work—he is pre-
sumed to have suffered from temporal lobe epilepsy—experts believe that
he succeeded despite his condition, not because of it. Several neurological
studies have examined whether temporal lobe epilepsy fosters greater creativity and have failed to find evidence that it does.

Jean-François Millet and Jules Breton. He learned to paint land-
scapes by copying the works of Charles Daubigny and Théodore
Rousseau. Through meticulous copywork, van Gogh worked backward to extract a wide range of lessons. He observed the way accomplished artists wield colors to convey emotion, the impact of
brushstroke length on the way the eye perceives movement, and
how shadows and reflections lend paintings nuance and depth.

Van Gogh was careful not to limit himself to art of a particular
genre and enjoyed sampling from a wide range of artists. He studied
his neo-impressionist contemporaries, scrutinized more established
Barbizon masters, and became enamored by Eastern artists, whose
works had only recently made their way into European markets.

Consuming a wide spectrum of influences sensitized van Gogh
to subtle differences between genres, helped him develop and refine
his palate, and exposed him to a range of artistic ideas. When he
found works he admired, he added their prints to his collection and
analyzed them intently. The simplicity of Japanese artwork, in particular, made an enormous impression on van Gogh. By the time of
his death, despite the fact that he was always incredibly poor, he had
more than one thousand Japanese prints to his name.

He also ventured outside his field for influences. Van Gogh was
a voracious reader and found inspiration in the works of George
Eliot, Émile Zola, and Charlotte Brontë. But he adored one writer
above all others: Charles Dickens. As he admitted to his brother
Theo, "My whole life is aimed at making the things from everyday
life that Dickens describes. . . ."

Drawing from this vast trove of influences, van Gogh was able
to combine distinct elements from disparate genres to produce
strikingly original work. From Millet, he developed a taste for
depicting the everyday lives of hardworking peasants. From Im-
pressionists like Claude Monet and Camille Pissarro, he borrowed
bright, vivid colors and the practice of applying tiny dabs of paint.
From Japanese art, he imported strong outlines and an absence of
shadows.

The intense, vibrant style we now recognize as uniquely van

Gogh's did not arrive fully formed. It emerged slowly, the product of years of incremental change. It gradually manifests as van Gogh encounters new influences, applies new discoveries, and conducts tiny experiments.

Van Gogh experimented with *everything*. He began by sampling different materials, going from charcoal to pencil to pen to brush. He attempted a range of styles, shifting from realism to Expressionism to Neo-impressionism. He tackled multiple techniques, starting with thin watercolors at first and over time gravitating toward dense layers of paint—a technique he is now recognized for called impasto. And perhaps most strikingly, he evolved in his use of colors, moving from dark, complementary colors in his early years to bright, contrasting colors that pop from across the room.

Van Gogh's growth and evolution as an artist would have been impossible had he continuously played it safe and avoided the ongoing challenges we now know are necessary for skill acquisition. Instead, he practiced relentlessly, producing more than two thousand paintings, drawings, and sketches in just ten years. Critically, he wasn't just productive. He deliberately focused on his perceived weaknesses, testing the limits of his abilities. It was not uncommon for him to work and rework the same image repeatedly. As he explained in his letter to a fellow artist, Anthon van Rappard, "I keep on making what I can't do yet in order to learn to be able to do it."

We know all of this because of van Gogh's long-standing commitment to stepping back, contemplating his progress, and committing his thoughts to paper. In so doing, he was benefiting from the many advantages of reflective practice.

Van Gogh did not become one of the most beloved and recognized artists in the world through inborn talent or decades of instruction from trained experts. He taught himself. How? By collecting works he admired, identifying crucial features that make them unique, and working to re-create them from scratch. But he didn't just copy—he evolved. He applied the formulas he uncovered and tweaked them by combining influences, experimenting with different tools, styles, and techniques, and taking lots of intelligent risks. Throughout his brief career, he practiced at the edge of his abilities, keyed in on opportunities for growth, and reflected deeply in ways that transformed casual observations into actionable insight.

Van Gogh stumbled across these strategies through a serendipitous mix of personality, circumstance, and luck. Fortunately, you don't have to.

The Lessons of Decoding Greatness

Over the course of *Decoding Greatness*, we've met dozens of standout performers from a wide range of diverse fields. We've detailed their methods, unpacked the reasons they work, and connected their techniques to crucial findings in the fields of creativity, motivation, skill acquisition, performance, and expertise.

How do you apply their strategies to your work? Let's review ten major lessons and identify ways we can all utilize them in everyday life.

1. **Become a collector.** The first step to achieving greatness is recognizing it in others. When you come across examples that move you, capture them in a way that allows you to revisit, study, and compare them to other items in your collection. When we think of collections, we tend to think of physical objects, like artworks, wine, or stamps. That definition is too limited. Copywriters collect headlines, designers collect logos, consultants collect presentation decks. Tour your collection as you would a private museum that you visit to find inspiration, study the greats, and remind yourself to think big.

2. **Spot the difference.** To learn from your favorite examples, you need to pinpoint what makes them unique. When you encounter works that resonate with you, make a habit of reflecting on a single question: "What's different about this example?" By comparing the stellar to the average, you can pinpoint key ingredients that give a work its flavor and identify particular elements that can be incorporated or evolved elsewhere.

3. **Think in blueprints.** Nearly every example you admire was developed using a blueprint: chefs utilize recipes, writers employ outlines, web designers work off site maps. Instead of attempting to re-create a fully realized work, inject a level of abstraction and draft a high-level outline. By working backward and crafting a blueprint, you will find patterns that demystify complex works.

4. **Don't mimic, evolve.** Copying someone else's wildly successful formula wholesale is the fastest route to being perceived as unoriginal while contributing to a genre's demise. It also won't earn you the same results because of the (likely) mismatch between your abilities and the demands of a formula, and because audiences' expectations evolve with time. Instead, chart your own path by adding new influences, adapting formulas from adjacent fields, or replacing elements you can't learn with those you naturally perform well.

5. **Embrace the vision-ability gap.** Studying the masters comes with a price: it raises the bar on the performance you deem necessary to be successful. Chances are, you will not be able to meet these expectations, at least not at first. It's natural to feel discouraged at this point or consider quitting, but remember: having great taste and a clear vision are strong indicators of potential. Often, simply recognizing that something is not yet great and having the drive and tenacity to revise for as long as it takes is the difference between an amateur and a professional.

6. **Keep score selectively.** Achieving at a high level is a lot easier when you're measuring the key elements that drive success. By scoring crucial aspects of your performance, you instantly motivate improvement, become less susceptible to wasted effort, and encourage more mindful decisions. Over the long term, the right metrics can hold you accountable, provide feedback, and reveal game-changing patterns. Just be careful not to obsess over any single metric or forget to update your metrics as you grow.

7. **Take the risk out of risk taking.** Risk taking is both essential to growth and inherently uncomfortable. One useful approach for making risk taking more palatable involves finding stretch opportunities that don't impose a high cost to failure. Here, businesses provide a useful road map—one that is applicable to individuals as well. You, too, can test your ideas and shrink the cost of failure by running tiny experiments, publishing your work under a pseudonym, preselling an idea before developing it, and diversifying your time investment over a range of projects. Stop wasting energy trying to build up the courage to take risks. It's far easier to take risks when the price of failure is negligible.

8. **Distrust comfort.** In most cases, emotions provide valuable real-time guidance on experiences worth pursuing and those to be avoided. One notable exception to that rule is the way we feel during skill acquisition. We don't grow when we're enjoying ourselves—we learn best when we are challenged, struggling, and occasionally failing. Whether at work or at home, top performers don't view comfort as an indication that they've made it. Rather, they regard it as a signal that their development has stalled.

9. **Harness the future and the past.** Repetition and feedback can help you elevate your performance, especially when used to target your weaknesses. But if that's the only practice you're getting, chances are you're only operating at a fraction of your potential. Two additional forms of practice are worth using: reflective practice, or analyzing your past experiences to extract important lessons, and imagery, or simulating a performance in advance. Both reflective practice and imagery provide a host of impressive cognitive and emotional benefits, and train you to anticipate more effectively—a hallmark of expertise.

10. **Ask wisely.** Despite what many of us assume, experts rarely make good instructors. Knowledge is a double-edged sword: knowing something makes it impossible to imagine not

knowing it. To get the most out of your conversations with experts, you need to come prepared with questions, elaborators, and clarifiers that prompt an expert to reveal his or her journey, process, and discoveries. Experts aren't the only people who can help you improve—nonexperts can be just as valuable. The trick is to invite the right audience, ask for advice instead of feedback, and arrive with a series of strategic questions geared toward improvement.

By applying these lessons, we all have the potential for building our skills, elevating our performance, and making lasting contributions. No matter what your field, your capacity for achieving at a high level need not be defined by whether or not you were fortunate enough to be born gifted or happened to receive the guidance of an expert.

Those at the peak of their profession earned their standing by nurturing an insatiable hunger for new ideas, perspectives, and solutions. They know you don't reach the top of the mountain by standing still. You get there by identifying concepts worth mastering, growing your arsenal of skills, and experimenting at the edge of your ability. Never before has that mind-set been more pivotal than it is today.

The good news is that stimulating ideas are everywhere. We live in an age of unparalleled creative abundance. The worlds of television, music, and publishing are bursting with content. Online magazines, blogs, and podcasts offer a wider range of ideas and perspectives than previous generations could have dreamed possible. Search engines, digitized journals, and online libraries allow anyone with an internet connection to discover cutting-edge theories, as well as ferret out overlooked gems.

The ingredients are readily available. Having read this book, you now know how to unlock, master, and evolve them in new directions.

It's time to see what you can do.

Acknowledgments

Not long after I began writing *Decoding Greatness*, when the excitement of signing a book deal was still fresh, a well-known author I know told me something in confidence that gave me pause. He and his wife had come to an understanding, he revealed. "The next time I tell her I'm thinking of writing a book, she has to punch me in the face." This, they agreed, was preferable to the anguish of completing another book.

My experience writing this book could not have been more different, thanks to a phenomenal network of colleagues, friends, and family whose support has made this work possible.

Thanks to Dr. James Fryer, Dorie Clark, Mitch Joel, Jon Iuzzini, Seth Godin, David Epstein, Danny Iny, Dr. Susan Pierce Thompson, Charles Benoit, David Tang, Dr. James Masciele, and Jon Itkin for reviewing drafts of this book and offering suggestions that improved the final product.

Thanks to Dr. Marina Tasopoulos-Chan, Justine Roth, Christy Kern, Dr. Miron Zuckerman, and Bethany Coates for contributing to the research.

Thanks to Dr. Dan Grodner, Greg Erway, Jane Manchun Wong, Alyssa Nathan, and Josh Yanover for generously making time for interviews.

Thanks to Kathy Hadzibajric, Kyle Young, Kate Wilcox, Miranda Wilcox, Roy McKenzie, Matthew McKeveny, Ethan Bence, and Pam Savage for being exceptional teammates, freeing up time for me to write.

Thanks to Tom Neillsen, Les Tuerk, Adam Kirschenbaum, Christine Teichmann, and Marge Hennesey for helping share my work with so many outstanding organizations.

This book would not have happened had I not met Lucinda Halpern. Lucinda is an exceptional literary agent with an impeccable radar for big ideas. She helped me rummage through a mountain of possibilities, spotted the gems, and constructed a plan for showcasing them in a compelling way. If you ever have the opportunity to work with Lucinda, you should pounce. She is preposterously good at her job. Thank you, Lucinda.

Lucinda introduced me to Stephanie Freirich, a gifted editor with the vision to sign this book when it was an overambitious encyclopedia on top performance, and the wisdom to suggest we narrow its focus. Stephanie: Every writer should have the good fortune of working with someone as strategic, discerning, and passionate as you.

Stephanie's team at Simon & Schuster has been uniformly outstanding. Thanks to Emily Simonson for her attention to detail, Jason Heuer and Jackie Seow for the striking cover design, and Lynn Anderson for the expert copyediting, and production editors Nate Knaebel and Lisa Healy.

Finally, my family. Thanks to my parents for the unwavering support (as evidenced by such motivational pearls as, "It's still not done?" and "You know, you don't have a lot of time . . ."), Maddy and Henry for being the perfect Maddy and Henry, and Anna for the love, patience, and inspiration.

Notes

Introduction: A Secret History from the Land of Innovation

xi **By the time Steve Jobs finds out:** The particulars of this historic exchange are drawn from Walter Isaacson, *The Innovators: How a Group of Hackers, Geniuses, and Geeks Created the Digital Revolution* (New York: Simon & Schuster Paperbacks, 2015), and Walter Isaacson, *Steve Jobs* (New York: Simon & Schuster Paperbacks, 2015). Additional sources include *Jobs vs. Gates: The Hippie and the Nerd*, directed by Nicolas Glimois and Karim Kamrani, Pulsations, 2017; Malcolm Gladwell, "Creation Myth," *New Yorker*, May 9, 2011, https://www.newyorker.com/magazine/2011/05/16/creation-myth; Emmie Martin, "Read Bill Gates' Answer to a Reddit Question About Whether He Copied Steve Jobs," *Business Insider*, March 13, 2017, https://www.businessinsider.in/read-bill-gates-answer-to-a-reddit-question-about-whether-he-copied-steve-jobs/articleshow/57622335.cms; Stewart Alsop II, "WUI: The War over User Interface," *P.C. Letter*, January 18, 1988; Tandy Trower, "The Secret Origin of Windows," Technologizer, March 9, 2010, https://www.technologizer.com/2010/03/08/the-secret-origin-of-windows/; Andy Hertzfeld, *Revolution in the Valley* (Sebastopol, CA: O'Reilly Books, 2004); Adam Fisher, *Valley of Genius: The Uncensored History of Silicon Valley* (New York: Hachette Book Group, 2018).

xiii **Xerox faced an existential crisis:** Isaacson, *The Innovators*; Isaacson, *Steve Jobs*; Gladwell, "Creation Myth"; Jim Memmott, "The Game-Changing Invention That Rochester Didn't Want," *Democrat and Chronicle*, October 14, 2019; Douglas K. Smith and Robert C. Alexander, *Fumbling the Future: How Xerox Invented, Then Ignored, the First Personal Computer* (San Jose: toExcel, 1999); Michael A. Hiltzik, *Dealers of Lightning: Xerox PARC and the Dawn of the Computer Age* (New York: HarperCollins, 2000); "A Legacy of Inventing the Future," PARC History, PARC, accessed October 8, 2020, https://www.parc.com/about-parc/parc-history/.

xv   **The laptop I am typing:** Rod Canlon, *Open: How Compaq Ended IBM's PC Domination and Helped Invent Modern Computing* (Dallas: BenBella Books, 2013).

xv   **Douglas Engelbart:** Isaacson, *The Innovators*; Isaacson, *Steve Jobs*; Hiltzik, *Dealers of Lightning*; Thierry Bardini, *Bootstrapping: Douglas Engelbart, Coevolution, and the Origins of Personal Computing* (Stanford: Stanford University Press, 2000).

xv   **Google Docs:** Ellis Hamburger, "Google Docs Began as a Hacked Together Experiment, Says Creator," The Verge, July 3, 2013, https://www.theverge .com/2013/7/3/4484000/sam-schillace-interview-google-docs-creator-box.

xv   **When Michael Dell received:** Michael Dell and Catherine Fredman, *Direct from Dell: Strategies That Revolutionized an Industry* (New York: Harper Business, 2006); Clayton M. Christensen, *The Innovator's Dilemma: When New Technologies Cause Great Firms to Fail* (Boston: Harvard Business Review Press, 2016).

xv   **Google's Larry Page was nine:** Christensen, *The Innovator's Dilemma*.

xv   **Jeff Bezos:** Christensen, *The Innovator's Dilemma*; John Cook, "Jeff Bezos' Mom: 'I Knew Early On That He Was Wired a Little Bit Differently," Geek Wire, May 8, 2011, https://www.geekwire.com/2011/jeff-bezos-mom-i-knew -early-wired-bit-differently/.

xvi   **the only way to write software:** Gary R. Ignatin, "Let the Hackers Hack: Allowing the Reverse Engineering of Copyrighted Computer Programs to Achieve Compatibility," *University of Pennsylvania Law Review* 140, no. 5 (May 1992): 1999–2050, https://doi.org/10.2307/3312440; Jonathan Band, "The Global API Copyright Conflict," *Harvard Journal of Law and Technology* 31, Special Issue (Spring 2018): 616–37.

xvi   **Jane Manchun Wong:** Zen Soo, "Jane Wong Uncovers Hidden App Features That Tech Giants Like Facebook Want to Keep Secret," *South China Morning Post*, November 26, 2018, https://www.scmp.com/tech/apps-social /article/2174875/jane-wong-explains-why-she-uncovers-hidden-app-features -tech-giants; Salvador Rodriguez, "Facebook Employees Turn to Rogue Hacker from Hong Kong to Learn What Other Teams are Building," CNBC, October 20, 2019, https://www.cnbc.com/2019/10/20/facebook-employees -turn-to-hong-kong-hacker-jane-manchun-wong-for-info.html; Alli Shultes, "Jane Manchun Wong: The Woman Scooping Silicon Valley," BBC, April 27, 2019, https://www.bbc.com/news/technology-47630849; Aaron Holmes, "This Rogue Hacker Digs up Unreleased Features on Instagram, Facebook, and Spotify—and She Often Finds Out About Them Before Other Employees at Those Companies Do," Business Insider, February 10, 2020, https://www.businessinsider.in/tech/news/this-rogue-hacker-digs-up-un released-features-on-instagram-facebook-and-spotify-and-she-often -finds-out-about-them-before-other-employees-at-those-companies-do

/articleshow/74068630.cms; Kaya Yurieff, "This 24-Year-Old Finds Unreleased Features in Your Favorite Apps," CNN Business, March 22, 2019, https://www.cnn.com/2019/03/22/tech/jane-wong-app-features/index.html.

xvii **a pair of Cornell and Duke University economists:** Robert H. Frank and Philip J. Cook, *The Winner-Take-All Society: Why the Few at the Top Get So Much More than the Rest of Us* (New York: Penguin, 1995).

xix **the majority of professionals are self-taught:** Michael J. Coren, "Two Out of Three Developers Are Self-Taught, and Other Trends from a Survey of 56,033 Coders," Quartz, March 30, 2016, https://qz.com/649409/two-out-of-three-developers-are-self-taught-and-other-trends-from-a-survey-of-56033-developers/.

xix **"Bill is basically unimaginative":** Isaacson, *Steve Jobs*, 173.

xx **In 2005, both he and Gates:** Isaacson, *Steve Jobs*, 467.

xx **"Oh my God":** Charles Arthur, "Bill Gates on the iPad—and His Envy of the iPhone," *The Guardian*, February 12, 2010, https://www.theguardian.com/technology/2010/feb/12/ipad-bill-gates-microsoft-opinion-iphone.

1: The Mastery Detectives

4 **Consider filmmaker Judd Apatow:** Judd Apatow, *Sick in the Head: Conversations About Life and Comedy* (New York: Random House, 2015); "Judd Apatow, The Man Behind Comedy, Returns to the Stage Himself," *The Leonard Lopate Show*, podcast, WNYC, July 12, 2017, https://www.wnyc.org/story/judd-apatow-comes-down-big-sick/.

4 **"I would call their agents":** Apatow, *Sick in the Head*, xiii.

5 **"I put my book aside":** Sara Plourde, "Workshop 18: Joe Hill," *10-Minute Writer's Workshop*, podcast, NHPR, May 18, 2017, https://www.nhpr.org/post/10-minute-writers-workshop-joe-hill#stream/0.

5 **Hill's father took to copying:** Nathaniel Rich and Christopher Lehmann-Haupt, "Stephen King, The Art of Fiction No. 189," *The Paris Review*, Fall 2006, https://www.theparisreview.org/interviews/5653/the-art-of-fiction-no-189-stephen-king.

5 **forms of copywork:** Angela Duckworth, *Grit: The Power of Passion and Perseverance* (New York: Scribner, 2016); Anders Ericsson and Robert Pool, *Peak: Secrets from the New Science of Expertise* (Boston: Houghton Mifflin Harcourt, 2016); Brett and Kate McKay, "Want to Become a Better Writer? Copy the Work of Others!," The Art of Manliness, March 27, 2014, https://www.artofmanliness.com/articles/want-to-become-a-better-writer-copy-the-work-of-others/.

6 **Many of the painters:** Cornelia Homburg, *The Copy Turns Original* (Amsterdam: John Benjamins Publishing Company, 1996); Bruce Johnston, "Van Gogh's £25m Sunflowers Is 'a Copy by Gauguin,'" *The Telegraph*, September 26, 2001, https://www.telegraph.co.uk/news/worldnews/europe/italy/1357627/Van-Goghs-25m-Sunflowers-is-a-copy-by-Gauguin.html;

Martin Bailey, "The Artist Whom Van Gogh Most Admired—and Whose Work fetched Record Prices," *The Art Newspaper*, October 4, 2019, https://www.theartnewspaper.com/blog/the-artist-whom-van-gogh-most-admired -and-whose-work-fetched-record-prices.

6 **Another, popular among nonfiction writers:** Malcolm Gladwell, "Malcolm Gladwell Teaches Writing," MasterClass, https://www.masterclass.com/classes /malcolm-gladwell-teaches-writing.

7 **"Exploring the index":** Chuck Klosterman, *X: A Highly Specific, Defiantly Incomplete History of the Early 21st Century* (New York: Blue Rider Press, 2017), 000.

7 **In *Poetics*, Aristotle:** Aristotle, *Poetics*, translated by Malcolm Heath (New York: Penguin Classics, 1997).

7 **Kurt Vonnegut:** Adrienne Lafrance, "The Six Main Arcs in Storytelling, as Identified by an A.I.," *The Atlantic*, July 12, 2016, https://www.theatlantic.com /technology/archive/2016/07/the-six-main-arcs-in-storytelling-identified-by -a-computer/490733/; Josh Jones, "Kurt Vonnegut Diagrams the Shape of All Stories in a Master's Thesis Rejected by U. Chicago," Open Culture, February 18, 2014, http://www.openculture.com/2014/02/kurt-vonnegut-masters-thesis -rejected-by-u-chicago.html; Ana Swanson, "Kurt Vonnegut Graphed the World's Most Popular Stories," *Washington Post*, February 9, 2015, https://www .washingtonpost.com/news/wonk/wp/2015/02/09/kurt-vonnegut-graphed-the -worlds-most-popular-stories/; "Part of Vonnegut's Legacy, *Cat's Cradle*, Also Earned Him Master's," *University of Chicago Chronicle* 26, no. 16 (May 2007), http://chronicle.uchicago.edu/070510/vonnegut.shtml; Kurt Vonnegut, *Palm Sunday: An Autobiographical Collage* (New York: Dial Press Trade, 2011).

7 **the hero's journey:** The term *hero's journey* belongs to the late Joseph Campbell, whose book *A Hero with a Thousand Faces* was published years after Vonnegut proposed his theory. Vonnegut identified a comparable emotional arc, which he termed "man in a hole." See Joseph Campbell, *The Hero with a Thousand Faces* (Novato, CA: New World Library, 2008); Joseph Campbell, *The Power of Myth*, edited by Betty Sue Flowers (New York: First Anchor Books, 1991).

8 **Cinderella:** image adapted from the blog of Derek Sivers. "Kurt Vonnegut Explains Drama," Derek Sivers, September 1, 2009. https://sive.rs/drama.

9 **data scientists crunched:** Marco Del Vecchio et al., "Improving Productivity in Hollywood with Data Science: Using Emotional Arcs of Movies to Drive Product and Service Innovation in Entertainment Industries," *Journal of the Operational Research Society*, March 2, 2020, https://doi.org/10.1080/016056 82.2019.1705194; Andrew J. Reagan et al., "The Emotional Arcs of Stories Are Dominated by Six Basic Shapes," *EPJ Data Science* 5, article 31 (November 2016), https://doi.org/10.1140/epjds/s13688-016-0093-1.

9 **an app called Capo:** Tyler Hayes, "How Do You Reverse Engineer a Song?," *Fast Company*, October 24, 2013, https://www.fastcompany.com/3020632/ how-do-you-reverse-engineer-a-song.

10   **Seasoned photographers:** Tom Miles, "Breaking Down a Photo: An Introduction to Reverse Engineering," New York Institute of Photography, January 6, 2014, https://www.nyip.edu/photo-articles/photography-tutorials /reverse-engineering-a-photo.

10   **Todd Wilbur:** "Who Is this Todd Wilbur Guy?," Todd Wilbur's Top Secret Recipes, https://topsecretrecipes.com/About-Top-Secret-Recipes.html; Todd Wilbur, *Top Secret Recipes Step-by-Step: Secret Formulas with Photos for Duplicating Your Favorite Famous Foods at Home* (New York: Plume, 2015).

11   **Michelle Bernstein:** Karen Page, *Kitchen Creativity: Unlocking Culinary Genius—with Wisdom, Inspiration, and Ideas from the World's Most Creative Chefs* (New York: Little, Brown and Company, 2017).

11   **Spend all your extra money:** Ibid., 198.

11   **This is when the inquisitive chef:** "Culinary Forensics," The Center for Genomic Gastronomy, December 8, 2012, https://genomicgastronomy.com /blog/culinary-forensics-draft/; Joyce Slaton, "6 Steps to Reverse-Engineer Any Restaurant Dish," *Chowhound*, October 19, 2011, https://www.chow hound.com/food-news/93995/how-to-reverse-engineer-any-restaurant -dish/#:~:text=%206%20Steps%20to%20Reverse-Engineer%20Any%20 Restaurant%20Dish,in%20question%2C%20Wilbur%20may%20cut%20 it. . .%20More%20; Sarah Spigelman, "Reverse Engineer Your Favorite Food with an App," Mashable, July 28, 2017, https://mashable.com/2017/07 /28/pic-2-recipe-app/; Rachel Whittaker, "How to Reverse Engineer Any Store-Bought Box, Can, or Package," Modern Alternative Kitchen, August 9, 2013, https://www.modernalternativekitchen.com/2013/08/how-to-reverse -engineer-any-store-bought-food/; Answer Fella, "How to Reverse-Engineer Food," *Esquire*, September 17, 2009, https://www.esquire.com/news-politics /q-and-a/a6332/ingredient-technology-1009/.

12   **Among the many principles:** Page, *Kitchen Creativity*; Andrew Dornenburg, *The Flavor Bible: The Essential Guide to Culinary Creativity, Based on the Wisdom of America's Most Imaginative Chefs* (New York: Little, Brown and Company, 2008); James Briscione, *The Flavor Matrix: The Art and Science of Pairing Common Ingredients to Create Extraordinary Dishes* (New York: Houghton Mifflin Harcourt, 2018).

13   **David Chang:** David Chang, "The Secret Code to Unleashing the World's Most Amazing Flavors," *Wired*, July 19, 2016, https://www.wired.com/2016 /07/chef-david-chang-on-deliciousness/. See also David Chang, *Eat a Peach: A Memoir* (New York: Random House, 2020).

13   **"Unified Theory of Deliciousness":** Chang, "The Secret Code to Unleashing the World's Most Amazing Flavors."

13   **Nostalgia researchers:** Jordan D. Troisi, "Threatened Belonging and Preference for Comfort Food Among the Securely Attached," *Appetite* 90, no. 1 (July 2005): 58–64, https://doi.org/10.1016/j.appet.2015.02.029; Charles Spence, "Comfort Food: A Review," *International Journal of Gastronomy and Food Science* 9 (October 2017): 105–09, https://doi.org/10.1016/j

.ijgfs.2017.07.001; Cari Romm, "Why Comfort Food Comforts," *The Atlantic*, April 3, 2015, https://www.theatlantic.com/health/archive/2015/04/why-comfort-food-comforts/389613/.

14 **The same can be said:** Robert A. Baron, "Opportunity Recognition as Pattern Recognition: How Entrepreneurs 'Connect the Dots' to Identify New Business Opportunities," *Academy of Management Perspectives* 20, no. 1 (February 2006): 104–19, https://doi.org/10.5465/amp.2006.19873412; Jeffrey H. Dyer, Hal B. Gregersen, and Clayton Christensen, "Entrepreneur Behaviors, Opportunity Recognition, and the Origins of Innovative Ventures," *Strategic Entrepreneurship Journal* 2, no. 4 (December 2008): 317–38, https://doi.org/10.1002/sej.59.

15 **Steve Ells:** Guy Raz, "Chipotle: Steve Ells," *How I Built This with Guy Raz*, podcast, NPR, October 30, 2017, https://www.npr.org/2017/12/14/560458221/chipotle-steve-ells#:~:text=Live%20Sessions-,Chipotle%3A%20Steve%20Ells%20%3A%20How%20I%20Built%20This%20with%20Guy%20Raz,open%20his%20own%20gourmet%20restaurant.

15 **By finding the underlying business strategies:** Oliver Gassmann, *The Business Model Navigator: 55 Models That Will Revolutionize Your Business* (Edinburgh: Pearson Education Limited, 2014).

16 **Starbucks:** Guy Raz, "Live Episode! Starbucks: Howard Schultz," *How I Built This with Guy Raz*, podcast, September 28, 2017, https://www.npr.org/2017/09/28/551874532/live-episode-starbucks-howard-schultz.

17 **Josef Stalin:** Walter J. Boyne, "Carbon Copy Bomber," *Air Force Magazine*, June 2009, 52–56, https://www.airforcemag.com/article/0609bomber/; Tim Bradford, "Industrial Espionage Is More Effective than R&D," *Harvard Business Review*, November 1, 2016, https://hbr.org/2016/11/industrial-espionage-is-more-effective-than-rd.

18 **Iran's military:** "Iran 'Foiled Plot to Assassinate Army Chief Behind Out-of-Country Operations,'" bne IntelliNews, October 3, 2019, https://www.intellinews.com/iran-foiled-plot-to-assassinate-army-chief-behind-out-of-country-operations-169067/?source=egypt-and-mena; David Axe, "Iran Unveils Copycat Arsenal," *Wired*, January 4, 2013, https://www.wired.com/2013/01/irans-copycat-arsenal/.

18 **generics:** Katherine Eban, *Bottle of Lies: The Inside Story of the Generic Drug Boom* (New York: HarperCollins, 2019); Erik Mogalian and Paul Myrdal, "What's the Difference Between Brand-Name and Generic Prescription Drugs?," *Scientific American*, December 13, 2004, https://www.scientificamerican.com/article/whats-the-difference-betw-2004-12-13/.

18 **"deformulation":** Jan W. Gooch, *Analysis and Deformulation of Polymeric Materials: Paints, Plastics, Adhesives, and Inks* (New York: Plenum Press, 1997); J. M. Oliveira Junior et al., "Deformulation of a Solid Pharmaceutical Form Using Computed Tomography and X-ray Fluorescence," *Journal of Physics: Conference Series* 630, no. 1 (2015): 15–24, https://doi.org/10.1088/1742-6596/630/1/012002; "Product Deformulation Service,"

Scientific Applications, Avomeen Analytical Services, https://www.avomeen
.com/scientific-applications/product-deformulation-service/.

19 **Kiichiro Toyoda:** "Kiichiro Toyoda," Inductees & Honorees, Automotive
    Hall of Fame, 2018, https://www.automotivehalloffame.org/honoree/kiichiro
    -toyoda/; Jon Gertner, "From 0 to 60 to World Domination," *New York Times*,
    February 18, 2007, https://www.nytimes.com/2007/02/18/magazine/18Toyota
    .t.html; "Kiichiro Toyoda, Founder of the Toyota Motor Corporation, Dies,"
    History, March 24, 2020, https://www.history.com/this-day-in-history/toyota
    -founder-dies.

19 **"competitive benchmarking":** Michael J. Cole, "Benchmarking: A Process
    for Learning or Simply Raising the Bar?," *Evaluation Journal of Australasia*
    9, no. 2 (January 2009): 7–15, https://doi.org/10.1177/1035719X0900900203;
    Dean Elmuti and Yunus Kathawala, "An Overview of Benchmarking Process: A Tool for Continuous Improvement and Competitive Advantage,"
    Benchmarking for Quality Management and Technology 4, no. 2 (1997):
    229–43, https://doi.org/10.1108/14635779710195087.

19 **A2Mac1:** Alexander Stoklosa, "This Independent Firm Helps Automakers
    Reverse Engineer Competing Cars," *Car and Driver*, December 4, 2018,
    https://www.caranddriver.com/features/a25393820/a2mac1-reverse-engi
    neer-competing-cars/; Lawrence J. Speer, "French Farm Is a Global Benchmarking Hotspot," Automotive News Europe, August 18, 2008, https://
    europe.autonews.com/article/20080818/ANE03/993621490/french-farm-is
    -a-global-benchmarking-hotspot; David Tracy, "The Fascinating Company
    That Tears Cars Apart to Find Out Exactly How They're Built," Jalopnik,
    October 3, 2016, https://jalopnik.com/the-fascinating-company-that-tears
    -cars-apart-to-find-o-1787205420; Carl Hoffman, "The Teardown Artists,"
    Wired, February 1, 2006, https://www.wired.com/2006/02/teardown/.

20 **the average price:** Nick Carley, "Rising Old Used Car Prices Help Push
    Poor Americans over the Edge," Reuters, October 11, 2019, https://www
    .reuters.com/article/us-autos-usa-used-analysis/rising-old-used-car-prices
    -help-push-poor-americans-over-the-edge-idUSKBN1WQ1AP.

20 **the wrong way of thinking:** Adam Grant, *Originals: How Non-Conformists Move the World* (New York: Penguin Books, 2017); Jon Birger, "Second-Mover Advantage," *Fortune*, March 13, 2006, https://money.cnn.com
    /magazines/fortune/fortune_archive/2006/03/20/8371782/index.htm; Theo
    Anderson, "The Second-Mover Advantage," KelloggInsight, November 4,
    2013,   https://insight.kellogg.northwestern.edu/article/the_second_mover
    _advantage; Marvin B. Lieberman and David B. Montgomery, "First-Mover (Dis)Advantages: Retrospective and Link with the Resource-Based
    View," *Strategic Management Journal* 19, no. 12 (December 1998): 1111–25,
    https://doi.org/10.1002/(SICI)1097-0266(1998120)19:12<1111::AID-SM
    -J21>3.0.CO;2-W; Constantinos C. Markides and Paul A. Geroski, "Fast Second," *Harvard Business Review*, February 6, 2008, https://hbr.org/2008/02
    /fast-second.

22　**a fascinating 2017 paper:** Takeshi Okada and Kentaro Ishibashi, "Imitation, Inspiration, and Creation: Cognitive Process of Creative Drawing by Copying Others' Artworks," *Cognitive Science* 41, no. 7 (September 2017): 1804–37, https://doi.org/10.1111/cogs.12442.

23　**Psychologists have a raft of terms:** Jessica J. Ellis and Eyal M. Reingold, "The Einstellung Effect in Anagram Problem Solving: Evidence from Eye Movement," *Frontiers in Psychology* 5, article 679 (July 2014), https://doi.org/10.3389/fpsyg.2014.00679; Abraham S. Luchins and Edith H. Luchins, "Einstellung Effects," *Science* 238, no. 4827 (1987): 598, https://doi.org/10.1126/science.238.4827.598-b; Karl Duncker, "On Problem-Solving," *Psychological Monographs* 58, no. 5 (1945): i–113, https://doi.org/10.1037/h0093599 [originally published in German in 1935]. See also David Epstein, *Why Generalists Triumph in a Specialized World* (New York: Riverhead Books, 2019).

2: Algorithmic Thinking

25　**Alyssa Nathan:** Lane Moore, "I Met My Husband on Tinder," *Cosmopolitan*, February 16, 2016, https://www.cosmopolitan.com/sex-love/news/a53737/i-met-my-husband-on-tinder/; personal interview with Alyssa Nathan and Josh Yanover, November 13, 2019.

25　**Tinder:** Cédric Courtois and Elisabeth Timmermans, "Cracking the Tinder Code," *Journal of Computer-Mediated Communication* 23, no. 1 (January 2018): 1–16, https://doi.org/10.1093/jcmc/zmx001; Kaitlyn Tiffany, "The Tinder Algorithm, Explained," Vox, February 6, 2019, https://www.vox.com/2019/2/7/18210998/tinder-algorithm-swiping-tips-dating-app-science; Dale Markowitz, "The Future of Online Dating Is Unsexy and Brutally Effective," Gizmodo, October 25, 2017, https://gizmodo.com/the-future-of-online-dating-is-unsexy-and-brutally-effe-1819781116.

25　**Studies suggest that nearly 40 percent:** Michael J. Rosenfeld, Reuben J. Thomas, and Sonia Hausen, "Disintermediating Your Friends: How Online Dating in the United States Displaces Other Ways of Meeting," *Proceedings of the National Academy of Sciences of the United States of America* 116, no. 36 (August 2019): 17753–58, https://doi.org/10.1073/pnas.1908630116.

27　**a central facet of high intelligence:** Mark P. Mattson, "Superior Pattern Processing Is the Essence of the Evolved Human Brain," *Frontiers in Neuroscience* 8, no. 9 (August 2014): 265, https://doi.org/10.3389/fnins.2014.00265; David J. Lick., Adam L. Alter, and Jonathan B. Freeman, "Superior Pattern Detectors Efficiently Learn, Activate, Apply, and Update Social Stereotypes," *Journal of Experimental Psychology: General* 147, no. 2 (July 2017): 209–27, https://doi.org/10.1037/xge0000349.

27　**Pattern recognition engines:** B. D. Ripley, *Pattern Recognition and Neural Networks* (Cambridge, UK: Cambridge University Press, 2009); Robert P. W. Duin and Elżbieta Pękalska, "The Science of Pattern Recognition.

Achievements and Perspectives," *Studies in Computational Intelligence* 68 (May 2007): 221–59, https://doi.org/10.1007/978-3-540-71984-7_10; Ariel Rosenfeld and Harry Wechsler, "Pattern Recognition: Historical Perspective and Future Directions," *International Journal of Imaging Systems and Technology* 11, no. 2 (July 2000): 101–16, https://doi.org/10.1002/1098 -1098(2000)11:2%3C101::AID-IMA1%3E3.0.CO;2-J; Ally Marotti, "Algorithms Behind Tinder, Hinge, and Other Dating Apps Control Your Love Life. Here's How to Navigate Them," *Chicago Tribune*, December 6, 2018, https://www.chicagotribune.com/business/ct-biz-app-dating-algorithms -20181202-story.html; Andrew W. Trask, *Deep Learning* (Shelter Island, NY: Manning Publications, 2019).

28 **It's here that computer algorithms:** Kartik Hosanagar, *A Human's Guide to Machine Intelligence: How Algorithms Are Shaping Our Lives and How We Can Stay in Control* (New York: Viking, 2019); Cade Metz, "How A.I. is Creating Building Blocks to Reshape Music and Art," *New York Times*, August 14, 2017, https://www.nytimes.com/2017/08/14/arts/design/google-how-ai-creates -new-music-and-new-artists-project-magenta.html; Laura Pappano, "Learning to Think like a Computer," *New York Times*, April 4, 2017, https://www.nytimes .com/2017/04/04/education/edlife/teaching-students-computer-code.html.

28 **"Chef Watson":** IBM and Institute of Culinary Education, *Cognitive Cooking with Chef Watson: Recipes for Innovation from IBM & the Institute of Culinary Education* (Naperville, IL: Sourcebooks, 2015); Laura Sydell, "I've Got the Ingredients. What Should I Cook? Ask IBM's Watson," NPR, October 27, 2014, https://www.npr.org/sections/alltechconsidered/2014/10/27/35 9302540/ive-got-the-ingredients-what-should-i-cook-ask-ibms-watson; Alexandra Kleeman, "Cooking with Chef Watson, I.B.M.'s Artificial Intelligence App," *New Yorker*, November 21, 2016, https://www.newyorker.com/maga zine/2016/11/28/cooking-with-chef-watson-ibms-artificial-intelligence-app; Sophie Curtis, "Cognitive Cooking: How Is A.I. Changing Foodtech?," Re-Work, April 19, 2016, https://blog.re-work.co/foodtech-ibm-chef-watson -florian-pinel-food-artificial-intelligence/.

30 **Andy Warhol collected artwork:** Brian Dillon, "Curios and Curiouser: The Weird and Wonderful Stuff That Artists Collect," *The Guardian*, February 6, 2015, https://www.theguardian.com/artanddesign/2015/feb/06/curios -and-curiouser-weird-wonderful-stuff-artists-collect.

30 **David Bowie collected records:** Marc Spitz, *Bowie: A Biography* (New York: Crown Publishing, 2009).

30 **Julia Child collected cookbooks:** Caroline Barta, "Why on Earth Did Julia Child Collect 5,000 Cookbooks?," Thinking in Public, June 13, 2018, https:// thinkinginpublic.org/story/why-on-earth-did-julia-child-collect-5000-cook books/.

30 **Quentin Tarantino spent so much time:** Lyn Hirschberg, "Quentin Tarantino, Pre-'Pulp Fiction,'" *Vanity Fair*, July 5, 1994, https://www.vanityfair .com/news/1994/07/tarantino199407.

30 **Ernest Hemingway possessed more than:** NPR Staff, "New Conservation Effort Aims to Protect Papa's Papers," *Weekend Edition Sunday*, NPR, December 27, 2015, https://www.npr.org/2015/12/27/460822063/new-conservation -effort-aims-to-protect-papas-papers.

30 **"A writer is a reader":** John Seabrook, "William Maxwell, The Art of Fiction no. 71," *Paris Review*, Fall 1982, https://www.theparisreview.org/interviews /3138/the-art-of-fiction-no-71-william-maxwell.

30 **"If you don't read":** Sara Plourde, "Workshop 8: Tom Perrotta," January 29, 2016, *10-Minute Writer's Workshop*, podcast, https://www.nhpr.org/post /10-minute-writers-workshop-tom-perrotta#stream/0.

30 *implicit learning:* Peter A. Frensch and Dennis Rünger, "Implicit Learning," *Current Directions in Psychological Science* 12, no. 1 (February 2003): 13–18, https://doi.org/10.1111/1467-8721.01213.

31 **The best ideas don't emerge:** For more on practice as necessary but insufficient for achieving greatness, particularly in fields involving creativity, see Scott Barry Kaufman, "Creativity Is Much More than 10,000 Hours of Deliberate Practice," *Scientific American*, April 17, 2016, https://blogs .scientificamerican.com/beautiful-minds/creativity-is-much-more-than-10 -000-hours-of-deliberate-practice/.

32 **Clayton Christensen:** Clayton M. Christensen, *The Innovator's Dilemma: When New Technologies Cause Great Firms to Fail* (Boston: Harvard Business Review Press, 2016); Jeff Dyer, Hal Gregersen, and Clayton M. Christensen, *The Innovator's DNA: Mastering the Five Skills of Disruptive Innovators* (Boston: Harvard Business Review Press, 2019).

34 **Wellington Mara:** Carlo DeVito, *Wellington: The Maras, the Giants, and the City of New York* (Chicago: Triumph Books, 2006); Kristopher Knox, "6 Ways Teams Have Hacked the NFL over the Years," Bleacher Report, November 2, 2016, https://bleacherreport.com/articles/2673516-6-ways-teams -have-hacked-the-nfl-over-the-years.

35 *reverse outlining:* David Starkey, *Academic Writing Now: A Brief Guide for Busy Students* (Calgary, AB: Broadview Press, 2017). See also Aaron Hamburger, "Outlining in Reverse," *New York Times*, January 21, 2013, https:// opinionator.blogs.nytimes.com/2013/01/21/outlining-in-reverse/; Curtis Sittenfeld, "Finally Write That Story," *New York Times*, July 18, 2020, https:// www.nytimes.com/2020/07/18/at-home/coronavirus-fiction-writing.html.

36 **Dorie Clark:** Dorie Clark, "Why I Created This Course," Rapid Content Creation MasterClass, https://learn.dorieclark.com/courses/content.

37 **the patterns that emerge:** For related research, see V. F. Reyna and C. J. Brainerd, "Fuzzy-Trace Theory: An Interim Synthesis," *Learning and Individual Differences* 7, no. 1 (1995): 1–75, https://doi.org/10.1016/1041-6080 (95)90031-4.

38 **what do the data tell us:** Rosebud Anwuri, "Billboard Hot 100 Analytics," Towards Data Science, June 15, 2018, https://towardsdatascience.com /billboard-hot-100-analytics-using-data-to-understand-the-shift-in-popular

-music-in-the-last-60-ac3919d39b49; Sarah McBride, "Applying Academic Formulae to Scripts Could Weed Out Hollywood Duds," NPR, August 17, 2010, https://www.npr.org/sections/money/2010/08/17/129261284/applying -academic-formulae-to-scripts-could-weed-out-hollywood-duds; Jodie Archer and Matthew L. Jockers, *The Bestseller Code: Anatomy of the Blockbuster Novel* (New York: St. Martin's Griffin, 2017); Michael Tauberg, "Anatomy of a Hit Song (2000–2018)," Medium, May 18, 2018, https://medium.com/@michaeltauberg/women-are-dominating-popular-music -43c5ed83534b; Dorien Herremans, David Martens, and Kenneth Sörensen, "Dance Hit Song Prediction," *Journal of New Music Research* 43, no. 3 (January 2014): 291–302, https://doi.org/10.1080/09298215.2014.881888; John Seabrook, *The Song Machine: Inside the Hit Factory* (New York: W. W. Norton, 2015).

41   **Ken Robinson:** Sir Ken Robinson, "Do Schools Kill Creativity?," February 2006, TED, https://www.ted.com/talks/sir_ken_robinson_do_schools_kill _creativity?language=en.

47   **What do the world's best websites:** Apple, home page, https://www.apple .com/; Samsung, home page, https://www.samsung.com/.

3: The Curse of Creativity

51   **Malcolm Gladwell:** For more on the elements that make Gladwell unique, see Adam Grant, "What Makes Malcolm Gladwell Fascinating," *Psychology Today*, October 8, 2013, https://www.psychologytoday.com/us/blog/give -and-take/201310/what-makes-malcolm-gladwell-fascinating.

52   **"I began as a writer":** "Being Malcolm Gladwell," Freakonomics Radio, May 1, 2016, https://freakonomics.com/podcast/malcolm-gladwell.

53   *Twilight:* Karen Valby, "The 'Twilight' Effect," *Entertainment Weekly*, November 16, 2012, https://ew.com/article/2012/11/16/twilight-effect/; "'Twilight' Author: It Started with a Dream," *The Oprah Winfrey Show*, CNN, November 18, 2009, https://edition.cnn.com/2009/LIVING/worklife/11/18/o.twilight .newmoon.meyer/.

53   **David Bowie was among the first:** Dylan Jones, *David Bowie: The Oral History* (New York: Three Rivers Press, 2018); Chris Welch, *David Bowie: Changes: A Life in Pictures 1947–2016* (London: Carlton Books, 2016).

54   **"Every moment in business":** Peter Thiel, *Zero to One: Notes on Startups, or How to Build the Future* (New York: Crown Business, 2014), 1.

54   **Jennifer Mueller:** Jennifer Mueller, *Creative Change: Why We Resist It . . . How We Can Embrace It* (New York: Mariner Books, 2018).

55   **Thom Yorke:** Steven Hyden, *This Isn't Happening: Radiohead's "Kid A" and the Beginning of the 21st Century* (New York: Hachette Books, 2020); Simon Reynolds, "Classic Reviews: Radiohead, 'Kid A,'" *Spin*, October 2, 2015, https://www.spin.com/2015/10/radiohead-kid-a-review-spin-magazine -simon-reynolds-2000/; "The Friday Interview: Thom Yorke," *The Guardian*,

September 22, 2000, https://www.theguardian.com/friday_review/story/0
„371289,00.html; "'I Don't Want to Be in a Rock Band Anymore,'" Citizen
Insane, December 2000, http://citizeninsane.eu/media/uk/select/04/pt_2000
-12_select.htm; Radiohead, "Kid A," released October 3, 2000, https://www
.metacritic.com/music/kid-a/radiohead; Rob Sheffield, "How Radiohead
Shocked the World: A 15th-Anniversary Salute to 'Kid A,'" *Rolling Stone*,
October 2, 2015, https://www.rollingstone.com/music/music-news/how-radio
head-shocked-the-world-a-15th-anniversary-salute-to-kid-a-49200/; Scott
Plagenhoef, "Thom Yorke," Pitchfork, August 16, 2006, https://pitchfork
.com/features/interview/6402-thom-yorke/; David Cavanaugh, "I Can See
the Monsters," Citizen Insane, October 2000, https://citizeninsane.eu/media
/uk/q/04/pt_2000-10_q.htm.

55   *"Kid A":* David Fricke, "People of the Year: Thom Yorke of Radiohead,"
Rolling Stone, December 14, 2000, https://www.rollingstone.com/music/music
-news/people-of-the-year-thom-yorke-of-radiohead-194004/.

56   **Kozmo.com:** Matthew Schwartz, "Kozmo Delivers No More," *Computer
World*, April 12, 2001, https://www.computerworld.com/article/2592097/kozmo
-delivers-no-more.html; Jayson Blair, "Behind Kozmo's Demise: Thin
Profit Margins," *New York Times*, April 13, 2001, https://www.nytimes.com
/2001/04/13/nyregion/behind-kozmo-s-demise-thin-profit-margins.html.

56   **Takeout Taxi:** Kristin Downey Grimsley, "The Takeoff of Takeout Taxi,"
Washington Post, November 21, 1994, https://www.washingtonpost.com
/archive/business/1994/11/21/the-takeoff-of-takeout-taxi/879b8c2a-3b90
-4d3b-8807-d263b72035c6/.

56   **Microsoft's SPOT watch:** Peter Bright, "Lessons Learned from Microsoft's
Pioneering—and Standalone—Smartwatches," Ars Technica, September 11,
2014, https://arstechnica.com/gadgets/2014/09/lessons-learned-from-micro
softs-pioneering-and-standalone-smartwatches/.

57   **In 2014, a group:** Kevin J. Boudreau et al., "The Novelty Paradox & Bias
for Normal Science: Evidence from Randomized Medical Grant Proposal
Evaluations," Harvard Business School, January 10, 2013, https://hbswk.hbs
.edu/item/the-novelty-paradox-bias-for-normal-science-evidence-from
-randomized-medical-grant-proposal-evaluations.

57   **Don Draper:** *Mad Men*, season 2, episode 4, "Three Sundays," directed by
Tim Hunter, written by Matthew Weiner et al., AMC, August 17, 2008.

58   **Karim Lakhani:** Derek Thompson, "The Four-Letter Code to Selling Just
About Anything," *The Atlantic*, January/February 2019, https://www.the
atlantic.com/magazine/archive/2017/01/what-makes-things-cool/508772/;
Kevin J. Boudreau et al., "The Novelty Paradox & Bias for Normal Science:
Evidence from Randomized Medical Grant Proposal Evaluations." For
more on Lakhani's work, see Derek Thompson, *Hit Makers: The Science of
Popularity in an Age of Distraction* (New York: Penguin Press, 2017).

58   **Tarantino's contributions were distinctive:** Ian Nathan, *Quentin Tarantino:
The Iconic Filmmaker and His Work* (London: White Lion Publishing,

2019); Alex Papaioannou, "Deconstructing Directors: Quentin Tarantino and Remaining Idiosyncratic," Popaxiom, February 21, 2019, https://pop axiom.com/deconstructing-directors-quentin-tarantino-and-remaining-idio syncratic/.

58 **When Doors guitarist Robby Krieger:** David Bianculli, "An Archival Interview with Ray Manzarek, Keyboardist for the Doors," *Fresh Air*, NPR, July 28, 2017, https://www.npr.org/2017/07/28/539989187/an-archival-interview -with-ray-manzarek-keyboardist-for-the-doors.

59 **Steve Jobs:** George Beahm, *I, Steve: Steve Jobs in His Own Words* (Evanston, IL: Agate Publishing, 2011).

59 **two Stanford University students:** John Battelle, "The Birth of Google," *Wired*, August 1, 2005, https://www.wired.com/2005/08/battelle/.

59 **the world's first printer:** John Man, *The Gutenberg Revolution: How Printing Changed the Course of History* (London: Transworld Publishers, 2010); Tom Wheeler, *From Gutenberg to Google: The History of Our Future* (Washington, DC: Brookings Institution, 2019).

59 **"Creativity is what happens":** Matt Ridley, "When Ideas Have Sex," TEDGlobal 2010, July 18, 2010, https://www.youtube.com/watch?v=OLH h9E5ilZ4.

59 **Barack Obama was immersed:** Edward McClelland, *Young Mr. Obama: Chicago and the Making of a Black President* (New York: Bloomsbury Press, 2010); Roy Peter Clark, "Why It Worked: A Rhetorical Analysis of Obama's Speech on Race," Poynter, October 20, 2017, https://www.poynter .org/reporting-editing/2017/why-it-worked-a-rhetorical-analysis-of-obamas -speech-on-race-2/; Linton Weeks, "The Art of Language, Obama Style," NPR, February 11, 2009, https://www.npr.org/templates/story/story.php ?storyId=100525275; Juraj Horváth, "Critical Discourse Analysis of Obama's Political Discourse," http://www1.cs.columbia.edu/~sbenus/Teaching/APTD /Horvath_CDO_Obama.pdf; "How Obama Learned His Pulpit Style," NBC Chicago, October 3, 2012, https://www.nbcchicago.com/news/local/how -obama-learned-his-pulpit-style/1940950/.

60 **"Motherfucker, you ain't goin'":** McClelland, *Young Mr. Obama*, 155.

60 **the Apple II:** Walter Isaacson, *Steve Jobs* (New York: Simon & Schuster Paperbacks, 2015).

61 **Steve Case:** Erik Blakemore, "Remember These Free AOL CDs? They're Collectibles Now," *Smithsonian Magazine*, October 13, 2015, https://www .smithsonianmag.com/smart-news/aol-cd-rom-collecting-thing-180956902/.

61 **Stan Lee:** Stan Lee, "Stan Lee Talks About How He Almost Quit on His Dream," Film Courage, April 5, 2012, https://www.youtube.com/watch?v=w swJDyxOnyk; Reed Tucker, *Slugfest: Inside the Epic, 50-Year Battle Between Marvel and DC* (New York: Da Capo Press, 2017).

61 **"My wife said if you're going to quit":** Ibid.

63 **In 2019, creativity researchers:** Spencer Harrison, Arne Carlsen, and Miha Škerlavaj, "Marvel's Blockbuster Machine: How the Studio Balances

Continuity and Renewal," *Harvard Business Review*, July–August 2019, https://hbr.org/2019/07/marvels-blockbuster-machine.

64 **Clayton Christensen:** Clayton M. Christensen, *The Innovator's Dilemma: When New Technologies Cause Great Firms to Fail* (Boston: Harvard Business Review Press, 2016); Jeff Dyer, Hal Gregersen, and Clayton M. Christensen, *The Innovator's DNA: Mastering the Five Skills of Disruptive Innovators* (Boston: Harvard Business Review Press, 2019); Jeffrey H. Dyer, Hal B. Gregersen, and Clayton Christensen, "Entrepreneur Behaviors, Opportunity Recognition, and the Origins of Innovative Ventures," *Strategic Entrepreneurship Journal* 2, no. 4 (December 2008): 317–38, https://doi.org/10.1002/sej.59.

65 **seeing a Disney logo:** Gráinne M. Fitzgerald, Tanya L. Chartrand, and Cavan J. Fitzsimons, "Automatic Effects of Brand Exposures on Motivated Behavior: How Apple Makes You 'Think Different,'" *Journal of Consumer Research* 35, no. 1 (June 2008): 21–35, https://doi.org/10.1086/527269.

65 **exposure to a Gatorade bottle:** Ron Friedman and Andrew J. Elliot, "Exploring the Influence of Sports Drink Exposure on Physical Endurance," *Psychology of Sport and Exercise* 9, no. 6 (November 2008): 749–59, https://doi.org/10.1016/j.psychsport.2007.12.001.

65 **images of Red Bull propel:** S. Adam Brasel and James Gips, "Red Bull 'Gives You Wings' for Better or Worse: A Double-Edged Impact of Brand Exposure on Consumer Performance," *Journal of Consumer Psychology* 21, no. 1 (January 2011): 57–64, https://doi.org/10.1016/j.jcps.2010.09.008.

67 **Tom Petty:** Paul Zollo, *More Songwriters on Songwriting* (Philadelphia: Da Capo Press, 2016).

67 **"I couldn't make a contemporary":** Chris Payne, "Billboard Cover Sneak Peek: 5 Ways Eddie Van Halen Breaks the Rock-Star Rules," *Billboard*, June 18, 2015, https://www.billboard.com/articles/columns/rock/6605222 /eddie-van-halen-billboard-cover-sneak-peek.

67 **Bill Maher:** Joel Keller, "Bill Maher: I Won't Watch John Oliver," Salon, September 12, 2014, https://www.salon.com/2014/09/12/bill_maher_i_refuse _to_watch_john_oliver/.

67 **Jimmy Fallon:** Judd Apatow, *Sick in the Head: Conversations About Life and Comedy* (New York: Random House, 2015).

67 **Judd Apatow:** Ibid.

68 **"The more often we read":** Chris Fenn, "Rereading: Authors Reveal Their Literary Addictions," *The Guardian*, April 7, 2012, https://www.theguardian .com/books/2012/apr/08/authors-reread-other-authors-novels.

69 **Take direct mail:** Kiri Masters, "Amazon's Toy Catalog Just Dropped— and It Shows Just How Much the Company Knows About Us," *Forbes*, November 5, 2019, https://www.forbes.com/sites/kirimasters/2019/11/05 /amazons-toy-catalog-just-dropped-and-shows-just-how-much-they-know -about-us/#2b30f6e9628f; Neil Patel, "4 Old-School Marketing Tactics Making a Comeback in 2018," Neilpatel, March 16, 2018, https://neilpatel.com /blog/old-school-marketing-tactics/.

69 **Roy Orbison:** Alan Clayson, *Only the Lonely: Roy Orbison's Life and Legacy* (New York: St. Martin's Press, 1989); Ellis Amburn, *Dark Star: The Roy Orbison Story* (City: Carol Publishing Group, 1990); Alex Orbison et al., *The Authorized Roy Orbison* (New York: Hachette Books, 2017); John Covach, *Sounding Out Pop: Analytical Essays in Popular Music* (Ann Arbor: University of Michigan Press, 2010); "About Joe Melson," Joe Melson, http://joemelson.com/bio/; Michael Fremer, "Recording Elvis and Roy with Legendary Studio Wiz Bill Porter—Part 2," Analog Planet, December 31, 2005, https://www.analogplanet.com/content/recording-elvis-and-roy-legendary-studio-wiz-bill-porter-part-ii-0.

72 **Absolut:** Richard W. Lewis, *Absolut Book: The Absolut Vodka Advertising Story* (Boston: Journey Editions, 1996); Natasha Frost, "How America Fell in Love with Vodka," Atlas Obscura, January 25, 2018, https://www.atlasobscura.com/articles/how-america-fell-in-love-with-vodka-smirnoff; David Giantasio, "How Bending Art and Commerce Drive Absolut Vodka's Legendary Campaigns," *AdWeek*, September 28, 2015, https://www.adweek.com/brand-marketing/how-blending-art-and-commerce-drove-absolut-vodka-s-legendary-campaigns-167143/; "Secrets of Successful Ad Campaigns: Lessons from Absolut, Nike and NASCAR," Knowledge@Wharton, September 25, 2002, https://knowledge.wharton.upenn.edu/article/secrets-of-successful-ad-campaigns-lessons-from-absolut-nike-and-nascar/; Expert commentator, "Absolut Vodka and Their Marketing Campaign Have Stood the Test of Time," Smart Insights, August 17, 2018, https://www.smartinsights.com/online-brand-strategy/international-marketing/campaign-of-the-week-the-longest-running-print-ad-marketing-campaign-in-history/.

73 **Michael Roux:** Richard Sandomir, "Michel Roux, Whose Vodka Success Was Absolut, Is Dead at 78," *New York Times*, May 10, 2019, https://www.nytimes.com/2019/05/10/obituaries/michel-roux-dead.html; George Lazarus, "Absolut Jumping Ship to Seagram," *Chicago Tribune*, October 13, 1993, https://www.chicagotribune.com/news/ct-xpm-1993-10-13-9310130040-story.html.

73 **"I grew this baby":** Lazarus, "Absolut Jumping Ship to Seagram."

73 **Amy Winehouse:** "Why Would More than 500 Artists Sample the Same Song?," *TED Radio Hour*, NPR, June 27, 2014, https://www.npr.org/2014/06/27/322721353/why-would-more-than-500-artists-sample-the-same-song.

74 **"I had no idea":** Ibid.

74 **Jacques Pépin:** Karen Page, *Kitchen Creativity: Unlocking Culinary Genius—with Wisdom, Inspiration, and Ideas from the World's Most Creative Chefs* (New York: Little, Brown and Company, 2017).

74 **"I would ask fifteen students":** Page, *Kitchen Creativity*, 413.

75 **Malcolm Gladwell:** Stephen J. Dubner, "Being Malcolm Gladwell," Freakonomics Radio, May 1, 2016, https://freakonomics.com/podcast/malcolm-gladwell/; "Episode 204: Malcolm Gladwell," *Longform*, podcast, August 3, 2016, https://longform.libsyn.com/episode-204-malcolm-gladwell.

75 **"All of a sudden":** "Episode 204: Malcolm Gladwell."

76 *David and Goliath:* Malcolm Gladwell, *David and Goliath: Underdogs, Misfits, and the Art of Battling Giants* (New York: Little, Brown and Company, 2013).

Part II: The Vision-Ability Gap

79 **"As a rule":** George Washington Walling, *Recollections of a New York Chief of Police* (New York: Claxon Books, 2017), 236.

80 **George Leonidas Leslie:** Walling, *Recollections of a New York Chief of Police*; J. North Conway, *King of Heists: The Sensational Bank Robbery of 1878 That Shocked America* (Guilford, CT: Lyons Press, 2009); Geoff Manaugh, *A Burglar's Guide to the City* (New York: Farrar, Straus and Giroux, 2016); Herbert Asbury, *The Gangs of New York: an Informal History of the Underworld* (New York, NY: Vintage Books, 2008); Allan Pinkerton, *Professional Thieves and the Detective: Containing Numerous Detective Sketches Collected From Private Records* (New York: G. W. Dillingham Co., Publishers, 1880); Carl Sifakis, *The Encyclopedia of American Crime* (New York: Smithmark, 1992).

83 **"What nobody tells people":** Glass's 2009 interview can be found at vimeo .com/85040589. See also "Episode 159: Ira Glass," *Longform*, podcast, September 23, 2015, https://longform.libsyn.com/episode-159-ira-glass; David Gianatasio, "How a 2009 Interview with Ira Glass Still Inspires Young Creatives Today," *AdWeek*, January 6, 2015, https://www.adweek.com/creativity /how-2009-interview-ira-glass-still-inspires-struggling-young-creatives-to day-162177/.

84 **"The book is my invisible friend":** Ann Patchett, *This Is the Story of a Happy Marriage* (New York: HarperCollins, 2013), 24-25.

84 **"When I can't think of another":** Ibid., 25.

85 **"The journey from the head":** Ibid., 25.

85 **human beings are born:** Judit Diószegi, Erand Llanaj, and Róza Ádány, "Genetic Background of Taste Preferences, and Its Nutritional Implications: A Systematic Review," *Frontiers in Genetics* 10, article 1272 (December 19, 2019), https://doi.org/10.3389/fgene.2019.01272; Nadia K. Byrnes and John E. Hayes, "Personality Factors Predict Spicy Food Liking and Intake," *Food Quality and Preference* 28, no. 1 (April 2013): 213–21, https://doi.org/10.1016/j.foodqual.2012.09.008; Marvin Zuckerman and D. Michael Kuhlman, "Personality and Risk-Taking: Common Biosocial Factors," *Journal of Personality* 68, no. 6 (December 2000): 999–1029, https:// doi.org/10.1111/1467-6494.00124; Kevin B. Smith et al., "Linking Genetics and Political Attitudes: Reconceptualizing Political Ideology," *Political Psychology* 32, no. 3 (June 2011): 369–97, https://doi.org/10.1111/j.1467 -9221.2010.00821.x; A.A.E. Vinkhuyzen et al., "Common SNPs Explain Some of the Variation in the Personality Dimensions of Neuroticism and

Extraversion," *Translational Psychiatry* 2, no. 4 (April 2012): e102, https://doi.org/10.1038/tp.2012.27; L. Bevilacqua and D. Goldman, "Genes and Addictions," *Clinical Pharmacological Therapy* 85, no. 4 (April 2009): 359–61, https://doi.org/10.1038/clpt.2009.6.

86 **Pierre Bourdieu:** Pierre Bourdieu, *Distinction: A Special Critique on the Judgment of Taste* (London: Routledge, 1984). See also Don Slater, *Consumer Culture and Modernity* (Cambridge, UK: Polity Press, 1997); Robert B. Ekelund, Jr., and Robert F. Hébert, *A History of Economic Theory and Method*, x ed. (New York: McGraw-Hill, 1990).

86 **Alain de Botton:** "Why Do Scandinavians Have Such Impeccable Taste in Interior Design?," The School of Life, May 11, 2017, https://www.theschooloflife.com/thebookoflife/why-do-scandinavians-have-such-impeccable-taste-in-interior-design/; Nancy Mitchell, "What Does It Mean to Have 'Bad Taste'? Here's One Fascinating Theory," Apartment Therapy, August 4, 2015, https://www.apartmenttherapy.com/good-taste-and-bad-taste-and-why-it-matters-221839; Melissa Block, "The Psychology of Taste, and Choice," *All Things Considered*, NPR, November 9, 2006, https://www.npr.org/templates/story/story.php?storyId=6463387; "On Good and Bad Taste," The School of Life, February 24, 2015, https://www.theschooloflife.com/thebookoflife/good-and-bad-taste/; Jacoba Urist, "Is Good Taste Teachable?," *New York Times*, October 4, 2017, https://www.nytimes.com/2017/10/04/style/design-good-taste.html. See also Alain de Botton, *Status Anxiety* (New York: Vintage Books, 2005).

86 **"What distinguishes, I think":** Sara Plourde, "Workshop 47: Jonathan Safran Foer," *10-Minute Writer's Workshop*, podcast, NHPR, June 28, 2017, https://www.nhpr.org/post/10-minute-writers-workshop-jonathan-safran-foer#stream/0.

87 **Theodore Sturgeon:** Theodore Sturgeon, "ON HAND. A Book," *Venture Science Fiction*, March 1958, 66.

4: The Scoreboard Principle

90 **the Ritz-Carlton:** Horst Schulze, *Excellence Wins: A No-Nonsense Guide to Becoming the Best in a World of Compromise* (Grand Rapids, MI: Zondervan, 2019); "Gold Standards," The Ritz-Carlton, https://www.ritzcarlton.com/en/about/gold-standards; Carmine Gallo, "Stop 'Listening' and Start Anticipating Your Customers' Needs," *Forbes*, May 28, 2014, https://www.forbes.com/sites/carminegallo/2014/05/28/stop-listening-and-start-anticipating-your-customers-needs/#7c9a70886b4f; Graham Robertson, "Ritz Carlton: Meeting the 'Unexpressed' Needs of Guests," LinkedIn, July 26, 2014, https://www.linkedin.com/pulse/20140726164857-13996180-ritz-carlton-meeting-the-unexpressed-needs-of-guests/; Jennifer Robinson, "How The Ritz-Carlton Manages the Mystique," Gallup, December 11, 2008, https://news.gallup.com/businessjournal/112906/how-ritzcarlton

-manages-mystique.aspx; Micah Solomon, "5 Wow Customer Service Stories from 5-Star Hotels: Examples Any Business Can Learn From," *Forbes*, July 29, 2017, https://www.forbes.com/sites/micahsolomon/2017/07/29/5-wow -customer-service-stories-from-5-star-hotels-examples-any-business-can -learn-from/#2337ab2033e6.

92   **Jobs instructed his team:** Walter Isaacson, *Steve Jobs* (New York: Simon & Schuster Paperbacks, 2015).

93   **In a 1,700-person clinical trial:** Kaiser Permanente, "Keeping a Food Diary Doubles Diet Weight Loss, Study Suggests," Science Daily, July 8, 2008, https://www.sciencedaily.com/releases/2008/07/080708080738.htm. For more on the efficacy of food diaries, see Raymond C. Baker and Daniel S. Kirschenbaum, "Self-Monitoring May Be Necessary for Successful Weight Control," *Behavior Therapy* 24, no. 3 (Summer 1993): 377–94, https://doi.org/10.1016 /S0005-7894(05)80212-6; Raymond C. Baker and Daniel S. Kirschenbaum, "Weight Control During the Holidays: Highly Consistent Self-Monitoring as a Potentially Useful Coping Mechanism," *Health Psychology* 17, no. 4 (July 1998): 367–70, https://doi.org/10.1037/0278-6133.17.4.367; K. N. Boutelle and D. S. Kirschenbaum, "Further Support for Consistent Self-Monitoring as a Vital Component of Successful Weight Control," *Obesity Research* 6, no. 3 (May 1998): 219–24, https://doi.org/10.1002/j.1550-8528.1998.tb00 340.x; Meghan L. Butryn et al., "Consistent Self-Monitoring of Weight: A Key Component of Successful Weight Loss Maintenance," *Obesity* 15, no. 12 (December 2007): 3091–96, https://doi.org/10.1038/oby.2007.368; Michele L. Patel et al., "Comparing Self-Monitoring Strategies for Weight Loss in a Smartphone App: Randomized Controlled Trial," *JMIR mHealth and uHealth*, 7, no. 2 (February 28, 2019): e12209, https://doi.org/10.2196/12209; Michele L. Patel, Taylor L. Brooks, and Gary G. Bennett, "Consistent Self-Monitoring in a Commercial App-Based Intervention for Weight Loss: Results from a Randomized Trial," *Journal of Behavioral Medicine* 43, no. 3 (June 2020): 391–401; Barbara Stiglbauer, Silvana Weber, and Bernad Batinic, "Does Your Health Really Benefit from Using a Self-Tracking Device? Evidence from a Longitudinal Randomized Control Trial," *Computers in Human Behavior* 94 (May 2019): 131–39, https://doi.org/10.1016/j .chb.2019.01.018.

95   **"metrics are incentives":** Ben Horowitz, *The Hard Thing About Hard Things: Building a Business When There Are No Easy Answers* (New York: HarperCollins, 2014), 132.

95   **Greg Erway:** Personal interview with Greg Erway, September 9, 2020. Greg's record of sixteen-plus hours was attained in a "marathon game" setting. The current world record exceeds twenty-four hours.

96   *numerical nudging:* Luxi Shen and Christopher K. Hsee, "Numerical Nudging: Using an Accelerating Score to Enhance Performance," *Psychological Science* 28, no. 8 (August 2017): 1077–86, https://doi.org/10.1177/09/56/79/76 /177/00497.

96 **three basic psychological needs:** Richard M. Ryan and Edward L. Deci, *Self-Determination Theory: Basic Psychological Needs in Motivation, Development, and Wellness* (New York: Guilford Press, 2017).

97 **Andreas Nieder:** Andreas Nieder, *A Brain for Numbers: The Biology of the Number Instinct* (Cambridge, MA: MIT Press, 2019).

98 **Eric Ries:** Eric Ries, *The Lean Startup: How Today's Entrepreneurs Use Continuous Innovation to Create Radically Successful Businesses* (New York: Currency, 2014).

99 **Roger Federer's tennis career:** Peter de Jonge, "How Roger Federer Upgraded His Game," *New York Times*, August 24, 2017, https://www.nytimes.com/interactive/2017/08/24/magazine/usopen-federer-nadal-backhand-wonder-year.html; ATP Staff, "Five Keys to Roger Federer's Wimbledon Domination, Eight Titles," ATP Tour, July 3, 2019, https://www.atptour.com/en/news/federer-wimbledon-infosys-insights-july-2019; "In Federer-Nadal Rivalry, Has the Federer Backhand Become a Weapon?," On the T, March 17, 2017, https://on-the-t.com/2017/03/17/federer-backhand-trends; Associated Press, "Roger Federer Blames Bath Mishap for Injury That Led to Surgery," ESPN, May 24, 2016, https://www.espn.com/tennis/story/_/id/15059810/roger-federer-blames-bath-mishap-injury-led-surgery; Jack de Menezes, "Roger Federer Reveals His Knee Injury Was Caused by Running a Bath for His Twin Daughters," *The Independent*, March 25, 2016, https://www.independent.co.uk/sport/tennis/roger-federer-reveals-his-knee-injury-was-caused-running-bath-his-twin-daughters-a6951971.html; Jeff Sackmann, "Will a Back-to-Normal Federer Backhand Be Good Enough?," Tennis Abstract, July 14, 2019, http://www.tennisabstract.com/blog/2019/07/14/will-a-back-to-normal-federer-backhand-be-good-enough/; "Roger Federer," ATP Stats Profile, Tennis Profiler, https://tennisprofiler.com/federer.

100 **"[I] was actually quite emotional":** ATP Staff, "When Federer Knew His Knee Might Not be the Same", *ATP Tour*, June 23, 2019, https://www.atptour.com/en/news/federer-reflects-on-2016-knee-injury-my-story-2019.

105 **Marshall Goldsmith:** Marshall Goldsmith, *Triggers: Creating Behavior That Lasts—Becoming the Person You Want to Be* (New York: Crown Publishing, 2015). Goldsmith's list of daily questions to ask oneself is available here: https://www.marshallgoldsmith.com/marshalls-daily-questions-spreadsheet/.

105 **Benjamin Franklin:** Edwin McDowell, "Darker Side to Franklin Is Reported," *New York Times*, August 18, 1987, https://www.nytimes.com/1987/08/18/arts/darker-side-to-franklin-is-reported.html; Amanda Cargill, "What Did the Founding Fathers Eat and Drink as They Started a Revolution?," *Smithsonian Magazine*, July 3, 2018, https://www.smithsonianmag.com/history/founding-fathers-july-4th-result-both-american-revolution-and-food-revolution-180969538/; Duckworth, *Grit*; Ericsson and Pool, *Peak*; Brett and Kate McKay, "Lessons in Manliness: Benjamin Franklin's Pursuit of the Virtuous Life," The Art of Manliness, February 24, 2008, https://www.artofmanliness.com/articles/lessons-in-manliness-benjamin-franklins

-pursuit-of-the-virtuous-life/; David G. Allan, "Ben Franklin's '13 Virtues' Path to Personal Perfection," CNN, March 1, 2018, https://www.cnn.com/2018/03/01/health/13-virtues-wisdom-project/index.html; James Wolcott, "Wired Up! Ready to Go!," *Vanity Fair*, January 8, 2013, https://www.vanityfair.com/culture/2013/02/quantified-self-hive-mind-weight-watchers.

107   **Daniel Humm:** *7 Days Out*, season 1, episode 2, "Eleven Madison Park," directed by Michael John Warren, Netflix, December 21, 2018.

108   **leading indicators:** For more on leading versus lagging indicators, see Philip A. Klein and Geoffrey H. Moore, "The Leading Indicator Approach to Economic Forecasting—Retrospect and Prospect," National Bureau of Economic Research, working paper no. 941, July 1982, https://doi.org/10.3386/w0941; Cal Newport, *Deep Work: Rules for Focused Success in a Distracted World* (New York: Grand Central Publishing, 2016).

109   **a mind-boggling 97 percent:** Amy Lundy, "When Federer Wins the First Point on Serve, It's Usually Game Over," FiveThirtyEight, July 10, 2018, https://fivethirtyeight.com/features/when-federer-wins-the-first-point-on-serve-its-usually-game-over/.

109   **"the embarrassment of a small tally":** Cal Newport, "From Deep Tallies to Deep Schedules: A Recent Change to My Deep Work Habits," Study Hacks Blog, December 7, 2016, https://www.calnewport.com/blog/2016/12/07/from-deep-tallies-to-deep-schedules-a-recent-change-to-my-deep-work-habits/.

110   **David Douglas:** Rebekah Kearn, "Man Complains of Forgery at Wells Fargo," Courthouse News Service, September 13, 2013, https://www.courthousenews.com/man-complains-of-forgery-at-wells-fargo/.

110   **Wells Fargo account fraud scandal:** Matt Egan, "Workers Tell Wells Fargo Horror Stories," CNN Money, September 9, 2016, https://money.cnn.com/2016/09/09/investing/wells-fargo-phony-accounts-culture/index.html; Michael Corkery, "Wells Fargo Killing Sham Account Suits by Using Arbitration," *New York Times*, December 6, 2016, https://www.nytimes.com/2016/12/06/business/dealbook/wells-fargo-killing-sham-account-suits-by-using-arbitration.html; E. Scott Reckard, "Wells Fargo's Pressure-Cooker Sales Culture Comes at a Cost," *Los Angeles Times*, December 21, 2013, https://www.latimes.com/business/la-fi-wells-fargo-sale-pressure-20131222-story.html; Randall Smith, "Copying Wells Fargo, Banks Try Hard Sell," *Wall Street Journal*, February 28, 2011, https://www.wsj.com/articles/SB10001424052748704430304576170702480420980; "Rules Amendments Effective in December: Wells Fargo Under Fire for Sales Practices," *American Bankruptcy Institute Journal* 35, no. 10 (October 2016): 8–9; Michael Harris and Bill Tayler, "Don't Let Metrics Undermine Your Business," *Harvard Business Review*, September–October 2019, https://hbr.org/2019/09/dont-let-metrics-undermine-your-business.

111   **"We were constantly told":** Reckard, "Wells Fargo's Pressure-Cooker Sales Culture Comes at a Cost."

112   **The remarkable thing:** Matt Levine, "Fake Accounts Still Haunt Wells Fargo,"

Bloomberg, October 23, 2018, https://www.bloomberg.com/opinion/articles
/2018-10-23/fake-accounts-still-haunt-wells-fargo.

112 **surrogation:** Jerry Z. Mueller, *The Tyranny of Metrics* (Princeton, NJ:
Princeton University Press, 2019); Willie Choi, Garu Hecht, and William B.
Tayler, "Strategy Selection, Surrogation, and Strategic Performance Mea-
surement Systems," *Journal of Accounting Research* 51, no. 1 (July 2012):
105–33, https://doi.org/10.1111/j.1475-679X.2012.00465.x; Yuji Ijiri, *The
Foundations of Accounting Measurement: A Mathematical, Economic,
and Behavioral Inquiry* (Englewood Cliffs, NJ: Prentice Hall, 1967); Will
Koehrsen, "Unintended Consequences and Goodhart's Law," Towards Data
Science, February 25, 2018, https://towardsdatascience.com/unintended
-consequences-and-goodharts-law-68d60a94705c.

113 **One example of balance:** For a fuller analysis of the motivational benefits of
short- and long-term goals, see Bettina Höchli, Adrian Brügger, and Claude
Messner, "How Focusing on Superordinate Goals Motivates Broad, Long-
Term Goal Pursuit: A Theoretical Perspective," *Frontiers in Psychology* 9
(October 2018), https://doi.org/10.3389/fpsyg.2018.01879; Edwin A. Locke
and Gary P. Latham, *New Developments in Goal Setting and Task Performance* (New York: Routledge, 2013).

114 **Andy Grove:** Andrew S. Grove, *High Output Management* (New York: Vintage Books, 2015). See also John Doerr, *Measure What Matters: OKRs—The
Simple Idea That Drives 10× Growth* (London: Portfolio Penguin, 2018).

114 **"For every metric":** "Building a Better Data-First Strategy: Lessons From
Top Companies," Knowledge @ Wharton, December 3, 2019, https://knowledge
.wharton.upenn.edu/article/building-better-data-first-strategy-lessons-top
-companies/. For more on paired metrics, see Grove, *High Output Management.*

5: How to Take the Risk Out of Risk Taking

116 **three deliciously esoteric facts:** Karen Page, *Kitchen Creativity: Unlocking
Culinary Genius—with Wisdom, Inspiration, and Ideas from the World's
Most Creative Chefs* (New York: Little, Brown and Company, 2017).

117 **Daniel Oppenheimer:** Pam A. Mueller and Daniel M. Oppenheimer, "The
Pen Is Mightier than the Keyboard: Advantages of Longhand over Laptop
Note Taking," *Psychological Science* 25, no. 6 (June 2014): 1159–68, https://
doi.org/10.1177/0956797614524581; Connor Diemand-Yauman, Daniel M.
Oppenheimer, and Erikka B. Vaughan, "Fortune Favors the Bold (and the
Italicized): Effects of Disfluency on Educational Outcomes," *Cognition* 118,
no. 1 (January 2011): 111–15, https://doi.org/0.1016/j.cognition.2010.09.012;
Anne Chemin, "Handwriting vs Typing: Is the Pen Still Mightier than the
Keyboard?," *The Guardian*, December 16, 2014, https://www.theguardian
.com/science/2014/dec/16/cognitive-benefits-handwriting-decline-typing;
Anne Quito, "Hard-to-Read Fonts Can Help Boost Your Memory," Quartz,

October 10, 2018, https://qz.com/1417818/hard-to-read-fonts-can-help-boost -your-memory/; NPR Staff and James Doubek, "Attention Students: Put Your Laptops Away," *Weekend Edition Sunday*, NPR, April 17, 2016, https:// www.npr.org/2016/04/17/474525392/attention-students-put-your-laptops-away.

118   **Robert A. Bjork:** Elizabeth Ligon Bjork and Robert A. Bjork, "Learning: Making Things Hard on Yourself, but in a Good Way: Creating Desirable Difficulties to Enhance Learning," in *Psychology and the Real World*, 2nd ed., edited by Morton Ann Gernsbacher and James R. Pomerantz (New York: Worth Publishers, 2014), 55–64; Nicholas C. Soderstrom and Robert A. Bjork, "Learning Versus Performance: An Integrative Review," *Perspectives on Psychological Science* 10, no. 2 (March 2015): 176–99, https://doi .org/10.1177/1745691615569000. See also Peter C. Brown, Henry L. Roediger III, and Mark A. McDaniel, *Make It Stick: The Science of Successful Learning* (Cambridge: Belknap Press of Harvard University Press, 2014); Barbara Oakley, *Mindshift: Break Through Obstacles to Learning and Discover Your Hidden Potential* (New York: TarcherPerigee, 2017); Ulrich Boser, *Learn Better: Mastering the Skills for Success in Life, Business, and School, or How to Become an Expert in Just About Anything* (New York: Rodale, 2017); Malcolm Gladwell, *David and Goliath: Underdogs, Misfits, and the Art of Battling Giants* (New York: Little, Brown and Company, 2013).

118   **Strain serves as an essential catalyst:** Brad Schoenfeld, *Science and Development of Muscle Hypertrophy* (Champaign, IL: Human Kinetics, 2016); Per Aagaard et al., "Increased Rate of Force Development and Neural Drive of Human Skeletal Muscle Following Resistance Training," *Journal of Applied Physiology* 93, no. 4 (October 2002): 1318–26, https://doi.org/10.1152 /japplphysiol.00283.2002; O. R. Seynnes, M. de Boer, and M. V. Narici, "Early Skeletal Muscle Hypertrophy and Architectural Changes in Response to High-Intensity Resistance Training," *Journal of Applied Physiology* 102, no. 1 (January 2007): 368–73, https://doi.org/10.1152/japplphysiol.00789.2006.

119   **Simone Biles:** Eren Orbey, "The International Federation of Gymnastics Needs to Keep Up with Simone Biles," *New Yorker*, October 11, 2019, https://www.newyorker.com/sports/sporting-scene/the-international-feder- ation-of-gymnastics-needs-to-keep-up-with-simone-biles; Nancy Armour, "Gymnastics Championships: Simone Biles Penalized for Having Skills Other Gymnasts Can't Pull Off," *USA Today*, October 4, 2019, https://www .usatoday.com/story/sports/columnist/nancy-armour/2019/10/04/gymnastics -simon-biles-penalized-championships-being-too-good/3866255002/; Dvora Meyers, "Why Simone Biles Is Even Better than Her Scores Tell," *The Guardian*, October 8, 2019, https://www.theguardian.com/sport/2019/oct/08 /simone-biles-skills-scoring-world-championships.

119   **the cost of workplace failure:** For more on the crippling cost of mistakes in the workplace and a variety of solutions, see Ron Friedman, *The Best Place to Work: The Art and Science of Creating an Extraordinary Workplace* (New York: Perigee, 2014).

121 **General Electric:** Vijay Govindarajan and Chris Trimble, *Reverse Innovation: Create Far from Home, Win Everywhere* (Boston: Harvard Business Review Press, 2012); Sarah Triantafillou, "GE Healthcare's MAC 800 Portable ECG Device Helps to Advance Physician Care of Athletes and Visitors at Vancouver 2010 Paralympic Winter Games," GE News, March 12, 2010, https://www.ge.com/news/press-releases/ge-healthcares-mac-800-portable-ecg-device-helps-advance-physician-care-athletes-and; Vijay Govindarajan, "A Reverse-Innovation Playbook," *Harvard Business Review*, April 2012, https://hbr.org/2012/04/a-reverse-innovation-playbook; Vijay Govindarajan and Ravi Ramamurti, *Reverse Innovation in Health Care: How to Make Value-Based Delivery Work* (Boston: Harvard Business Review Press, 2018; "'Reverse Innovation': GE Makes India a Lab for Global Markets," Knowledge@Wharton, May 20, 2010, https://knowledge.wharton.upenn.edu/article/reverse-innovation-ge-makes-india-a-lab-for-global-markets/; Vinod Mahanta, "How GE Got Out of the GE Way to Create the Nano of ECGs," *Economic Times*, March 11, 2011, https://economictimes.india times.com/how-ge-got-out-of-the-ge-way-to-create-the-nano-of-ecgs/article show/7673404.cms; "GE Healthcare Launches Low-Cost Portable ECGs," Business Standard, November 24, 2009, https://www.business-standard.com/article/companies/ge-healthcare-launches-low-cost-portable-ecg-10911 2400032_1.html; Brian Dolan, "GE's 1st Portable ECG Includes Medical Texting," Mobi Health News, March 13, 2009, https://www.mobihealthnews.com/903/ges-1st-portable-ecg-includes-medical-texting/; Amos Winter et al., "Engineering Reverse Innovations," *Harvard Business Review*, July 1, 2015, https://hbr.org/2015/07/engineering-reverse-innovations; Chris Trimble, Jeffrey R. Immelt, and Vijay Govindarajan, "How GE Does Reverse Innovation," *Harvard Business Review*, podcast, October 23, 2009, https://hbr.org/podcast/2009/10/how-ge-does-reverse-innovation; "Reverse Innovation Gets Real: Announcing the McKinsey Award Winners," McKinsey & Company, March 22, 2016, https://www.mckinsey.com/about-us/new-at-mckinsey-blog/innovating-for-the-world.

123 **reverse innovation is an approach:** Natalie Zmuda, "P&G, Levi's, GE Innovate by Thinking in Reverse," *Ad Age*, June 13, 2011, https://adage.com/article/global-news/p-g-levi-s-ge-innovate-thinking-reverse/228146.

123 **Aziz Ansari:** Aziz Ansari, *Modern Romance* (New York: Penguin Books, 2016); Sridhar Pappu, "A Hit Netflix Show. A Best-Selling (and Scholarly!) Book. A Powerful 'S.N.L.' Monologue. Can You Blame Him for Wanting to Hide?," *New York Times*, June 8, 2017, https://www.nytimes.com/spotlight/master-of-none.

123 **Peter Sims:** Peter Sims, *Little Bets: How Breakthrough Ideas Emerge from Small Discoveries* (New York: Simon & Schuster Paperbacks, 2011).

123 **Zig Ziglar:** Skip Hollandsworth, "How Many of You Have Heard of Zig Ziglar Before—or Is This Your First Time-uh?," *Texas Monthly*, July 1, 1999, https://www.texasmonthly.com/articles/how-many-of-you-have-heard

-of-zig-ziglar-before-or-is-this-your-first-time-uh/; dallasnews Administrator, "Zig Ziglar, Dallas Motivational Speaker of 'See You at the Top' Fame, Dies at 86," *Dallas Morning News*, November 28, 2012, https://www.dallasnews.com/news/obituaries/2012/11/29/zig-ziglar-dallas-motivational-speaker-of-see-you-at-the-top-fame-dies-at-86/; "Motivational Speaker Zig Ziglar Dead at Age 86," *New York Daily News*, November 28, 2012, https://www.nydailynews.com/news/national/zig-ziglar-dies-age-86-article-1.1209642.

124 **Scott Adams:** Scott Adams, *How to Fail at Almost Everything and Still Win Big: Kind of the Story of My Life* (New York: Penguin Group, 2013).

124 **Lizz Winstead:** Adam Grant, *Originals: How Non-Conformists Move the World* (New York: Penguin Books, 2017).

125 **Jeff Kinney:** Gillian Zoe Segal, *Getting There: A Book of Mentors* (New York: Abrams Books, 2015).

125 **Atul Gawande:** Sara Plourde, "Workshop 54: Atul Gawande," *10-Minute Writer's Workshop*, NHPR, podcast, October 6, 2017, https://www.nhpr.org/post/10-minute-writers-workshop-atul-gawande#stream/0.

126 **Tim Ferriss:** Cory Doctorow, "HOWTO Use Google AdWords to Prototype and Test a Book Title," BoingBoing, October 24, 2010, https://boingboing.net/2010/10/25/howto-use-google-adw.html; wei danger, "64) The 4-Hour Workweek—Smoke Test in the Physical World," Thulme.com, October 25, 2010, http://thulme.com/weiji/64-the-4-hour-workweek-escape-9-5-live-anywhere-and-join-the-new-rich/.

127 **the Cockroaches:** David Bidini, "The Hidden History of How the Rolling Stones Pulled Off Their Legendary Secret El Mocambo Show," *National Post*, May 12, 2015, https://nationalpost.com/entertainment/music/the-hidden-history-of-how-the-rolling-stones-pulled-off-their-legendary-secret-el-mocambo-show; Chet Flippo, "Rolling Stones Gather Momentum," *Rolling Stone*, July 27, 1978, https://www.rollingstone.com/music/music-news/rolling-stones-gather-momentum-236799/; "Rolling Stones—Mick Jagger's Handwritten Set List for 1981 Secret Show as 'The Cockroaches,'" Record Mecca, accessed December 16, 2019, https://recordmecca.com/item-archives/rolling-stones-mick-jaggers-handwritten-set-list-for-1981-secret-show-as-the-cockroaches/.

127 **the Gap:** Garin Pirnia, "Facts About the Gap," Mental Floss, September 2, 2019, https://www.mentalfloss.com/article/596712/the-gap-facts; Bethany Biron, "The Rise and Fall of Gap, One of the Most Iconic and Beloved American Retailers," Business Insider, November 12, 2019, https://www.businessinsider.com/gap-company-history-rise-and-fall-pictures-2019-11.

128 **Target manages:** Gary Mortimer, "Phantom Brands Haunting Our Supermarket Shelves as Home Brand in Disguise," The Conversation, October 27, 2016, https://theconversation.com/phantom-brands-haunting-our-supermarket-shelves-as-home-brand-in-disguise-67774.

128 **established brands often disguise:** Annie Gasparro and Laura Stevens,

"Brands Invent New Lines for Only Amazon to Sell," *Wall Street Journal*, January 25, 2019, https://www.wsj.com/articles/food-makers-invent-brands -for-only-amazon-to-sell-11548414001.

129 **Palessi:** Jordan Vallinsky, "Payless Fools Influencers with a Fake Store," CNN Business, November 29, 2018, https://www.cnn.com/2018/11/29/bus iness/payless-fake-store/index.html; Megan Cerullo, "Payless Sold Discount Shoes at Luxury Prices—and It Worked," CBS News, November 29, 2018, https://www.cbsnews.com/news/payless-sold-discount-shoes-at-luxury-prices -and-it-worked/.

129 **Agatha Christie:** Agatha Christie, *An Autobiography* (New York: William Morrow Paperbacks, 2012); "The Mary Westmacotts," Agatha Christie, https://www.agathachristie.com/about-christie/family-memories/the-mary -westmacotts.

130 **David Johansen:** "Singer and Musician David Johansen," *Fresh Air*, pod-cast, NPR, February 22, 2001, https://www.npr.org/templates/story/story .php?storyId=1118947; "Singer David Johansen: Return of the N.Y. Dolls," *Fresh Air*, podcast, NPR, December 7, 2004, https://www.npr.org/templates /story/story.php?storyId=4206764; Margot Dougherty, "David Johansen Used to Bare It with the Dolls, but Alter Ego Buster Poindexter Is a Bigger Grin," *People*, January 25, 1988, https://people.com/archive/david-johansen -used-to-bare-it-with-the-dolls-but-alter-ego-buster-poindexter-is-a-bigger-grin -vol-29-no-3/; Colin Larkin, ed., *The Virgin Encyclopedia of Popular Music* (London: Virgin Books, 1997), 676.

130 **Nick Swinmurn:** Dinah Eng, "Nick Swinmurn: Zappos' Silent Founder," *Fortune*, September 5, 2012, https://fortune.com/2012/09/05/nick-swinmurn -zappos-silent-founder/; "Who We Are," Zappos, https://www.zappos.com /about/who-we-are.

131 **Bill Gates:** Walter Isaacson, *The Innovators: How a Group of Hackers, Geniuses, and Geeks Created the Digital Revolution* (New York: Simon & Schuster Paperbacks, 2015).

132 **Elon Musk generates $14 billion:** Andrew J. Hawkins, "Tesla Has Re-ceived 325,000 Preorders for the Model 3," The Verge, April 7, 2016, https://www.theverge.com/2016/4/7/11385146/tesla-model-3-preorders -375000-elon-musk.

133 **Irving "Swifty" Lazar:** Michael Korda, "The King of the Deal," *New Yorker*, March 22, 1993, https://www.newyorker.com/magazine/1993/03/29/the-king -of-the-deal; Amy Wallace, "Agent Swifty Lazar, Pioneer Deal-Packager, Dies at 86: Hollywood: He Parlayed Boldness into a Star-Studded Client List and Hosted Legendary Oscar Night Parties," *Los Angeles Times*, De-cember 31, 1993, https://www.latimes.com/archives/la-xpm-1993-12-31-mn -7149-story.html.

134 **it was fishing that ignited:** Tom Nicholas, *VC: An American History* (Cam-bridge, MA: Harvard University Press, 2019).

135 **Disney:** John-Erik Koslosky, "Walt Disney Co.'s Biggest Strength:

Diversification," The Motley Fool, October 29, 2018, https://www.fool.com
/investing/general/2015/07/31/disneys-biggest-strength-diversification.aspx;
Constantinos C. Markides, "To Diversify or Not to Diverify," *Harvard Business Review*, November–December 1997, https://hbr.org/1997/11/to-diversify
-or-not-to-diversify.

135 **Berkshire Hathaway:** Matthew Frankel, "3 Big Competitive Advantages of
Berkshire Hathaway," The Motley Fool, March 10, 2016, https://www.fool
.com/investing/general/2016/03/10/3-big-competitive-advantages-of-berkshire
-hathaway.aspx.

135 **BuzzFeed:** Jonah Peretti, "9 Boxes: Building Out Our Multirevenue Model,"
BuzzFeed, December 12, 2017, https://www.buzzfeed.com/jonah/9-boxes;
Jonah Peretti, "BuzzFeed in 2020," BuzzFeed, January 3, 2020, https://www
.buzzfeed.com/jonah/buzzfeed-in-2020.

135 **Lynda Weinman:** Rachel Emma Silverman and Nikki Waller, "Lynda.com:
A 60-Year-Old Earns Internet Glory," *Wall Street Journal*, November 10,
2015, https://www.wsj.com/articles/lynda-com-a-60-year-old-earns-internet
-glory-1428625176; Jane Porter, "From Near Failure to a $1.5 Billion Sale:
The Epic Story of Lynda.com," *Fast Company*, April 27, 2015, https://www
.fastcompany.com/3045404/from-near-failure-to-a-15-billion-sale-the-epic
-story-of-lyndacom.

137 **researchers at the University of Wisconsin:** Joseph Raffiee and Jie Feng,
"Should I Quit My Day Job?: A Hybrid Path to Entrepreneurship," *Academy of Management Journal* 57, no. 4 (2014): 936–63, https://doi.org/10.5465
/amj.2012.0522. See also Adam Grant, "Entrepreneurs, Don't Give Up Your
Day Jobs (Yet)," *Wired*, February 19, 2016, https://www.wired.co.uk/article
/entrepreneurs-dont-quit-your-day-job.

6: Practicing in Three Dimensions

140 **Tony Romo:** Michelle R. Martinelli, "Tony Romo Is Statistically Better
at Predicting NFL Plays than Completing NFL Passes," *USA Today*, January 30, 2019, https://ftw.usatoday.com/2019/01/tony-romo-nfl-prediction
-accuracy-super-bowl; Harry Lyles, Jr., "Tony Romo's First Season in the
Broadcast Booth Was an Incredible Success," SBNation, January 23,
2018, https://www.sbnation.com/2018/1/23/16918858/tony-romo-broadcast
-nfl-cbs-2017-season; Zach Helfand, "Why Tony Romo Is a Genius at
Football Commentary," *New Yorker*, January 28, 2019, https://www.new
yorker.com/sports/sporting-scene/why-tony-romo-is-a-genius-at-football
-commentary; Richard Dietsch, "How Did Tony Romo Do in His CBS
Broadcast Debut?," *Sports Illustrated*, September 11, 2017, https://www.si
.com/media/2017/09/11/tony-romo-broadcast-debut-cbs-former-cowboys-
qb-impresses; David Barron, "On TV/Radio: CBS' Tony Romo Riding High
Entering First Super Bowl Broadcast," *Houston Chronicle*, January 24,
2019, https://www.houstonchronicle.com/texas-sports-nation/texans/article

/On-TV-Radio-CBS-Tony-Romo-riding-high-entering-13558717.php; Tom Goldman, "How Former NFL Quarterback Tony Romo Got His Broadcast Break," NPR, February 1, 2019, https://www.npr.org/2019/02/01/690822731 /how-former-nfl-quarterback-tony-romo-got-his-broadcast-break.

141 **Enhanced anticipation is a common feature:** K. Anders Ericsson et al., eds., *The Cambridge Handbook of Expertise and Expert Performance*, 2nd ed. (Cambridge, UK: Cambridge University Press, 2018); Eduardo Salas, Michael A. Rosen, and Deborah DiazGrenados, "Expertise-Based Intuition and Decision Making in Organizations," *Journal of Management* 36, no. 4 (July 2010): 941–73, https://doi.org/10.1177/0149206309350084; Merim Bilalić, "The Brains of Experts," *The Psychologist* 31 (March 2015): 24–29, https://thepsychologist.bps.org.uk/volume-31/march-2018/brains-experts; Jaeho Shim et al., "The Use of Anticipatory Visual Cues by Highly Skilled Tennis Players," *Journal of Motor Behavior* 37, no. 2 (April 2005): 164–75, https://doi.org/10.1.1.526.1345; Kevin Woodley, "Goalies Rely on Reading Shooter Before Reacting," NHL, April 8, 2016, https://www.nhl.com /news/nhl-goalies-react-to-shots-unmasked/c-280181412; Wilfried Kunde, Katrin Elsner, and Andrea Kiesel, "No Anticipation—No Action: The Role of Anticipation in Action and Perception," *Cognitive Processes* 8, no. 2 (June 2007): 71–78, https://doi.org/10.1007/s10339-007-0162-2; Chris Berdik, *Mind over Mind: The Surprising Power of Expectations* (New York: Penguin, 2012).

141 **his brain is *less* active:** Ericsson et al., *The Cambridge Handbook of Expertise and Expert Performance*; Robert L. Solso, "Brain Activities in a Skilled Versus Novice Artist: An fMRI Study," *Leonardo* 34, no. 1 (February 2001): 31–34, https://doi.org/10.1162.002409401300052479; K. Anders Ericsson, Michael J. Prietula, and Edward T. Cokely, "The Making of an Expert," *Harvard Business Review*, July–August 2007, https://hbr.org/2007/07/the-making -of-an-expert.

141 **In 1978, British psychologists published:** C. M. Jones and T. Miles, "Use of Advance Cues in Predicting the Flight of a Lawn Tennis Ball," *Journal of Human Movement Studies* 4, no. 4 (1978): 231–35.

142 **they consider fewer options:** Ericsson et al., *The Cambridge Handbook of Expertise and Expert Performance*; A. M. Williams and R. C. Jackson, "Anticipation in Sport: Fifty Years On, What Have We Learned and What Research Still Needs to Be Undertaken?," *Psychology of Sport and Exercise* 42 (May 2019): 16–24, https://doi.org/10.1016/j.psychsport.2018.11.014; Philip E. Ross, "The Expert Mind," *Scientific American*, August 2006, https:// wimse.fsu.edu/media/expert-mind.pdf.

142 **"In the beginner's mind":** Shunryu Suzuki, *Zen Mind, Beginner's Mind* (New York: John Weatherhill, 1970), 21.

142 **more widely dispersed:** Merim Bilalić, "The Double Take of Expertise: Neural Expansion Is Associated with Outstanding Performance," *Current Directions in Psychological Science* 27, no. 6 (December 2018): 462–69, https://doi.org/10.1177/0963721418793133.

142 **Certain features of Tony Romo's brain:** Eleanor A. Maguire et al., "Navigation-Related Structural Change in the Hippocampi of Taxi Drivers," *Proceedings of the National Academy of Sciences of the United States of America* 97, no. 8 (April 2000): 4398–403, https://doi.org/10.1073/pnas.070039597; Katherine A. Woollett and Eleanor A. Maguire, "Acquiring 'the Knowledge' of London's Layout Drives Structural Brain Changes," *Current Biology* 21, no. 24 (December 2011): 2109–14, https://doi.org/10.1016/j.cub.2011.11.018; Ursula Debarnot et al., "Experts Bodies, Experts Minds: How Physical and Mental Training Shape the Brain," *Frontiers in Human Neuroscience* 8, article 280 (May 2014), https://doi.org/10.3389/fnhum.2014.00280.

144 **Robert Zemeckis:** Caseen Gaines, *We Don't Need Roads: The Making of the* Back to the Future *Trilogy* (New York: Plume, 2015); Susannah Gora, *You Couldn't Ignore Me if You Tried: The Brat Pack, John Hughes, and Their Impact on a Generation* (New York: Three Rivers Press, 2010).

146 **ESPN asked John Harbaugh:** Heather J. Rice and David C. Rubin, "I Can See It Both Ways: First- and Third-Person Visual Perspectives at Retrieval," *Consciousness and Cognition* 18, no. 4 (September 2009): 877–90, https://doi.org/10.1016/j.concog.2009.07.004.

146 **Steve Kerr:** Baxter Holmes, "Inside the Warriors' Most Devastating Quarter," ESPN, June 7, 2018, https://www.espn.com/nba/story/_/id/23719065/nba-breaking-warriors-incredible-third-quarter-runs; Marc Stein and Scott Cacciola, "Why Do the Warriors Dominate the 3rd Quarter? Consider Their Halftime Drill," *New York Times*, May 31, 2018, https://www.nytimes.com/2018/05/31/sports/warriors-third-quarter.html.

147 **That's the exercise Harvard researchers:** Giada Di Stefano et al., "Learning by Thinking: How Reflection Aids Performance," Harvard Business School, March 25, 2014, http://www.sc.edu/uscconnect/doc/Learning%20by%20Thinking,%20How%20Reflection%20Aids%20Performance.pdf.

149 **John Dewey:** John Dewey, *How We Think: A Restatement of the Relation of Reflective Thinking to the Educative Process* (Boston: Houghton Mifflin, 1998); Donald A. Schön, *The Reflective Practitioner: How Professionals Think in Action* (New York: Basic Books, 1983); Carol Rogers, "Defining Reflection: Another Look at John Dewey and Reflective Thinking," *Teachers College Record* 104, no. 4 (June 2002): 842–66.

150 **journaling:** Karen A. Baikie and Kay Wilhelm, "Emotional and Physical Health Benefits of Expressive Writing," *Advances in Psychiatric Treatment* 11, no. 5 (September 2005): 338–46, https://doi.org/10.1192/apt.11.5.338; James W. Pennebaker, *Opening Up by Writing It Down: How Expressive Writing Improves Health and Eases Emotional Pain* (New York: Guilford Press, 2016); K. Klein and A. Boals, "Expressive Writing Can Increase Working Memory Capacity," *Journal of Experimental Psychology* 130, no. 3 (September 2001): 520–33, https://doi.org/10.1037//0096-3445.130.3.520; Joshua M. Smyth and James W. Pennebaker, "Exploring the Boundary Conditions in Expressive Writing: In Search of the Right Recipe," *British*

Journal of Health Psychology 13, no. 1 (February 2008): 1–7, https://doi
.org/10.1348/135910707X260117; James W. Pennebaker, "Writing About
Emotional Experiences as a Therapeutic Process," *Psychological Science* 8, no. 3 (May 1997): 162–66, https://doi.org/10.1111/j 1467-9280.1997.
tb00403.x; James W. Pennebaker and Cindy K. Chung, "Expressive Writing:
Connections to Physical and Mental Health," in *The Oxford Handbook
of Health Psychology*, edited by Howard S. Friedman (New York: Oxford
University Press, 2011), 000–000, https://c3po.media.mit.edu/wp-content
/uploads/sites/45/2016/01/PennebakerChung_FriedmanChapter.pdf; Ting
Zhang et al., "A 'Present' for the Future: The Unexpected Value of Redis-
covery," *Psychological Science* 25, no. 10 (October 2014): 1851–60, https://
doi.org.10.1177/0956797614542274; Dan Ciampa, "The More Senior Your
Job Title, the More You Need to Keep a Journal," *Harvard Business Review*, July 7, 2017, https://hbr.org/2017/07/the-more-senior-your-job-title-the
-more-you-need-to-keep-a-journal, Oliver Burkeman, "Consumed by Anxiety? Give It a Day or Two," *The Guardian*, September 15, 2017, https://www
.theguardian.com/lifeandstyle/2017/sep/15/consumed-by-anxiety-give-it
-day-or-two; Colin Patterson and Judith A. Chapman, "Enhancing Skills of
Critical Reflection to Evidence Learning in Professional Practice," *Physical Therapy in Sport* 14, no. 3 (April 2013): 133–38, https://doi.org/10.1016/j
.ptsp.2013.03.004; D. Scott DeRue et al., "A Quasi-Experimental Study of
After-Event Reviews and Leadership Development," *Journal of Applied
Psychology* 97, no. 5 (September 2012): 997-1015, https://doi.org/10.1037
/a0028244.

150 **Navy SEALs:** Jocko Willink and Leif Babin, *Extreme Ownership: How U.S.
Navy SEALs Lead and Win* (New York: St. Martin's Press, 2017).

151 **five-year journal:** An example of a five year journal can be found at https://
amzn.to/3nNhrnK.

152 **memory is not the precise:** Donna J. Bridge and Joel L. Voss, "Active Retrieval Facilitates Across-Episode Binding by Modulating the Content
of Memory," *Neuropsychologia* 63 (October 2014): 154–64, https://doi
.org/10.1016/j.neuropsychologia.2014.08.024; Kimberly S. Chiew et al., "Motivational Valence Alters Memory Formation Without Altering Exploration
of Real-Life Spatial Environment," *PLOS ONE* 13, no. 3 (March 2018):
e0193506, https://doi.org/10.1371/journal.pone.0193506; Johannes Gräff et
al., "Epigenetic Priming of Memory Updating During Reconsolidation to
Attenuate Remote Fear Memories," *Cell* 156, nos. 1–2 (January 2014): 261–
76, https://doi.org/10.1016/j.cell.2013.12.020; Daniel Kahneman, *Thinking,
Fast and Slow* (New York: Farrar, Straus and Giroux, 2011).

152 **Michael Phelps:** Michael Phelps and Alan Abrahamson, *No Limits: The
Will to Succeed* (New York: Free Press, 2008); Duncan White, "London
2012 Olympics: Michael Phelps Sets Mind's Eye on Triumphant Role
in Final Part of Lord of the Rings Trilogy," *The Telegraph*, July 15, 2012,
https://www.telegraph.co.uk/sport/olympics/swimming/9401518/London

-2012-Olympics-Michael-Phelps-sets-minds-eye-on-triumphant-role-in
-final-part-of-Lord-of-the-Rings-trilogy.html.

153 **Lindsey Vonn:** Tim Layden, "Ready to Rock," *Sports Illustrated*, February 17, 2010, https://www.si.com/more-sports/2010/02/17/vonn.

153 **Pelé:** D. C. Gonzalez, *The Art of Mental Training: A Guide to Performance Excellence* (CreateSpace Independent Publishing Platform, 2013).

154 **Wayne Rooney:** Mark Bailey, "Sports Visualisation: How to Imagine Your Way to Success," *The Telegraph*, January 22, 2014, https://www.telegraph.co.uk/men/active/10568898/Sports-visualisation-how-to-imagine-your-way-to-success.html.

154 **Jack Nicklaus:** "Jim Flick and Jack Nicklaus: Go to the Movies," *Golf Digest*, April 27, 2010, https://www.golfdigest.com/story/flick-nicklaus-film.

154 **Wayne Gretzky:** Wayne Gretzky and Rick Reilly, *Gretzky: An Autobiography* (New York: HarperCollins, 1990).

154 **Mike Tyson:** David Sammel, *Locker Room Power: Building an Athlete's Mind* (Great Britain: Westbrook Publishing, 2019).

154 **Research indicates that the value:** Sheryl Ubelacker, "Surgeons Study Benefits of Visualizing Procedures," *Globe and Mail*, January 28, 2019, https://www.theglobeandmail.com/life/health-and-fitness/health/surgeons-study-benefits-of-visualizing-procedures/article22681531/; Joe Ayres and Tim Hopf, "Visualization: Reducing Speech Anxiety and Enhancing Performance," *Communication Reports* 5, no. 1 (Winter 1992): 1–10, https://doi.org/10.1080/08934219209367538; Nicolò F. Bernardi et al., "Mental Practice Promotes Motor Anticipation: Evidence from Skilled Music Performance," *Frontiers in Human Neuroscience* 7 (August 2013): 451, https://doi.org/10.3389/fnhum.2013.00451; John Perry, *Sport Psychology: A Complete Introduction* (London: Hodder & Stoughton, 2016).

155 **Bianca Andreescu:** "Andreescu Wins US Open; Serena Still Stuck on 23," ESPN, September 7, 2019, https://www.espn.com/tennis/story/_/id/27562153/andreescu-wins-us-open-serena-stuck-23.

155 **Jim Carrey:** "What Oprah Learned from Jim Carrey," *Oprah's Life Class*, Oprah Winfrey Network, https://www.youtube.com/watch?v=nPU5bjzLZX0.

155 **researchers at UCLA led:** Lien B. Pham and Shelley E. Taylor, "From Thought to Action: Effects of Process- Versus Outcome-Based Mental Simulations on Performance," *Personality and Social Psychology Bulletin* 25, no. 2 (February 1999): 250–60, https://doi.org/10.1177/0146167299025002010.

156 **Mentally rehearsing the specific actions:** Robert M. G. Reinhart, Laura J. McClenahan, and Geoffrey F. Woodman, "Visualizing Trumps Vision in Training Attention," *Psychological Science* 26, no. 7 (May 2015): 1114–22, https://doi.org/10.1177/0956797615577619; Maamer Slimani et al., "Effects of Mental Imagery on Muscular Strength in Healthy and Patient Participants: A Systematic Review," *Journal of Sports Science & Medicine* 15, no. 3 (September 2016): 434–50; Sophie M. A. Wallace-Hadrill and Sunjeev K. Kamboj, "The Impact of Perspective Change as a Cognitive Reappraisal Strategy

on Affect: A Systematic Review," *Frontiers in Psychology*, November 4, 2016, https://doi.org/10.3389/fpsyg.2016.01715; Sonal Arora et al., "Mental Practice Enhances Surgical Technical Skills: A Randomized Control Study," *Annals of Surgery* 253, no. 2 (February 2011): 265–70, https://doi.org/10.1097 /SLA.0b013e318207a789; Rachel J. Bar and Joseph F. X. DeSouza, "Tracking Plasticity: Effects of Long-Term Rehearsal in Expert Dancers Encoding Music to Movement," *PLOS ONE* 11, no. 1 (January 2016): e0147731, https://doi.org/10.1371/journal.pone.0147731; Heather J. Rice and David C. Rubin, "I Can See It Both Ways: First- and Third-Person Visual Perspectives at Retrieval," *Consciousness and Cognition* 18, no. 4 (September 2009): 877–90, https://doi.org/10.1016/j.concog.2009.07.004; Brain C. Clark et al., "The Power of the Mind: The Cortex as a Critical Determinant of Muscle Strength/Weakness," *Journal of Neurophysiology* 112, no. 12 (December 2014): 3219–26, https://doi.org/10.1152/jn.00386.2014; Giuliano Fontani et al., "Effect of Mental Imagery on the Development of Skilled Motor Actions," *Perceptual and Motor Skills* 105, no. 3 (December 2007): 803–26, https://doi .org/10.2466/PMS.105.7.803-826; Caroline J. Wright and Dave Smith, "The Effect of PETTLEP Imagery on Strength Performance," *International Journal of Sport and Exercise Psychology* 7, no. 1 (2009): 18–31, https://doi .org/10.1080/1612197X.2009.9671890.

159 **Billie Jean King:** Dave Davies, "Pioneer Billie Jean King Moved the Baseline for Women's Tennis," *Fresh Air*, NPR, January 31, 2004, https://www .npr.org/transcripts/269423125.

159 **Research suggests that the optimal length:** Bianca A. Simonsmeier et al., "The Effects of Imagery Interventions in Sports: A Meta-analysis," *International Review of Sport and Exercise Psychology*, June 2020, https://doi.org/1 0.1080/1750984X.2020.1780627, Adam J. Toth et al., "Does Mental Practice *Still* Enhance Performance? A 24 Year Follow-up and Meta-analytic Replication and Extension," *Psychology of Sport and Science* 48 (May 2020): 101672, https://doi.org/10.1016/j.psychsport.2020.101672; J. E. Driskell, Carolyn Copper, and Aidan Moran, "Does Mental Practice Enhance Performance?," *Journal of Applied Psychology* 79, no. 4 (August 1994): 481–92, https://doi.org/10.1037/0021-9010.79.4.481.

159 **coaching malpractice:** David Waldstein, "Batting Practice: Cherished Tradition or a Colossal Waste of Time?," *New York Times*, August 16, 2012, https:// www.nytimes.com/2012/08/17/sports/baseball/batting-practice-cherished -tradition-or-colossal-waste-of-time.html; Brandon Hall, "Why Traditional MLB Batting Practice Is Dying a Slow Death," Stack, March 7, 2019, https://www.stack.com/a/why-traditional-mlb-batting-practice-is-dying-a -slow-death; Joe Lemire, "A Novel Idea in the Majors: Using Batting Practice to Get Better," *New York Times*, May 23, 2019, https://www.nytimes .com/2019/05/23/sports/batting-practice.html.

161 **certain actions start to occur:** Mary Brabeck, Jill Jeffrey, and Sara Fry, "Practice for Knowledge Acquisition (Not Drill and Kill)," American

Psychological Association, 2010, https://www.apa.org/education/k12/practice
-acquisition.

162 **automaticity can make:** Ericsson et al., *The Cambridge Handbook of Expertise and Expert Performance*; Wayne D. Gray and John K. Lindstedt, "Plateaus, Dips, and Leaps: Where to Look for Inventions and Discoveries During Skilled Performance," *Cognitive Science* 41, no. 7 (September 2017): 1838–70, https://doi.org/10.1111/cogs.12412; Jeff Huang et al., "Master Maker: Understanding Gaming Skill Through Practice and Habit From Gameplay Behavior," *Topics in Cognitive Science* 9, no. 9 (April 2017): 437–66, https://doi.org/10.1111/tops.12251; Gordon D. Logan, "Skill and Automaticity: Relations, Implications, and Future Directions," *Canadian Journal of Psychology* 39, no. 2 (1985): 367–86, https://core.ac.uk/download/pdf/208483003 .pdf; Gordon D. Logan, "Toward an Instance Theory of Automatization," *Psychological Review* 95, no. 4 (1988): 492–527, https://citeseerx.ist.psu.edu /viewdoc/download?doi=10.1.1.418.1417&rep=rep1&type=pdf; see also Atul Gawande, *The Checklist Manifesto: How To Get Things Right* (New York: Picador, 2011); Josh Waitzkin, *The Art of Learning: An Inner Journey to Optimal Performance* (New York: Free Press, 2008); Joshua Foer, *Moonwalking with Einstein: The Art and Science of Remembering Everything* (New York: Penguin, 2011).

162 **K. Anders Ericsson:** ERICSSON TEXT; Anders Ericsson and Robert Pool, *Peak: Secrets from the New Science of Expertise* (Boston: Houghton Mifflin Harcourt, 2016); Brabeck, Jeffrey, and Fry, "Practice for Knowledge Acquisition (Not Drill and Kill)." For popular accounts and applications of Ericsson's work, see Daniel Coyle, *The Little Book of Talent: 52 Tips for Improving Your Skills* (New York: Bantam Books, 2012); Matthew Syed, *Bounce: Mozart, Federer, Picasso, Beckham, and the Science of Success* (New York: HarperCollins, 2010); Geoff Colvin, *Talent Is Overrated: What Really Separates World-Class Performers from Everybody Else* (New York: Portfolio/Penguin, 2018); Malcolm Gladwell, *Outliers: The Story of Success* (New York: Little, Brown and Company, 2008); David Epstein, *The Sports Gene: Inside the Science of Extraordinary Athletic Performance* (New York: Penguin Group, 2014).

164 **Dan Knights:** "Inside the World of Competitive Rubik's Cube Solving," *The Leonard Lopate Show*, podcast, WNYC, December 29, 2016, https://www .wnyc.org/story/ian-scheffler-cracking-cube/. See also Ian Scheffler, *Cracking the Cube: Going Slow to Go Fast and Other Unexpected Turns in the World of Competitive Rubik's Cube Solving* (New York: Touchstone, 2016). A recording of Knights's solving in free fall is available at https://www.you tube.com/watch?v=dtRsKWAECbs.

164 **pressure acclimatization training:** Stewart Cotterill, *Performance Psychology: Theory and Practice* (London: Routledge, 2017); Tripp Driskell, Steve Sciafani, and James E. Driskell, "Reducing the Effects of Game Day Pressures Through Stress Exposure Training," *Journal of Sport Psychology in*

Action 5, no. 1 (January 2014): 28–43, https://doi.org/10.1080/21520704.2013.866603.

165 **Novelty, on the other hand:** Tomonori Takechu et al., "Locus Coeruleus and Dopaminergic Consolidation of Everyday Memory," *Nature* 537, no. 7620 (September 2016): 357–62, https://doi.org/10.1038/nature19325; Steven C. Pan, "The Interleaving Effect: Mixing It Up Boosts Learning," *Scientific American*, August 4, 2015, https://www.scientificamerican.com/article/the-interleaving-effect-mixing-it-up-boosts-learning/; Chandramallika Basak and Margaret A. O'Connell, "To Switch or Not to Switch: Role of Cognitive Control in Working Memory Training in Older Adults," *Frontiers in Psychology* 7, article 230 (March 2, 2016), https://doi.org/10.3389/fpsyg.2016.00230; Nicholas F. Wymbs, Amy J. Bastian, and Pablo A. Celnik, "Motor Skills Are Strengthened Through Reconsolidation," *Current Biology* 23, no. 3 (February 2016): 338–43, https://doi.org/10.1016/j.cub.2015.11.066.

165 **Among the first studies:** Dennis Landin, Edward P. Hebert, and Malcolm Fairweather, "The Effects of Variable Practice on the Performance of a Basketball Skill," *Research Quarterly for Exercise and Sport* 64, no. 2 (July 1993): 232–37, https://doi.org/10.1080/02701367.1993.10608803; Ulrich Boser, *Learn Better: Mastering the Skills for Success in Life, Business, and School, or How to Become an Expert in Just About Anything* (New York: Rodale, 2017).

166 **Bill Bradley:** John McPhee, "A Sense of Where You Are," *New Yorker*, January 25, 1965, https://www.newyorker.com/magazine/1965/01/23/a-sense-of-where-you-are.

166 **Stephen Curry:** Daniel Chao, "Human Athletes Are Using Training Technology from the Future to Become More like Robots," *Quartz*, August 7, 2016, https://qz.com/749746/human-athletes-are-using-training-technology-from-the-future-to-become-more-like-robots/; Max Whittle, "The Pre-Game Routine That Makes Steph Curry the Best in the NBA," *The Guardian*, April 18, 2016, https://www.theguardian.com/sport/2016/apr/18/steph-curry-golden-state-warriors-nba-pre-game.

166 **At the 2012 Beijing Olympics:** Michael Phelps and Brian Cazaneuve, *Beneath the Surface: My Story* (New York: Sports Publishing, 2016). See also Charles Duhigg, *The Power of Habit: Why We Do What We Do in Life and Business* (New York: Random House, 2012).

167 **Herschel Walker:** Thomas C. Hayes, "Walker Balances Bulk with Ballet," *New York Times*, April 11, 1988, https://www.nytimes.com/1988/04/11/sports/walker-balances-bulk-with-ballet.html; Josh Katzowitz, "Steve McLendon: Ballet Is 'Harder than Anything Else I Do,'" CBS Sports, July 31, 2013, https://www.cbssports.com/nfl/news/steve-mclendon-ballet-is-harder-than-anything-else-i-do/; "Lynn Swann Lake?," *Pittsburgh Post-Gazette*, August 2, 2013, https://newsinteractive.post-gazette.com/thedigs/2013/08/02/lynn-swann-lake/.

167 **cross-training:** Hirofumi Tanaka and Thomas Swensen, "Impact of Resistance Training on Endurance Performance," *Sports Medicine* 25, no. 3

(March 1998): 191–200, https://doi.org/10.2165/00007256-199825030-00005; Matt Fitzgerald, "Eight Benefits of Cross-Training," *Runner's World*, November 22, 2004, https://www.runnersworld.com/training/a20813186/eight -benefits-of-cross-training/; "Mixing in Martial Arts to Improve On-Field Performance," NFL News, October 28, 2015, https://www.nfl.com/news /mixing-in-martial-arts-to-improve-on-field-performance-0ap3000000567511.

168   **Haruki Murakami:** Haruki Murakami, *What I Talk About When I Talk About Running: A Memoir* (New York: Vintage Books, 2009).

168   **Jon Stewart:** *Wordplay*, directed by Patrick Creadon, April 6, 2006; "Will Shortz," *The Daily Show with Jon Stewart*, August 20, 2003, http://www .cc.com/video-clips/e8ixc0/the-daily-show-with-jon-stewart-will-shortz; "1-Across and 2-Down: The History and Mysteries of the Crossword Puzzle," *The Sunday Edition*, CBC Radio, May 15, 2020, https://www.cbc.ca /radio/sunday/the-sunday-edition-for-may-17-2020-1.5564926/1-across-and -2-down-the-history-and-mysteries-of-the-crossword-puzzle-1.5564972.

168   **business leaders enrolling in improv classes:** Jesse Scinto, "Why Improv Training Is Great Business Training," *Forbes*, June 27, 2014, https://www .forbes.com/sites/forbesleadershipforum/2014/06/27/why-improv-training -is-great-business-training/#16e935ea6bcb; Elizabeth Doty, "Using Improv to Transform How You Lead," Strategy+Business, May 24, 2018, https:// www.strategy-business.com/blog/Using-Improv-to-Transform-How-You -Lead?gko=afcc2.

7: How to Talk to Experts

169   **Marlon Brando:** Benjamin Svetkey, "Marlon Brando's Real Last Tango: The Never-Told Story of His Secret A-List Acting School," *Hollywood Reporter*, June 11, 2015, https://www.hollywoodreporter.com/news/marlon-brandos -real-last-tango-801232; William J. Mann, *The Contender: The Story of Marlon Brando* (New York: HarperCollins, 2019).

171   **Magic Johnson and Isiah Thomas:** Elliott Pohnl, "Magic Johnson, Wayne Gretzky, and 13 Great Players Who Couldn't Coach," Bleacher Report, November 17, 2010, https://bleacherreport.com/articles/520877-magic-johnson -wayne-gretzky-and-13-great-players-who-couldnt-coach.

171   **Wayne Gretzky:** Ibid.

171   **Tony La Russa:** "Tony La Russa Stats," Baseball Reference, https://www .baseball-reference.com/players/l/larusto01.shtml.

171   **A comprehensive analysis:** John Hattie and H. W. Marsh, "The Relationship Between Research and Teaching: A Meta-analysis," *Review of Educational Research* 66, no. 4 (Winter 1996): 507–42, https://doi.org/10.2307/1170652. See also Jordan Weissmann, "Study: Tenured Professors Make Worse Teachers," *The Atlantic*, September 9, 2013, https://www.theatlantic.com/business /archive/2013/09/study-tenured-professors-make-worse-teachers/279480/; Adam Grant, "A Solution for Bad Teaching," *New York Times*, February 5,

2014, https://www.nytimes.com/2014/02/06/opinion/a-solution-for-bad
-teaching.html.

172 **Jimmy Fallon:** "Charades with Gal Gadot and Miley Cyrus," *The Tonight
Show Starring Jimmy Fallon*, October 5, 2017, https://www.youtube.com
/watch?v=qXH1dVI8Jic&feature=youtu.be.

173 **a Stanford experiment:** Elizabeth Louise Newton, "The Rocky Road
from Actions to Intentions," PhD diss., Stanford University, 1990, https://
creatorsvancouver.com/wp-content/uploads/2016/06/rocky-road-from
-actions-to-intentions.pdf. See also Chip Heath and Dan Heath, *Made to
Stick: Why Some Ideas Survive and Others Die* (New York: Random House,
2008).

174 **our brains evolved:** Siba E. Ghrear, Susan A. J. Birch, and Daniel M. Bernstein, "Outcome Knowledge and False Belief," *Frontiers in Psychology*,
February 12, 2016, https://doi.org/10.3389/fpsyg.2016.00118; Colin Camerer,
George Loewenstein, and Martin Weber, "The Curse of Knowledge in Economic Settings: An Experimental Analysis," *Journal of Political Economy*
97, no. 5 (October 1989): 1232–54, https://doi.org/10.1086/261651.

175 **a fraction of the required time:** Pamela J. Hinds, "The Curse of Expertise:
The Effects of Expertise and Debiasing methods on Predictions of Novice
Performance," *Journal of Experimental Psychology: Applied* 5, no. 2 (1999):
205–21, https://doi.org/10.1037/1076-898X.5.2.205; Susan A. J. Birch et al.,
"A 'Curse of Knowledge' in the Absence of Knowledge? People Misattri-
bute Fluency When Judging How Common Knowledge Is Among Their
Peers," *Cognition* 166 (September 2017): 447–58, https://doi.org/10.1016/j
.cognition.2017.04.015.

175 **Richard Clark:** Richard E. Clark et al., "Cognitive Task Analysis," in *Hand-
book of Research on Educational Communications and Technology*, 3rd ed.,
edited by J. Michael Spector et al. (New York: Routledge, 2007), 1801–56;
Richard E. Clark et al., "The Use of Cognitive Task Analysis to Improve
Instructional Descriptions of Procedures," *Journal of Surgical Research* 173,
no. 1 (March 2012): e37–42, https://doi.org/10.1016/j.jss.2011.09.003; Maura
E. Sullivan et al., "Cognitive-Task-Analysis," in *Textbook of Simulation,
Skills, and Team Training*, edited by Shawn T. Tsuda, Daniel J. Scott, and
Daniel B. Jones (Woodbury, CT: Ciné-Med, 2012), 000–000.

176 **In 2008, researchers:** Kristin E. Flegal and Michael C. Anderson, "Overthinking Skilled Motor Performance: Or Why Those Who Teach Can't Do,"
Psychonomic Bulletin & Review 15, no. 5 (November 2008): 927–32, https://
pubmed.ncbi.nlm.nih.gov/18926983/.

176 **communicating in ways:** Matthew Fisher and Frank C. Keil, "The Curse
of Expertise: When More Knowledge Leads to Miscalibrated Explanatory
Insight," *Cognitive Science* 40, no. 5 (2015): 1–19, https://onlinelibrary.wiley
.com/doi/full/10.1111/cogs.12280.

180 **focus group moderators:** These insights are drawn from my professional experiences moderating focus groups.

181   **Kate Murphy's recommended clarifier:** Kate Murphy, *You're Not Listening: What You're Missing and Why It Matters* (New York: Celadon Books, 2020).

181   **studies show that starting:** Tamara van Gog and Nikol Rummel, "Example-Based Learning: Integrating Cognitive and Social-Cognitive Research Perspectives," *Educational Psychology Review* 22, no. 2 (June 2010): 155–74, https://doi.org/10.1007/s10648-010-9134-7; Alexander Renkl, "Toward an Instructionally Oriented Theory of Example-Based Learning," *Cognitive Science* 38, no. 1 (January–February 2014): 1–37, https://doi.org/10.1111/cogs .12086; Ruth Colvin Clark, *Building Expertise: Cognitive Methods for Training and Performance Improvement* (San Francisco: John Wiley & Sons, 2008); Ruth Colvin Clark, *Evidence-Based Training Methods: A Guide for Training Professionals* (Alexandria, VA: ATD Press, 2020); James Geary, *I Is an Other: The Secrets of Metaphor and How It Shapes the Way We See the World* (New York: HarperCollins, 2011).

181   **Analogies explain the unfamiliar:** Dedre Gentner and Christian Hoyos, "Analogy and Abstraction," *Topics in Cognitive Science* 9, no. 3 (2017): 672–93, https://doi.org/10.1111/tops.12278; Clark, *Building Expertise*; Clark, *Evidence-Based Training Methods*.

182   **repeat back:** Wojciech Kulesza et al., "The Echo Effect: The Power of Verbal Mimicry to Influence Prosocial Behavior," *Journal of Language and Social Psychology* 33, no. 2 (March 2014): 182–201, https://doi.org/10.1177/02619 27X13506906; Roderick I. Swaab, William W. Maddux, and Marwan Sinaceur, "Early Words That Work: When and How Virtual Linguistic Mimicry Facilitates Negotiation Outcomes," *Journal of Experimental Social Psychology* 47, no. 3 (May 2011): 616–21, https://doi.org/10.1016/j.jesp.2011.01.005; Rick B. van Baaren et al., "Mimicry and Prosocial Behavior," *Psychological Science* 15, no. 1 (January 2004): 71–74, https://doi.org/10.1111/j.0963-7214.2004.01501012.x.

183   **one solution researchers found:** Clark et al., "Cognitive Task Analysis"; Clark, *Building Expertise*.

183   **"What language is this written in?":** Askold W., customer review, Amazon, December 27, 2018, https://www.amazon.com/gp/customer-reviews/R1LRV 1GEV2MH4/ref=cm_cr_arp_d_rvw_ttl?ie=UTF8&ASIN=B00BO4GSA2.

184   **"This book is [a] bloated":** "War and Peace," Emma's Reviews, Goodreads, September 3, 2020, https://www.goodreads.com/review/show/119972526.

184   **"Overrated, Overwrought, Overhyped":** Flying Scot, customer review, Amazon, July 18, 2018, https://www.amazon.com/gp/customer-reviews/R15605 MMCOE2OW?ASIN=0312421273.

184   **"One Hundred Hours of Boredom":** Michael R. Gallagher, customer review, Amazon, May 22, 2014, https://www.amazon.com/gp/customer-reviews /R37ACXID9Q86VD/ref=cm_cr_arp_d_rvw_ttl?ie=UTF8&ASIN= B00MOQOFJK.

184   **"Beloved - Not!":** mbryson, customer review, Amazon, June 13, 2012, https:// www.amazon.com/gp/customer-reviews/R1IPG4Q2YBC8KR/ref=cm_cr _getr_d_rvw_ttl?ie=UTF8&ASIN=1400033411.

184 *User Friendly:* Cliff Kuang and Robert Fabricant, *User Friendly: How the Hidden Rules of Design Are Changing the Way We Live, Work, and Play* (New York: Farrar, Straus and Giroux, 2019).

185 **A comprehensive analysis:** Avraham N. Kluger and Angelo DeNisi, "The Effects of Feedback Interventions on Performance: A Historical Review, a Meta-Analysis, and a Preliminary Feedback Intervention Theory," *Psychological Bulletin* 119, no. 2 (March 1996): 254–84, https://doi.org/10.1037/0033 -2909.119.2.254.

186 **Quentin Tarantino:** Mark Seal, "Cinema Tarantino: The Making of *Pulp Fiction*," *Vanity Fair*, February 13, 2013, https://www.vanityfair.com/holly wood/2013/03/making-of-pulp-fiction-oral-history.

186 **Jerry Seinfeld:** Oliver Burkeman, "Jerry Seinfeld on How to Be Funny Without Sex and Swearing," *The Guardian*, January 5, 2014, https://www.the guardian.com/culture/2014/jan/05/jerry-seinfeld-funny-sex-swearing-sitcom -comedy; *Dying Laughing*, directed by Lloyd Stanton and Paul Toogood, released June 4, 2016.

187 **"I always think":** Dan Amira, "Jerry Seinfeld Says Jokes Are Not Real Life," *New York Times Magazine*, August 15, 2018, https://www.nytimes.com/2018 /08/15/magazine/jerry-seinfeld-says-jokes-are-not-real-life.html.

187 **"The timbre of it":** Burkeman, "Jerry Seinfeld on How to Be Funny Without Sex and Swearing."

187 **David Sedaris:** Colin Marshall, "David Sedaris Breaks Down His Writing Process: Keep a Diary, Carry a Notebook, Read Out Loud, Abandon Hope," Open Culture, June 27, 2017, http://www.openculture.com/2017/06 /david-sedaris-breaks-down-his-writing-process.html.

188 **In 2019, a team:** Jaewon Yoon et al., "Framing Feedback Giving as Advice Giving Yields More Critical and Actionable Input," Harvard Business School, working paper 20-021, August 2019, https://www.hbs.edu/faculty /Publication%20Files/20-021_b907e614-e44a-4f21-bae8-e4a722babb25.pdf.

189 **Mike Birbiglia:** Mike Birbiglia, "6 Tips for Getting Your Solo Play to Broadway," *New York Times*, October 30, 2018, https://www.nytimes.com/2018 /10/30/theater/mike-birbiglia-broadway-the-new-one.html; Mike Birbiglia, "Mike Birbiglia's 6 Tips for Making It Small in Hollywood. Or Anywhere," *New York Times*, August 30, 2016, https://www.nytimes.com/2016/09/04 /movies/mike-birbiglias-6-tips-for-making-it-small-in-hollywood-or-any where.html.

190 **Twitter users—particularly those:** Stephan Wojcik and Adam Hughes, "Sizing Up Twitter Users," Pew Research Center, April 24, 2019, https://www .pewresearch.org/internet/2019/04/24/sizing-up-twitter-users/; "National Politics on Twitter: Small Share of U.S. Adults Produce Majority of Tweets," Pew Research Center, October 23, 2019, https://www.pewresearch.org/politics /2019/10/23/national-politics-on-twitter-small-share-of-u-s-adults-produce -majority-of-tweets/.

190 **Ongoing feedback breaks:** Nakkyeong Choi and Rohae Myung, "Feedback

Frequency Effect on Performance Time in Dynamic Decision Making Task," *Proceedings of the Human Factors and Ergonomics Society Annual Meeting*, September 28, 2017, https://doi.org/10.1177/1541931213601531; Chak Fu Lam et al., "The Impact of Feedback Frequency on Learning and Task Performance: Challenging the 'More Is Better' Assumption," *Organizational Behavior and Human Decision Processes* 116, no. 2 (November 2011): 217–28, https://doi.org/10.1016/j.obhdp.2011.05.002.

191   *concept testing:* David J. Bland and Alexander Osterwalder, *Testing Business Ideas: A Field Guide for Rapid Experimentation* (Hoboken, NJ: Wiley, 2019).

191   **Chobani:** Clint Fontanella, "Everything You Need to Get Started with Concept Testing," HubSpot, August 5, 2019, https://blog.hubspot.com/service /concept-testing.

191   **Salman Rushdie:** Alison Beard, "Life's Work: An Interview with Salman Rushdie," *Harvard Business Review*, September 2015, https://hbr.org/2015 /09/lifes-work-salman-rushdie.

191   **"I think young writers":** Salman Rushdie, "10-Minute Writer's Workshop: Salman Rushdie," NHPR, October 9, 2015, https://www.nhpr.org/post/10 -minute-writers-workshop-salman-rushdie#stream/0.

191   **"[In later drafts,] I become":** Salman Rushdie, "10-Minute Writer's Workshop: Salman Rushdie," NHPR, October 9, 2015, https://www.nhpr.org/post /10-minute-writers-workshop-salman-rushdie#stream/0.

192   **Criticism triggers the release:** Yoichi Chida and Mark Hamer, "Chronic Psychosocial Factors and Acute Physiological Responses to Laboratory-Induced Stress in Healthy Populations: A Quantitative Review of 30 Years of Investigations," *Psychological Bulletin* 134, no. 6 (December 2008): 829–85, https://doi.org/10.1037/a0013342; Sally S. Dickerson and Margaret E. Kemeny, "Acute Stressors and Cortisol Responses: A Theoretical Integration and Synthesis of Laboratory Research," *Psychological Bulletin* 130, no. 3 (May 2004): 355–91, https://doi.org/10.1037/0033-2909.130.3.355.

193   **In 2015, researchers:** Stefano Palminteri et al., "Contextual Modulation of Value Signals in Reward and Punishment Learning," *Nature Communications* 6, article 8096 (August 25, 2015), https://doi.org/10.1038/ncomms9096.

194   **introduce psychological distance:** Jennifer N. Belding, Karen Z. Naufel, and Kentaro Fujita, "Using High-Level Construal and Perceptions of Changeability to Promote Self-Change over Self-Protection Motives in Response to Negative Feedback," *Personality and Social Psychology Bulletin* 41, no. 6 (April 2015): 1250–63, https://doi.org/10.1177/0146167215580776.

194   **Research suggests that taking time:** Noelle Nelson, Selin A. Malkoc, and Baba Shiv, "Emotions Know Best: The Advantage of Emotional Versus Cognitive Responses to Failure," *Journal of Behavioral Decision Making* 31, no. 1 (January 2018): 40–51, https://doi.org/10.1002/bdm.2042.

194   **In Western cultures:** Janine Bempechat, Jin Li, and Samuel Ronfard, "Relations Among Cultural Learning Beliefs, Self-Regulated Learning, and Academic Achievement for Low-Income Chinese American Adolescents," *Child*

Development 89, no. 3 (December 2016): 851–61, https://doi.org/10.1111 /cdev.12702; Jin Li et al., "How European American and Taiwanese Mothers Talk to Their Children About Learning," *Child Development* 85, no. 3 (May–June 2014): 1206–21, https://doi.org/10.1111/cdev.12172; Jin Li, "Mind or Virtue: Western and Chinese Beliefs About Learning," *Current Directions in Psychological Science* 14, no. 4 (August 2005): 190–94, https:// doi.org/10.1111/j.0963-7214.2005.00362.x; Jin Li, "U.S. and Chinese Cultural Beliefs About Learning," *Journal of Educational Psychology* 95, no. 2 (June 2003): 258–67, https://doi.org/10.1037/0022-0663.95.2.258; Jin Li, "Learning Models in Different Cultures," *New Directions for Childhood and Adolescent Development* 2002, no. 96 (Summer 2002): 45–64, https:// doi.org/10.1002/cd.43; Alix Spiegel, "Struggle Means Learning: Difference in Eastern and Western Cultures," KQED, November 15, 2012, https://www .kqed.org/mindshift/24944/struggle-means-learning-difference-in-eastern -and western-cultures; Kathryn Schulz, *Being Wrong: Adventures in the Margin of Error* (New York: HarperCollins, 2010).

195 **"I've bombed so many times":** "Worst I Ever Bombed: John Oliver," *Late Night with Jimmy Fallon*, August 21, 2013, https://www.youtube.com/watch ?v=gaLRhx1znF4&list=FL3YEnKSND_ZWHcakqCQzewQ&index=4.

195 **"Five of us toured":** Judd Apatow, *Sick in the Head: Conversations About Life and Comedy* (New York: Random House, 2015), 55.

195 **"You get to a point":** Terry Gross, "Aziz Ansari on 'Master of None' and How His Parents Feel About Acting," *Fresh Air*, NPR, May 24, 2017, https:// www.npr.org/transcripts/529815176.

195 **Research conducted at Columbia University:** Stacey R. Finkelstein and Ayelet Fishbach, "Tell Me What I Did Wrong: Experts Seek and Respond to Negative Feedback," *Journal of Consumer Research* 39, no. 1 (June 2012): 22–38, https://doi.org/10.1086/661934.

196 **"If you want to avoid criticism":** Chuck Klosterman, *I Wear the Black Hat: Grappling with Villains (Real and Imagined)* (New York: Scribner, 2014), 000.

Conclusion: Stumbling on Greatness

197 **Vincent van Gogh:** Steven Naifeh and Gregory White Smith, *Van Gogh: The Life* (New York: Random House Trade Paperbacks, 2012); "Distant Beauty: How van Gogh Bent Japanese Art to His Own Will," BBC Arts, March 20, 2018, https://www.bbc.co.uk/programmes/articles/14cB7k5NY w3YRDtLQ2ftnMF/distant-beauty-how-van-gogh-bent-japanese-art-to-his -own-will; Nina Siegal, "He Was More than His Madness," *New York Times*, December 9, 2014, https://www.nytimes.com/2014/12/10/arts/design/changes -at-the-van-gogh-museum-in-amsterdam.html; William Cook, "Where Van Gogh Learned to Paint," *The Spectator*, February 14, 2015, https:// www.spectator.co.uk/article/where-van-gogh-learned-to-paint; Henry Adams, "Seeing Double: Van Gogh the Tweaker," *New York Times*, October 2, 2013,

https://www.nytimes.com/2013/10/06/arts/design/seeing-double-van-gogh
-the-tweaker.html; Alastair Sooke, "Van Gogh and Japan: The Prints That
Shaped the Artist," BBC Arts, June 11, 2018, https://bbc.com/culture/story
/20180611-van-gogh-and-japan-the-prints-that-shaped-the-artist; "Vincent
van Gogh Copies," Van Gogh Studio, https://www.vangoghstudio.com/;
"Practice Makes Perfect," Van Gogh Museum, https://vangoghmuseum
.com/en/vincent-van-gogh-life-and-work/practice-makes-perfect; Kathryn
Hughes, "How Dickens, Brontë, and Eliot Influenced Vincent van Gogh,"
The Guardian, April 5, 2019, https://www.theguardian.com/books/2019
/apr/05/how-dickens-bronte-and-eliot-influenced-vincent-van-gogh; Vincent
van Gogh, *The Letters of Vincent van Gogh*, translated by Arnold Pomerans,
edited by Ronald de Leeuw (New York: Penguin Classics, 1998); Takeshi
Okada and Kentaro Ishibashi, "Imitation, Inspiration, and Creation: Cognitive Process of Creative Drawing by Copying Others' Artworks," *Cognitive Science* 41, no. 7 (September 2017): 1804–37, https://doi.org/10.1111
/cogs.12442; Victoria Moore, "Letters from the Edge: Van Gogh's Poignant
Story Revealed Through His Writing," *Daily Mail*, January 23, 2010, https://
www.dailymail.co.uk/news/article-145373/Van-Goghs-poignant-story
-revealed-writing.html; "Getting to Know van Gogh: Steven Naifeh," Columbia Museum of Art, October 18, 2019, https://www.youtube.com/watch?v=R
1zUpp6UzYc; "The Starry Night," Vincent van Gogh, MoMA Learning,
https://www.moma.org/learn/moma_learning/vincent-van-gogh-the-starry
-night-1889/; "Inspiration from Japan," Van Gogh Museum, https://www
.vangoghmuseum.nl/en/stories/inspiration-from-japan#8; Kristin Bonk Fong,
"Sharing van Gogh's Creative Process," Denver Art Museum, February
14, 2013, https://www.denverartmuseum.org/en/blog/sharing-van-goghs
-creative-process; "Letters," Van Gogh Museum, https://www.vangoghmuseum
.nl/en/highlights/letters/528; Colta Ives and Susan Alyson Stein, "Vincent
van Gogh (1853–1890): The Drawings," Heilbrunn Timeline of Art History,
Metropolitan Museum of Art, October 2005, https://www.metmuseum.org
/toah/hd/gogh_d/hd_gogh_d.htm; Cornelia Homburg, *The Copy Turns
Original* (Amsterdam: John Benjamins Publishing Company, 1996).

198 **Several neurological studies:** John R. Hughes, "A Reappraisal of the Possible Seizures of Vincent van Gogh," *Epilepsy Behavior* 6, no. 4 (June 2005):
504–10, https://doi.org/10.1016/j.ybeh.2005.02.014; Paul Wolf, "Creativity and Chronic Disease Vincent van Gogh (1853–1890)," *Western Journal of Medicine* 175, no. 5 (November 2001): 348, https://doi.org/10.1136
/ewjm.175.5.348; Martin Cartwright et al., "Temporal Lobe Epilepsy and
Creativity: A Model of Association," *Creativity Research Journal* 16, no. 1
(March 2004): 27–34, https://doi.org/10.1207/s15326934crj1601_3.

199 **"My whole life is aimed":** Kathryn Hughes, "How Dickens, Brontë, and Eliot
Influenced Vincent van Gogh," *The Guardian*, April 5, 2019, https://www.the
guardian.com/books/2019/apr/05/how-dickens-bronte-and-eliot-influenced
-vincent-van-gogh.

Index

About the Author

RON FRIEDMAN, PHD, is an award-winning psychologist who has served on the faculty of the University of Rochester, Nazareth College, and Hobart and William Smith Colleges, and has consulted for political leaders, nonprofits, and many of the world's most recognized brands. Popular accounts of his research have appeared on NPR and in major newspapers, including the *New York Times*, *Washington Post*, *Boston Globe*, *Globe and Mail*, and *The Guardian*, as well as magazines like the *Harvard Business Review*, *Fast Company*, and *Psychology Today*.

Ron is the founder of ignite80, a learning and development company that translates research in neuroscience, human physiology, and behavioral economics into practical strategies that help working professionals become healthier, happier, and more productive. His first book, *The Best Place to Work*, was selected an *Inc. Magazine*'s Best Business Book of the Year.